PASTELS AND PEDOPHILES

PASTELS *and* PEDOPHILES

INSIDE THE MIND OF QANON

Mia Bloom *and* Sophia Moskalenko

REDWOOD PRESS
Stanford, California

Stanford University Press
Stanford, California

Printed in the United States of America on acid-free, archival-quality paper
Library of Congress Cataloging-in-Publication Data is available.
ISBN 9781503630291 (cloth)
ISBN 9781503630611 (ebook)
Cover photograph: Evelyn Hockstein
Cover design: Rob Ehle

CONTENTS

ACKNOWLEDGMENTS

This book is the brainchild of the director of Stanford University Press, Alan Harvey. After eight months of trying to solicit a manuscript about QAnon and either getting no response from journalists covering the Q beat (whom I—Mia—will not name, but you know who you are) or being ghosted by a prospective author, Alan joked that at this point I probably knew enough about QAnon to write a book myself.

He was half right. Having the opportunity to work with the most brilliant psychologist on radicalization, Dr. Sophia Moskalenko, allowed us to get this book finished in record time. We both thank SUP for turning this manuscript around so quickly. Thank you, Alan Harvey, Caroline McKusick, Tim Roberts, and Jennifer Gordon for your helpful insights and editing.

I want to thank my colleagues in the Department of Criminology at Georgia State University and especially Volkan Topalli and David Maimon at the Evidence-Based Cybersecurity Research Group, whose access to the dark net allowed us to glean unique insights for this book.

We are beholden to the Minerva Research Initiative, and especially to David Montgomery, Rebecca Goolsby, Harold Hawkins, and Toni Haynes. My ability to write and conduct new research is directly correlated to the fact that Minerva's 12-plus years of support has reduced my teaching load, allowing me to focus more on research than teaching. This research was funded in part by the Office of Naval Research Grant #13275485—SC1000013887. We do not represent the Department of the Navy or the Minerva Research Initiative; any mistakes or errors are exclusively our own.

The GSU grad students working on the project have been extremely helpful, and while we thank all of them, two in particular deserve special mention: Kristian Warpinski created graphic representations to help shape the models for "becoming involved with" and "exiting QAnon"; and Bhashithe Abeysinghe, in response to a text message late one Saturday night, was able to scrape almost all of Parler before Amazon stopped web hosting—generating a database of materials that scholars will be able to use in the future. We thank Cynthia Miller-Idriss for her support and endorsement of this project.

Having to explain the addictive qualities of conspiratorial thinking to my seminar students forced me to articulate convoluted and complex processes in a digestible fashion. To that end I also owe Kari Pricher, Sophie Varon, Susan Chun, Jennifer Griffiths, and Danelle Garcia a debt of gratitude for allowing us the opportunity to present this research to a massive audience—and, to Anderson Cooper, for being as obsessed with QAnon as it is with him.

I, Sophia, would like to thank: Mia Bloom, for setting me up on a blind date with an idea that I ended up falling in love with; Alan Harvey, for his visionary support for this project; Isabelle, Kai, and Erik, for putting up with Mom writing day and night for a few weeks; Kristian Warpinski, for giving my graphic ideas a digital form; Caroline McKusick and Jennifer Gordon, for helping to make the book a much smoother read; Tim Roberts, for keeping this unusually brisk production organized and streamlined.

Last, but not least, we thank our friends and their spouses for their friendship and encouragement.

We dedicate this book to Albus, Margosha, and Mimi.

Mia Bloom
Sophia Moskalenko

CHAPTER 1

LOONY LIES AND CONSPIRACIES

Making Sense of QAnon

Background and Context

The screen is dark with eerie music playing in the background. The music reaches a crescendo, and a flaming Q appears as a deep voice reveals, "8 million children are missing!" According to the video, the children are being bred specifically for their blood and body parts, they are missing birth certificates so there is no way to trace them, and our (U.S.) government is doing nothing about it—in fact they are participating in the blood lust. The only person on the planet, who can save the children, is Donald John Trump.[1]

Welcome to the universe of QAnon.

QAnon is a baseless conspiracy theory from the darkest underbelly of the Internet. Named after the Department of Energy's highest level of security clearance, a Q clearance is related to access to nuclear weapons' designs but not to other national security concerns.[2] The conspiracy theory conceives that former President Trump is fighting a battle against a "deep-state" cabal of Democratic saboteurs who worship Satan and traffic children for sex or for their blood.[3]

QAnon burst onto the scene in October 2017 with predictions that the National Guard was about to arrest Hillary Clinton. On October 28, an anonymous user browsing the /pol/ section of 4chan, a notorious alt-right imageboard, saw a post that read, "Hillary Clinton will be arrested between 7:45 AM — 8:30 AM EST on Monday — the morning on Oct 30, 2017." This user would later adopt the name "Q Clearance Patriot" (shortened to "Q"). Q hinted that they were a military officer in former President Trump's inner circle; their writings—almost 5,000—gave birth to the QAnon conspiracy theory.[4]

This original Q post was on the 4chan site, which was launched in 2003. There have been several "chans," including 2chan, 4chan, and 8chan. Historically, the chans, which originated in Asia, were the purview of involuntary celibates (incels), anarchists, and nihilists before spreading to the United States. The 4chan site hosts discussion boards dedicated to different topics, from anime and manga to video games and porn.[5]

As QAnon evolved, it moved from 4chan to other social media platforms, and its messages spread to Facebook, Instagram, Parler, TikTok, and even to Nextdoor and Peloton. In a short four years, QAnon metastasized from a fringe movement on anonymous message boards into a cultlike movement, with millions of followers around the world—one that has captured the imagination and practically seized control of the Republican Party.[6] More surprisingly, it has ensnared many women, causing incalculable damage to families and resulted in murders, kidnappings, and intense partisanship in U.S. politics, as you will read in this book.

There were 97 QAnon-supporting candidates in the 2020 primaries, of which 22 Republicans and 2 Independents were victorious and ran in the November 2020 elections. In 2021 a freshman senator from Georgia was removed from her committee assignments; a second freshman senator from Colorado is being investigated for aiding and abetting a failed coup. And, instead of shunning the baseless conspiracy, the Republican Party appears to have embraced it. Statistics show a steady climb in the percentage of QAnon believers in the United States from 5 percent in 2019[7] to 10 percent in 2020 to 17 percent in February 2021. An NPR/Ipsos poll revealed 17 percent of Americans believe a group of Satan-worshipping, child-enslaving elites want to control the world. Equally disturbing is that another 37 percent aren't sure whether the allegations are completely false.[8]

David Gilbert from Vice News explained that:

> QAnon followers come from all walks of life—they are liberals, conservatives, PhDs, lawyers, doctors. There are highly educated people that fall into these movements and it is dangerous and remiss to pigeon-hole QAnon followers according to educational attainment or social status.[9]

Marc-André Argentino, a PhD candidate from Montreal who studies the conspiracy, criticized the Democratic National Committee when they launched a $500,000 ad campaign in February 2021 that offered the GOP a choice between being "the party of QAnon or appealing to college educated voters." Argentino insisted that QAnon comprises people of *all* educational levels, and he railed on Twitter: "Can we stop saying these are uneducated people, that they are crazy and wear tinfoil hats?"[10]

The increasing number of people who believe in QAnon and the range of socioeconomic and educational strata to which it appeals mean that it is highly likely someone in your family or among your friends believes that QAnon is real.

What is QAnon? Why do ordinarily sane people believe something so outrageous? How did we get here? And can we fix the problem?

This book seeks to answer all of these questions. We examine the possible identity of Q, trace the origins of QAnon to long-entrenched anti-Semitic tropes, explore why women have been especially vulnerable to QAnon, and explain psychologically how Q has managed to take root in the U.S. body politic.

What Is QAnon?

By now, you have probably seen and heard about QAnon: a baseless conspiracy theory that claims there is a secret cabal of devil-worshipping Democrats and elites that feed off the blood of children. Like its predecessor Pizzagate (discussed in Chapter 2), which was another social media rumor alleging that Hillary Clinton was operating a child-trafficking scheme from Comet Ping Pong pizzeria, QAnon began on the chans in a series of forum posts. Its origins are hotly debated: Did it start as a puzzle, or a joke, or even as the basis for a live-action role-playing (LARP) game? The nature of QAnon and the complexity of the posts changed as it moved through different areas of the Internet before ending up on the Facebook feed of your family and coworkers. The core conspiracy claim of QAnon is that there is a "deep state," and the only person who is capable of fighting it and preventing a dystopian future (like the one depicted in film *The Purge*) is Donald Trump.

Who Is Q?

No one really knows definitively who Q is.[11] Theories vary widely, according to Vice News and HBO documentaries tracking down the identity of Q. Some say that it is Edward Snowden, retired U.S. Army Lieutenant General Michael Flynn, or even Alex Jones.[12] The HBO documentary *Q: Into the Storm* settled on Ron Watkins, the son of Jim Watkins—known by his computer alias "CodeMonkeyZ."

Q began posting in October 2017, feigning that they were a high-level intelligence operative with a Q-level security clearance. Based on months of research by Vice News, there appeared to be several possibilities for Q's identity, four of which we present below.

As researchers have sought to identify who Q is and debate the likely identities, it is equally plausible that whoever was posting as Q might have changed a few times—a literary ruse used in shows like *Gossip Girl* or *Bridgerton*. Terrorism expert Clint Watts has likened Q to the fictional character "Dread Pirate Roberts" in the film *The Princess Bride*.[13] In the film there is no ONE pirate named Roberts, but the name is passed down every few years to someone else. Westley explains this baton passing to Buttercup:

> Roberts had grown so rich, he wanted to retire . . . he told me his secret. "I am not the Dread Pirate Roberts, . . . my name is Ryan; I inherited the ship from the previous Dread Pirate Roberts. . . . He was not the real Dread Pirate Roberts either. His name was Cummerbund. The real Roberts has been retired fifteen years and living like a king in Patagonia." It was the name that mattered.[14]

It is also possible that the original Q began posting for the LOLs or "lolz"—as they call "shit posting"—by adding vague Nostradamus-like predictions. This is what most people without much experience with 4chan might have misunderstood: that much of the content was meant to be sarcastic or not serious. At the outset it was not clear whether Q was real or a fictional game. But its gamelike characteristics were precisely what appealed to the 4chan audience and kept them engaged. Vice News investigated and observed:

> Part of the QAnon appeal lies in its game-like quality. Followers wait for clues left by "Q" on a message board. When the clues appear, believers dissect the riddle-like posts alongside Trump's speeches and tweets and news articles in an effort to validate the main narrative that Trump is winning a war against evil.[15]

So let's begin with the first person claiming to be Q.

Manuel Chavez III (aka Defango)

Manny Chavez, whose gamer avatar goes by the name Defango, claims that he invented the idea for Q but only as a live-action role-playing (LARP) game.[16] These games are popular online and in real life, and the players all know that it is a game. People dress up as soldiers from the Civil War and re-enact famous battles at Gettysburg or dress up as knights and joust at medieval fairs. In LARPs, usually everyone knows they are fake and just for fun.[17]

Chavez claims that Q was a LARP game that grew out of an online puzzle, Cicada 3301. These complex online puzzles began on 4chan in 2012, and they captivated their audience of hackers and online gamers. The challenging puzzles were designed to sustain the user on the platform for hours at a time. There is some speculation even today that these Cicada puzzles were actually created by U.S intelligence agencies as a kind of audition to help them identify talented young people to for recruitment into the CIA. The puzzles leveraged valuable skills in hacking, cryptography, or code breaking in order to succeed.[18]

Not long after Chavez claims to have developed the idea for Q, a rival named Thomas Schoenberger (who has also been suggested as being Q) stole the puzzle out from under Manny. Schoenberger allegedly created a new Cicada puzzle in which he could "radicalize smart people."[19] After Schoenberger took over the Cicada puzzles, the images and references grew darker. Schoenberger employed iconography from the occult and Nazi symbolism. In Schoenberger's puzzle, one of the greatest prizes you could win was the "Spear of Destiny" (the weapon that Roman soldiers used to torture Jesus Christ on the Cross), which was also a treasured Nazi symbol.[20]

QAnon has been compared to LARPs because it employs many of the same design structures and intermittent rewards. According to game designer Reed Berkowitz, QAnon "has a game-like feel to it that is evident to anyone who has ever played an online role-play (RP) or LARP before."[21] Like online platforms whose goal is to sustain user engagement and keep them online by offering a variable schedule of reinforcement, the Cicada puzzles ensured people would remain engaged for hours and hours at a time, figuring out the solution to the next level and the next.

In the early 2010s, there were many anonymous characters online. 4chan was full of posts that claimed to be from some (likely fictional) "highly placed government official." QAnon was not the first "anon" poster on the message boards in cyberspace; there had been others like High level anon, FBI-anon, CIA-anon, White House insider-Anon, and many more. But those other anons failed to catch on in the same way that QAnon did, nor did they successfully migrate to other platforms, becoming accessible to non-techie gamers or LARPers. So while the Cicada puzzles became increasingly popular after 2012, in 2017 an influential Twitter handle @snowwhite7Iam (the anonymous account of Lisa Clapier) encouraged people to leave the Cicada puzzle and to "follow the white rabbit" to participate in a new game. QAnon used the familiar metaphor from *Alice in Wonderland.*

Clapier, a media producer from Los Angeles, was a longtime activist and conspiracy theorist who had been involved with several left-wing movements including Occupy Wall Street, Julian Assange, Anonymous, the original Cicada 3301 puzzle, and finally QAnon.[22] Her persuasive tactics successfully pulled people out of the Cicada puzzle and directed them down the proverbial rabbit hole to the world of QAnon. In the first 10 days, after November 8, 2017, over 100,000 tweets containing the hashtag #FollowTheWhiteRabbit were posted to Twitter.[23]

Women on social media helped push the move to QAnon. In November 2018, 24 of the 29 accounts promoting the move from Cicada to Q (83%) used female avatars (although this is no guarantee that they were women). One, a YouTube influencer named Tracy Beanz (real name Tracy Diaz), played a major role. She posted a dozen YouTube videos in which she deciphered Q posts for her audience. Her videos were watched over 8 million times. Beanz provides some early insight into the profit motive for amplifying Q, as she included links to her Patreon or PayPal accounts in all her videos.[24]

In 2018 several high-profile Republican politicians and "celebrity" Trump supporters like James Woods, Governor Ron DeSantis of Florida, and disgraced "historian" Dinesh D'Souza were key nodes pushing the hashtag #FollowtheWhiteRabbit or other Q-affiliated slogans.[25]

> Q became the narrator of a tale that cast Trump as the central hero in an epic global struggle, doling out the story in thousands of posts known as "Q drops," first on 4chan, then on the even more outré 8chan and its successor site, 8kun.[26]

In his interview with Vice News, Manny Chavez explained that the paradigm of leaving clues or breadcrumbs, known as Q-drops, originating from the Cicada puzzles.[27] People familiar with puzzles would recognize the similarity with QAnon right away. Then devoted QAnon enthusiasts, called "bakers," would gather together the various Q-drops and post their findings on aggregator sites, with open APIs (application programming interfaces) like Facebook and Twitter.

It is worth clarifying that the Internet is comprised of open APIs (things you can find and view on Google), encrypted and semi-encrypted platforms (WhatsApp, Telegram, Hoop Messenger messenging sites), and the dark net. We hear more now about the encrypted and semi-encrypted platforms because they have been used by terrorist groups like ISIS or the Proud Boys to plan attacks. Encrypted sites are only accessible to members of channels or chatrooms, and navigating these semi-encrypted platforms is challenging. The dark net, or dark web, is not easily searchable and is often the venue for illegal activities like buying drugs, human trafficking, or other shady activities. Most of what happened with QAnon occurred first on the message boards and only later moved to sites like Facebook, Twitter, and Instagram.

The technique of leaving little clues as Q-drops enabled QAnon influencers to convince their audience that they were "figuring it out for themselves" when in fact the clues or Q-drops were pre-seeded in such a way that the conclusion was predetermined, just as it had been in the Cicada puzzles. This could be compared to a therapist guiding their patient or a lawyer leading a witness. Chavez explained:

> Basically all of the methods and systems used within QAnon are direct copies of weapons grade psychological warfare tools embedded into a puzzle. I mean who gets their information from a shady guy posting on a pedofile [sic] board?[28]

QAnon operated anonymously on the message boards and maximized this anonymity by using automated accounts. QAnon also used "sock accounts," intended for deception by using fake names, as well as automated algorithms that could share content to hundreds or even thousands of people simultaneously, called "bots." While we know now that Facebook algorithms suggested QAnon groups, even before QAnon used Facebook it had tweaked the algorithms to amplify QAnon content so that it might appear at the top of any search result. We also now know that there was "malign foreign influencers" that amplified the QAnon messages by boosting the hashtags and "liking" the posts to game the algorithms.

Going back to the online gamers and the Cicada puzzles, these were the same people initially involved with Q when it began leaving cryptic posts on 4chan.[29] However, not everyone believes Manny invented Q, partly because he has mocked the QAnon movement. Chavez claims that he has also been the target of multiple accusations of stalking, harassment, and even pedophilia by Tom Schoenberger.[30] Schoenberger was interviewed extensively in the HBO documentary *Q: Into the Storm* and pointed to a number of possible QAnon influencers that drove the movement from the message boards to the mainstream, but they also might have shared information with Trump loyalists to leverage QAnon support for the president.

Jim and Ron Watkins, Father & Son

The next possible candidate for who might be Q is the father and son duo of Jim and Ron Watkins. Cullen Hoback, the HBO documentarian, claims that Ron Watkins let it "slip" that he was Q, although the fact that Watkins was controlling the Q-drops and had already been identified by Fredrick Brennan made the revelation somewhat anti-climactic.

After its emergence on 4chan, whoever was posting as Q found himself in need of a new platform when 4chan became inhospitable because of the Gamergate backlash in 2014. You may recall that Gamergate was a controversy on 4chan in which female game developers were horribly cyber-bullied and harassed. The harassment campaign included doxxing (publishing personal details or emails and addresses) as well as death threats and threats of sexual violence. Gamergate is the origin of many of the worst elements from the Internet's repulsive underbelly that we see today, including incels (involuntary celibates), men's rights activists, misogyny, and racism. It is likely that many of the QAnon posts were problematic for the 4chan moderators, who kicked off thousands of accounts because of Gamergate. Many of the people who were de-platformed by this expulsion migrated to 8chan, a new message board that had been created by Fredrick Brennan, a disabled teenager from Brooklyn. Brennan created 8chan in 2014. One assessment of 8chan was that it was a fringe Internet image board best known for pornography, racism, and assorted illegal content.[31] Jim Watkins, a former helicopter repairman for the U.S. Army, alleged that 4chan had been "infiltrated by enemies"[32] and rationalized the departure from 4chan to 8chan.

An alternative explanation for why QAnon moved from 4chan to 8chan was that Jim Watkins was looking for an excuse to seize control. Watkins was trying to persuade the original founder of 8chan, Fredrick Brennan, to work with him in 2014. Jim and his son Ron became Brennan's partners once the 8chan message board became too large for Brennan to handle by himself. One reason why people assume that the Watkins father and son might be Q is that Brennan claims that he can read the computer code on the boards that point to Ron Watkins leaving the Q-drops.[33] According to Brennan, in the HBO documentary *Q: Into the Storm*, the irony that Jim Watkins might be Q (given that QAnon fancies itself as saving children from sexual exploitation) is Watkins's own history as a pornographer. [34]

For some people, QAnon is more of a religious movement than a conspiracy theory. Like most of the Judeo-Christian faiths, there is a core set of beliefs that stem from revelations in a text. "In this case, that text didn't appear on stone tablets handed from a mountaintop or on golden plates buried in the ground in upstate New York, but through a series of cryptic postings on a website best known for racist memes and the manifestoes of mass shooters."[35]

In 2016 Brennan quit 8chan. In doing so he gave complete control of the platform over to Jim and Ron. In the aftermath of Donald Trump's 2016 electoral victory, Jim Watkins sought to capitalize on Trump's victory and create his own right-wing news channel to compete with Breitbart. Watkins called it *The Goldwater* and posted stories about the Clinton body count (following the allegations of their murder of Seth Rich) and pedophilia and the FBI impounding Democrats' laptops (sound familiar?).[36] The online news channel didn't succeed, hilariously because it was named after the Republican Senator Barry Goldwater, and many of the 8chan members assumed it was a Jewish site. In an interview with BuzzFeed News, Watkins admitted: "They all think we're a bunch of Jews, because [Goldwater] is a Jewish name. There's [sic] a lot of people who think that the Jews are running the world."[37]

Q began posting on a dedicated 8chan sub-board called CBTS_Stream (Calm Before the Storm)[38] beginning in December 2017. At this time, the CBTS board was managed by a South African conspiracy theorist named Paul Furber. Furber would later feud with Jim Watkins over control of the board and its content. Q portrayed itself as being the most incredible intelligence insider in history. But accessing these message boards was primarily the purview of the young and the technologically adept. To enable easier access to the materials for a broader audience, Furber decided to use Reddit to post QAnon information. Reddit is a popular website that aggregates content based on users' likes. Users can submit posts, and members vote up or down, which changes its rankings. If the users "upvote" a post, it will appear to be higher on the rankings and get more visibility. Subreddits are smaller versions of Reddit. Furber created a new Subreddit devoted exclusively to

Q content and called it "r/thegreatawakening." The move to Reddit was the first pivotal move that allowed QAnon to tap into a larger audience of likeminded conspiracy theorists. Being on Reddit also meant that discussions about Q-drops were no longer the purview of the fringe message boards. Reddit was a more accessible platform.

As QAnon moved from fringe message board sites to more mainstream ones, it found a new audience: Not the 20-year-old gamers who frequented the chans or Reddit, but the over-65 boomers on Facebook via posts on dozens of public and private Facebook groups.[39]

From Reddit, QAnon supporters began to ardently proselytize their "truth" on Facebook and other social media platforms to their friends and family. QAnon became so popular it produced a dedicated YouTube channel; Facebook was flooded with Q-related posts, memes, and images and found an ever-increasing audience receptive to its messages.

Once QAnon became more popular, Jim Watkins observed other people were able to monetize it.[40] During this period, the story gets complicated. There were several apparent sources for the Q-drops, and they often reflected the author—changing tone, punctuation, style, and even spelling. Paul Furber felt that since he created the original message boards, they were "his." Anyone connected to the message board could post as Q, and several people at the time did. This included the couple responsible for "Patriot Soapbox," a round-the-clock YouTube channel for QAnon information and discussions.[41] Coleman Rogers and his wife Christina Urso ran Patriot Soapbox and were dedicated Trump supporters. The password for the 8chan site (which was "mattock") was easily hacked, allowing the couple, Furber, or Watkins to post what appeared to be competing or contradictory Q-drops.[42] As journalists have attempted to identify who Q is, they have been unable to determine who was responsible for the materials on the QAnon Subreddits.

For the most part, the HBO docuseries *Q: Into the Storm* presents the elder Watkins seeking to control the QAnon message boards without interference from Rogers, Urso, Furber, or anyone else.[43] Once the Q account had been hacked, Jim Watkins had the excuse he needed to create a brand new message board for which he maintained sole control. Using his unique access as the owner of 8chan, Jim had his son Ron (known on the channel as "CodeMonkeyZ") exclusively authenticate Jim's posts as "coming from Q." In doing so, Watkins delegitimized anything Furber, Rogers, or Urso had posted previously on CBTS. QAnon followers watched in real time as Q announced that "he" was abandoning the CBTS board for a new message board—created by Jim Watkins, the owner of 8chan and authenticated by Ron Watkins (the site's administrator).

When Jim created the new board, Q's writing style changed. Q began using all caps and incomplete sentences, posting acronyms and abbreviations instead of full sentences. The HBO documentary alleged that Watkins's posts attempted to implicate Trump's ally Steve Bannon. The "Great Awakening" Subreddit had over 70,000 followers, but in 2018 Reddit banned Q for "posting content that incites violence, disseminates personal information, or harasses . . . [All of which got] users and communities banned from Reddit."[44] Reddit moderators to the Q Subreddits—Tracy Beanz (Diaz), Coleman Rogers, his wife

Christina Urso, and even Paul Furber—were all banned from the site.[45]

While Reddit had banned QAnon content, moderators, and Subreddits in 2018, 8chan remained a cesspool where racists and right-wing extremists congregated. Even though he had originally created it, Fredrick Brennan began calling for 8chan to be shut down once it became the platform of choice for mass casualty shooters and terrorist attackers to live stream their deadly operations.[46] Brennan did not want to be associated with this material.[47] In contrast, Jim Watkins advocated for limitless protections for free speech. This included hate speech and even the live streaming of 17 minutes of killings in March 2019. Brenton Tarrant, the mass killer in New Zealand, had posted his manifesto to 8chan before carrying out his deadly shooting attacks in Christchurch, New Zealand, that left 51 people dead. After the massacres in New Zealand, Watkins refused to take Tarrant's 74-page manifesto down, even after it became clear what had transpired and that people might emulate this kind of attack.[48] New Zealand and France jointly declared in the "Christchurch Call," which committed the signatories to the elimination of terrorist and violent extremist content online.[49]

As the conspiracy picked up more followers and new converts, locating Q-drops became a cottage industry. Apps were designed to provide push notifications the moment a new Q-drop was released. Nevertheless, the message boards remained very difficult to navigate for people who were not as tech savvy.

In the fall of 2018, Q followers began showing up at Trump rallies brandishing Q signs or wearing Q-branded clothing.

Up until 2018, Jim Watkins had been unable to profit off of 8chan's QAnon posts; however, he did eventually monetize QAnon to a degree. Jim Watkins initially wanted power and influence, but after seeing how some of the influencers were benefiting financially from QAnon, he might have wanted "in on the action." While Watkins was posting on 8chan, Jason Gelinas, a Citibank executive, became an ardent QAnon supporter.[50] Gelinas's descent into QAnon was prompted, as we explain in Chapter 3, by a feeling of something being "not quite right."

> Like many of you, I felt that something wasn't right in the world, that our country was headed in the wrong direction," he wrote. "Then something magical happened in 2016 that defied expectations—a complete outsider to the political establishment, Donald J. Trump, won the presidential election! Amazing. A glimmer of light in the darkness.[51]

The message boards and Subreddits were still challenging to navigate for the uninitiated. In April 2018 while working at Citibank, Gelinas designed a website dedicated to offering Q-drops in a user-friendly setting. Gelinas called it Qmap.pub. Qmap was designed for people who had little to no computer experience. In contrast to the message boards, Qmap used a minimalist design with pull-down menu options, a search function, and icon buttons for curated content. This new venue increased the popularity of QAnon. Each Q-drop was titled (rather than numbered as it was on the message boards), and tabs across the top of the screen enabled users to sort drops by theme, hashtag, or a category such as "suspicious deaths." On the left side of the screen Jason had placed icons: chess pieces, a globe, or a skull for quick access.[52] Gelinas generated thousands of dollars every month with donations to his Patreon account thanks to a site that allowed people with limited technological skills to do their own research without having to read through the chan message boards and collect them. Once Gelinas was unmasked as the owner of Qmap in 2020, Citicorp fired him.

By 2020, Qmap.pub drew 10 million visitors a month and played a pivotal role in turning the obscure and incoherent fringe conspiracy into a cult-like following with political repercussions.[53] During this same period in the leadup to the 2020 election, Jim Watkins launched a super-PAC called Disarm the Deep State, where people could donate to him to help spread the QAnon message and offer financial support to QAnon-supporting political candidates such as Marjorie Taylor Greene and Lauren Boebert.[54] In the 2020 primaries, there were 97 QAnon-affiliated candidates in 30 states.[55] Twenty-four went on to compete in the November 2020 election.

ABC News has reported that Ron Watkins was most likely Q, since Jim and Ron were the "two most clearly associated" with the Q-drops.[56] The theory that Watkins is Q has been popularized in the "Reply All" podcast, episode 166.[57] In the summer of 2019, Cloudflare, 8chan's cybersecurity provider, cut ties with the platform, and 8chan went dark for three months.[58] For as long as 8han was down, QAnon did not post any drops or updates. Then QAnon flickered back to life as 8chan was reborn as 8kun and now was completely under Watkins's control.[59] The only account able to post to 8kun was Q, and the three-month

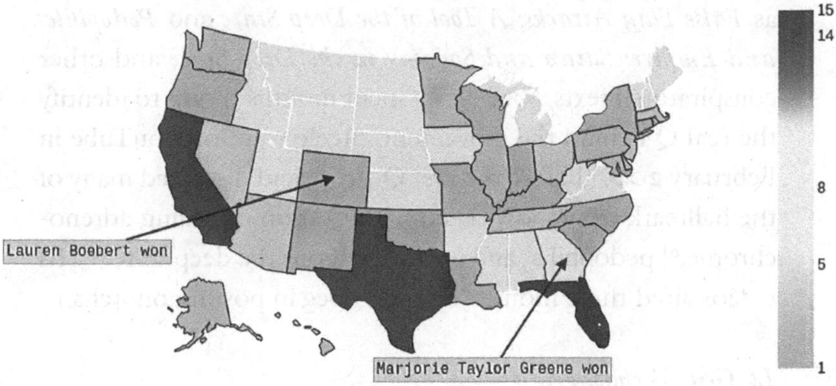

Figure 1.1. Number of QAnons supporting congressional primary candidates. Source: Bhashithe Abeysinghe.

lag resulted, according to Cullen Hoback, in only the QAnon supporters sticking with the new site.

Robert David Steele

Another identity floated for Q is Robert David Steele, an alleged CIA analyst with years of intelligence experience:[60] "alleged" because when we had CIA colleagues look him up, they found nothing. Because of the secrecy around someone in the CIA in either the DO (Directorate of Operations like Valerie Plame) or the DA (Directorate of Analysis like the fictional character Jack Ryan) there is no way for anyone to check if someone had a 20-year career in the agency or was in Langley for a few weeks as a low-level analyst. Steele claims to have been a high-level operative and told Vice News that QAnon was "the most sophisticated intelligence operation in history." Steele has authored multiple conspiracy-oriented books with titles such as *False Flag Attacks: A Tool of the Deep State* and *Pedophiles and Empire: Satan and Sodomy in the Deep State* and other conspiratorial texts. Vice News spent months trying to identify the real Q behind the movement. Steele went on YouTube in February 2017, before the first Q-drop, and discussed many of the hallmark tropes associated with QAnon including adrenochrome,[61] pedophilia, and warnings about the deep state.[62] His videos aired three months before Q began posting on 4chan.

Lt. Gen. Michael Flynn

The fourth candidate for Q is that he is a high-level White House insider, like Lt. Gen. Michael Flynn (or someone closely connected to him). There is a great deal of speculation as to why President Trump refused to disavow the QAnon conspiracy during the 2020 campaign. There are an additional set of allegations that QAnon supporters point to statements from President Trump that could not possibly be a coincidence. In one Q-drop, Q suggested that Trump would use the term "tip top" and shortly thereafter, Trump appeared on the balcony of the White House with First Lady Melania Trump and the Easter Bunny. Trump called the bunny "Tippy Top." For QAnon believers, this was proof.[63]

The reason why people might suspect that General Flynn was involved with Q is because by 2019, most QAnon-related posts on the encrypted app Telegram, the right-wing social media platform Parler, or on other sites included a (now disabled) link to Flynn's legal defense fund.[64] As Q often hinted, "follow the money." General Flynn himself pledged allegiance to QAnon on July 4, 2020, in which he added the phrase to the standard oath of office "Where we go one we go all." Flynn then posted the video to Facebook, Twitter, and other platforms ensuring that his oath of allegiance went viral. On General Flynn's website, he sold Q-branded items, T shirts, and other merchandise evem after this material was banned from Etsy and Amazon.[65]

"Where we go one we go all": This phrase is usually used as a hashtag in an acronym #WWG1WGA. In QAnon mythology, cited in Martin Geddes's writings (and their posts on social media), the phrase comes from an inscription on the bell[66] on John F. Kennedy's sailboat. The boat, *Victura,* is now part of the JFK Library on the campus of UMass Boston. There is no inscription on the bell (in fact, there is no bell). We checked. Nor is it on the Kennedy family's other boat, the *Honey Fitz.* The phrase on the bell is a fabrication from the mind of Martin Geddes, a British QAnon conspiracist. This lie, like so much of QAnon lore, was ripped off from a Hollywood film: the 1996 movie *White Squall* starring Jeff Bridges, in which there is a bell on their boat with that very inscription. The screenshot from the film is widely circulated among the QAnon supporters as evidence of JFK's connection to Q.

We may never know definitively who Q really is or was or whether Q has been different people at different times. The Vice News documentary leaves the question unanswered, whereas the HBO documentary settles on Ron Watkins. That said, most followers of QAnon don't necessarily care who he (or she) actually is since the movement has spread beyond any one individual. According to Adrienne LaFrance of *The Atlantic*, QAnon has grown beyond its identity.[67] A (now) deleted Twitter account expressed this view succinctly: "NO ONE cares who Q is. WE care about the TRUTH."[68]

Q's Origin Story

As you read this book, you might wonder where on earth did these ideas come from? You might also be surprised as you read here that many of the most outlandish QAnon claims have existed for hundreds of years and found a warm reception in Catholicism, Protestantism, and Russian Orthodoxy.

QAnon emerged in the aftermath of Pizzagate when Edgar Welch drove from North Carolina to Washington, DC, to liberate the hypothetical children from the basement of the pizzeria Comet Ping Pong. Pizzagate was a 2016 conspiracy theory revolving around suspicions of Democratic politicians trafficking in children. Like QAnon, Pizzagate was a conspiracy theory born on the 4chan message boards and spread by far-right media influencers like Alex Jones's *InfoWars* show, Jerome Corsi, and Michael Flynn Jr., son of disgraced General Flynn. In 2016, after driving from North Carolina to DC, Edgar Welch found no children in the basement—in fact, the building did not have a basement. We discuss Pizzagate in greater detail in Chapter 2.

Despite the fact that Welch testified that he was wrong, the same people who believe in QAnon believe that Pizzagate was real. It is worth noting that much of the controversy and rumor mill about Pizzagate was spread by far-right websites and promoted by alt-right activists like Mike Cernovich and the Flynns.[69] Foreign actors—such as troll farms in Vietnam, the Czech Republic, and Cyprus—further amplified the false allegations.[70]

Pizzagate received a rebirth in 2020 on the social media platform TikTok. Michael Flynn Jr. continues to promote Pizzagate till today. Several conspiracies have merged into QAnon, many of which existed prior to 2017. For example, QAnon believes that in addition to the blood-drinking cabal of Democrats, there are lizard people who inhabit this earth in human form. Anna Merlan has likened QAnon to a "conspiracy singularity," where many conspiracies are merged into a melting pot of unimaginable density. Instead of Q absorbing the adjacent conspiracies, she describes that all the conspiracies come together and overlap, drawing upon one another's constituents.[71]

Watching anything about QAnon you will undoubtedly hear that it is a "baseless conspiracy theory with anti-Semitic overtones." But what exactly does that mean? To appreciate how much of QAnon is old wine in new bottles, we need to briefly explore the history of anti-Semitism.

The Anti-Semitic Roots of QAnon

In order to understand where QAnon derived its most shocking claims, we need to delve into the history of European anti-Semitism and the even longer history of hostility to Jews by the Catholic, Protestant, and Russian Orthodox (Eastern branch) Church.

Russian Czar Nicholas II looked upon the Jewish population in his empire with disdain. The Jews had been a troublesome lot not only because they had rejected the Lord Jesus Christ but also because they posed a danger to czarist rule over all of Mother Russia. A generation earlier, Jews had been blamed for the assassination of Czar Alexander II in 1881. Between 1880 and 1910, Russian authorities amplified anti-Semitic conspiracies in order to distract the people from their poor living conditions or from imperial corruption; Russian authorities encouraged violence against the Jewish residents of the Pale of Settlement, a geographic area where Jews were permitted to live as they could not freely live anywhere they chose. These paroxysms of violence were called pogroms. They erupted periodically but were perfectly timed around Ash Wednesday and Easter and emboldened by fiery sermons from the pulpit.

In 1900 during the reign of Czar Nicholas II, a new lie emerged that claimed the Jews sought to rule the world by leveraging their (ill-gotten) money and their intelligence to manipulate trusting Christians. As with any anti-Semitism, such views were oxymoronic: Jews were simultaneously strong but weak, manipulative yet easily duped, to be feared and to be scorned.

In 1902, the czarist secret police forged a document to support the fiction about this Jewish plot to take over the world that built upon existing conspiratorial beliefs about the Jewish need for blood and the danger Jews posed to unbaptized babies. Originally published in 1902–1903 under the title *Anti-Christ* in Russian, *The Protocols of the Elders of Zion* (*The Protocols*) became one of the most widely disseminated anti-Semitic tracts of all time.

The Protocols Were the Original Fake News

The Protocols, published as a pamphlet, are allegedly the minutes of meetings held by Jewish elders in Prague, which took place at a Jewish cemetery. The cabal came together to discuss how they would carry out their plan to rule the world. Several themes in *The Protocols* remain full of tropes that exist today: that Jews seek to rule the world; that they control the media; that Jews are responsible for pornography; and that this secret cabal controlled the politicians. Overall Jews had a corrosive and corrupting effect on everyone and everything around them.

The implications in the tract rendered every negative event traceable back to the Jews. Every disaster, emergency, or political upheaval could likewise be traced back to the Jews' evil plan. Events that had nothing to do with Jews—such as the French Revolution—were still blamed on the Jews as part of their devious scheme. Jews could be simultaneously blamed for both capitalism and socialism (these are diametrically opposed ideologies).

In allocating blame for emerging political movements to the Jews, the czar sought to insulate himself from the political upheaval that was spreading throughout Europe in favor of representative democracy and diminishing the power of antiquated monarchies. By attacking Jews, the Russian secret police was really attacking secular ideologies that threatened to overthrow the czar.

As the pamphlet circulated throughout Central and Western Europe, its origins were revealed to be fake. The tract had plagiarized sections of Maurice Joly's *The Dialogue in Hell Between Machiavelli and Montesquieu*, a satirical French novel attacking the monarchy, and Hermann Goedsche's 1868 novel *Biarritz*. In one chapter, Goedsche envisioned a nocturnal Jewish meeting in a cemetery where they discussed plans to rule the world. In 1872, the chapter from *Biarritz* was published in St. Petersburg as a freestanding document (not as part of a fictional novel). As the chapter made its rounds through various capitals in Europe, different authors added more details to the narrative. Eventually the chapter was combined with Joly's material and became the basis of the Russian secret police's forgery. The fact that parts of the story had been plagiarized from two different novels and merged was temporarily forgotten. In so many ways, the same way that QAnon lore has been constructed from bits of literature and film storylines is mirrored in the way that *The Protocols* came together.

The *Times* of London unmasked *The Protocols* as a fake; nevertheless, anti-Semites propagated the forgery as documentary evidence of Jewish malfeasance. The first non-Russian edition was a German translation published in 1920, followed by translations to Polish, French, and English. That same year, automobile mogul and well-known anti-Semite, Henry Ford published an Americanized version of *The Protocols* under the title *The International Jew*. It remains the most widely disseminated work of anti-Semitism, translated into every language and in circulation throughout the world until today.

Adolf Hitler folded *The Protocols* into his own writings, specifically *Mein Kampf*. During the rise of Nazism, what previously had been justification for hating Jews for religious reasons (for having killed Christ) was substituted with a more sophisticated justifications for hating Jews for scientific reasons. Hatred of Jews was no longer simply a function of them being Christ killers but Germans considered Jews to be a race set apart by genetically different and inferior characteristics. These inferior elements could not be overcome via assimilation into society or even by conversion to Christianity. Jews were dangerous or threatening because of their blood.

As Hitler rose to power after 1933, the Nazis published 23 different versions of *The Protocols*. Its ideas and themes were folded into Nazi and Soviet propaganda. Hitler's worldview reaffirmed there existed a racial struggle (*Kampf*) for survival of the fittest. For Hitler, Jews were the source of evil, disease, social injustice, and cultural decline. Capitalism and all forms of Marxism, especially communism, were blamed on Jews and their global conspiracy.

After 1948, *The Protocols* found welcome reception in Arabic translation, and it became a bestseller in the Middle East. Stories of Saudi princes handing out leather-bound illuminated copies to distinguished visitors was a longstanding joke within the State Department, as visiting U.S. politicians had to find ever-more creative ways to get rid of the gift since they could not be caught with this material without ruining their political careers.

Conspiracy theories are a common way to explain a precarious world. People seek plausible explanations when things go wrong. Conspiracies offer comfort and reassurance that there is a higher power behind seemingly random events. While *The Protocols* might have been inspired by elite political ambitions, they resonated with the rank and file because they harkened back to historic religious anti-Semitism that blamed Jews for rejecting Christ as their savior and Lord.

The Catholic Church shifted its emphasis from preaching that Jews had rejected Christ to alleging that they had murdered God. Characteristic of most conspiracy theories, there were innate contradictions—Jews were both weak and powerful. They were inferior but also dangerous. The Church's accusation of deicide was not renounced until the second Vatican Council (1962–1965) finally repudiated the fallacious charge that the Jews had killed Christ.[72] Throughout Europe, Jews were treated as unwanted aliens and every few years would be blamed for the spread of disease or some other black swan event like a plague. The Church continued to promote the idea that the Jews were in league with the devil and portrayed them as using the blood of Christian children for ritual sacrifice.[73]

Trump's Dog Whistles

Anti-Semitism did not disappear with the second Vatican Council. It is alive and well in the United States. During Trump's first presidential campaign, he aired a two-minute ad, entitled Trump's "Argument for America," that was full of anti-Semitic tropes. The ad focused on billionaire George Soros, then Federal Reserve Chair Janet Yellin (now secretary of the Treasury), and Goldman Sachs CEO Lloyd Blankfein—all of whom are Jewish—juxtaposed with images of Wall Street and Washington, DC, to convey to allegedly "economically anxious" Trump supporters that Jews were to blame for the financial state they were in.[74] One consistent feature of many of the conspiracies that are now a part of the QAnon meta conspiracy is that George Soros is almost always the bogeyman. Soros, the billionaire investor and philanthropist, is the common thread from Pizzagate, to QAnon, to Dominion voting machines. Soros appears to be the villain in every conspiracy narrative.

Even in the hours before the failed insurrection of 2021, Trump supporters gathered at the Ellipse, flanked by Rudy Giuliani and Don Junior, to watch a video. The propaganda in the film used subtle images to imply that it was Jews who controlled the Democrats and manipulated social justice campaigns like Black Lives Matter to undermine white America.[75] The imagery in the video played to people's worst fears and featured prominent Jewish representatives and senators in order to hammer the message. The star of the video was, naturally, George Soros.

Disinformation about Soros is the one common feature across several conspiracies including Pizzagate, QAnon, and a variety of additional conspiracies in Europe. Roger Stone and Alex Jones disseminated disinformation about George Soros for years on *InfoWars*, and social media—and the right-wing media bubble of Fox News, One America News, and NewsMax—till today seem obsessed.[76] Soros has been the persistent bogeyman for the right wing and target of conspiracy theorists for years. Cesar Sayoc—who sent pipe bombs to CNN, Barack Obama, Hillary Clinton, and movie stars in 2019—also targeted George Soros.[77] QAnon's obsession with Soros and the allegations about a powerful cabal of Satanists is derived from *The Protocols of the Elders of Zion*.

The other focal point for QAnon is the chemical substance adrenochrome, allegedly harvested from terrified or tortured children. QAnon promoter and alleged intelligence operative Robert David Steele has hundreds of videos posted to YouTube discussing adrenochrome. Recall, the Church under Pope Pius initiated the fiction about Jews' need for blood as part of ritual sacrifice (called blood libel) to achieve two self-serving goals. One was to encourage families to baptize their children. This benefited the Church financially regardless of a family's ability to pay. Convincing parishioners that unbaptized children might be used for ritual sacrifice ensured a continued stream of income. The other motive was the expediency of having a reliable scapegoat. When disaster strikes and people might question the existence of God, the Church had a villain to blame, ensuring their flock's continued devotion.

Adrenochrome: The Modern-Day Blood Libel

According to QAnon, Adrenochrome is the chemical compound that is produced from children's blood when their adrenalin is activated during pain or torture. QAnon has convinced its followers that the evil cabal of Democrats and their Hollywood proxies who oppose Donald Trump torture children and extract this chemical from their bodies, which they then use as a recreational drug, or to maintain their youth, or get high. Or, after Tom Hanks announced in March 2020 that he had contracted coronavirus, adrenochrome was touted as a cure for COVID-19.

The only thing that is true about this conspiracy is that adrenochrome is a real chemical substance: $C_9H_9NO_3$. It is the metabolic byproduct produced by the oxidation of adrenaline (more commonly known as epinephrine). It is what is in an EpiPen if you are allergic to bees or peanuts. Science writer Brian Dunning explains that "Adrenochrome has some limited pharmacological use in a few countries. It is easily synthesized, widely available, and inexpensive—there is no need to harvest it from children or anyone else."[78]

Although by no means a narcotic substance (it is not listed as a controlled substance by the U.S. government), adrenochrome has appeared in works of fiction over the years. Aldous Huxley mentioned its alleged effects, which he likened it to mescaline intoxication in the *The Doors of Perception* (1954), although he never tried it. Adrenochrome is also mentioned at the beginning of *A Clockwork Orange* (1962), and Hunter S. Thompson portrayed adrenochrome as having hallucinogenic properties in his 1971 novel *Fear and Loathing in Las Vegas.* "Taking full literary license, Thompson decided to depict adrenochrome as some kind of wild psychedelic drug."[79] Like so many other parts of the conspiracy, QAnon blends elements from fiction with historic anti-Semitism.

As part of the QAnon conspiracy, they believe children are being sacrificed for their blood. QAnon is a modern-day blood libel[80] that leverages many of the historic anti-Semitic stereotypes about Jews and the blood of babies. The first mention of adrenochrome as part of the Q conspiracy is traced to a 4chan post of a video (which is no longer available) entitled "Jew Ritual BLOOD LIBEL Sacrifice is #ADRENOCHROME Harvesting." Copies of this video are still on YouTube.[81] From 4chan the idea of adrenochrome spread to Alex Jones's *InfoWars* to build on the narrative.

The accusation of Jewish malfeasance resulted in blood libels from the middle ages up until the twentieth century.[82] Blood libels originated with the Catholic Church that disseminated the falsehood that Jews needed Christian blood to bake unleavened bread (matzo) for Passover, or alternatively that they drank the blood as medicine or used it as an aphrodisiac.[83] In the twentieth century, Nazi propagandists used blood libels as proof that Jews were a threat to Germany. Their newspaper *Der Stürmer* devoted an entire issue to blood libels and accusations of the master Jewish plan to murder non-Jews.[84]

A blood libel even occurred in the United States. In September 1928, 4-year-old Barbara Griffiths went missing in Massena, New York. A rumor that Jews had kidnapped and killed her as part of a religious ritual gained traction, leading police to question local Jewish leaders and the town's rabbi about her disappearance. The theory quickly caught fire, finding believers not just among the townsfolk but also in powerful figures such as state police officers and Massena's mayor. The girl was found the following day alive and unharmed.[85]

Blood libels flourished in Europe during the nineteenth and twentieth centuries in part because of explicitly anti-Semitic newspapers and political parties whose *raison d'etre* was to diminish Jewish influence. With the exception of Henry Ford's *Dearborn Independent*, not many U.S. newspapers were dedicated to attacking Jews. In contrast, almost a hundred years later, social media and the Internet provide ample opportunities to express the most hateful views and disseminate racist materials. The allegations that QAnon makes about adrenochrome are the modern manifestation of a blood libel.

Consider for a moment how completely nonsensical this allegation is. Anyone familiar with Jewish dietary laws, called ***kashrut*** (kosher), knows that Jews have an antipathy toward blood.[86] As part of the koshering process, the proteins are subject to a kind of brining, salting and soaking in water three times. The only reason to process meat in this way is to extract the residual blood.

The antipathy toward blood might have been a reaction to the pagan religions that existed during early antiquity as Judaism evolved into a faith. In the sixth century Jewish dietary laws began to be codified in the Babylonian Talmud, although the first dietary exclusion is found in Exodus, commanding "do not boil a kid in its mother's milk" (Exodus 23:19), thereby prohibiting the mixing of milk and meat. The prohibition against consuming blood appears in Leviticus 7:26–27: "Moreover you shall eat no blood whatever, whether of fowl or of animal, in any of your dwellings. Whoever eats any blood, that person shall be cut off from his people."[87]

Jewish religious law forbids the consumption of any blood, human or animal. But accusations of ritual murder vilified Jews and have been used to justify the pillaging, torture, burning alive, and expulsion of countless Jews throughout the history of European anti-Semitism.[88]

The Storm, Lizard People, and Dominion Voting Machines

QAnon is a meta conspiracy theory that folds in adjacent or complementary conspiracies. People who believe in QAnon are more likely to believe that COVID-19 is a hoax or are anti-5G, anti-mask, anti-vaxx; believe that the moon landing was faked and that 9/11 was an inside job. *Daily Beast* reporter Will Sommer explains:

> As a sort of mega-conspiracy theory, QAnon can encompass a wide array of other, often conflicting conspiratorial beliefs. Not every QAnon believer holds to the same tenets of QAnon, and the most committed are often engaged in furious online battles with each other over the exact meaning of a QAnon clue.[89]

QAnon believers are eager for the day of reckoning they call "the Storm," in which Trump will arrest his political opponents and send them to Guantanamo Bay or execute them. QAnon devotees believe that they will play a role in this purge by educating everyone else about QAnon and celebrate the "Great Awakening."[90] Many believed this "storm" would come on January 20, 2021, and that Joseph R. Biden would not be sworn in as the 46th U.S. president. Instead he, Vice President Kamala Harris, and the attendees of the inauguration would be marched down Pennsylvania Avenue and shot or hanged.

Most all of the Q predictions over the years have not materialized: Hillary Clinton is not in jail, Barack Obama was not indicted and wearing an ankle monitor, nor was Michelle Obama discovered to be a man. However, supporters were able to suspend their disbelief with every failed prediction. The inauguration was a particularly difficult prophecy to get wrong, and the result has been that some QAnon believers experienced deep melancholy, suicidal ideation, or engaged in self-harm. While many people have left QAnon, others doubled or tripled down despite the failed prophecies.

One of the more unusual adjacent theories involves Donald Trump being a time traveler and that some of the blood-drinking members of the cabal are actually lizard people.[91] The lizard people conspiracy emerged in the UK. David Icke, a former football (soccer) star and news presenter for the BBC, wrote 20 books about the presence of lizard people beginning with his 1999 *The Biggest Secret*, in which blood-drinking shape-shifting reptilians from the Alpha Draconis star system were plotting again humankind. Icke alleged that many global leaders such as the Rothschild family, the British royal family and the Bush family were all actually a race of Anunnaki lizards. According to his many books on the subject, an alien race of reptilians has altered human DNA, and lizard people live among us.

Interestingly enough, there was a feedback loop between this conspiracy theory and science fiction. When Icke was writing about lizard people, the previous decade a show appeared on ABC called *V* (1983). In the show, a race of reptilians had come to earth under the pretense of being peaceful, but under their exquisite human disguises, they were evil rodent-eating lizards. Icke had watched the show and added details to his books about lizard people inspired by the science fiction plotlines. In another book, Icke referred to the alien lizards as Archons. This name was then used in the film series, *Men In Black*. Icke identified the Draco constellation from which the lizard people had evolved. J. K. Rowling named her villain

Draco Malfoy of the Slytherin House, represented not by a lizard but by a snake.

When *V* returned to television in 2009, the show's writers allegedly read Icke's books to get ideas for plotlines,[92] including the aliens' having sent sleeper agents decades before their arrival to access the highest levels of government and undermine human society. Thus there is a reciprocal loop between the lizard conspiracy theory and science fiction about lizard people.

One possible explanation for why conspiracy thoeries resonate is that there is an element of familiarity. If someone has watched a film or a TV show that includes some element or detail echoed in the conspiracy theory, they might be more inclined to believe it because some part of their memory fails to distinguish between a fictional memory and a factual memory.

Take, for example, the QAnon adjacent belief in the Dominion voting machine conspiracy. The owners of 8chan and likely one of several Q posters, Jim and Ron Watkins both aggressively pushed the falsehood that Dominion machines deliberately switched 2020 general election votes intended for Trump to Biden through a manipulated algorithm.[93] Seventy-five percent of Republicans believe there were voting irregularities, and social media (amplified again by foreign actors) intensified the conspiracy around a campaign to "Stop the Steal." Further, the conspiracy theory intimates that Dominion did this deliberately and would silence any whistleblowers who came forward to present evidence of their wrongdoing.

One possible reason why this explanation was disseminated is that it sounded plausible. In 2006 there had been a film entitled *Man of the Year* with that exact same storyline. The film, starring Robin Williams as a Jon Stewart-like comedian, runs for president as a joke but wins. A computer programmer discovers that the voting machine algorithm confused by double consonants or vowels defaulted votes to Williams's character. The voting machine company, worried that the revelation would hurt the company's bottom line and its ability to sell the machines globally, moves to silence the programmer. The people who fabricated the Dominion voting machine controversy didn't have much imagination and seemingly copied the storyline from a movie that was not widely seen and received 21 percent on Rotten Tomatoes. In the comment section of reviews online, someone writing in 2020 commented, "wow life imitating art."

Like the unscientific allegations about adrenochrome's hallucinogenic properties that originated in literary fiction, the Dominion voting machine scandal was pulled from a Hollywood plotline. The myth about the bell on JFK's boat is drawn from a Hollywood movie. For a group that claims to hate Hollywood as much as it does and refers to it as "Pedowood," it certainly plagiarizes a lot of their mythology from Hollywood scripts.

To underscore Q's dependence on Hollywood, on Election Day 2020, the Q account posted a photo of an American flag, an Abraham Lincoln quote, and a link to a clip of a song from the 1992 movie *Last of the Mohicans*.[94] Then Q went silent.

There is a pressing need to understand why millions of people believe in this baseless conspiracy theory in which so many of their key tropes can be so easily and quickly debunked. Not only is QAnon a threat to the United States, but the conspiracy theory is spreading globally faster than the coronavirus that has amplified its popularity. This book will explain why people choose to believe in conspiracies and what psychological strings QAnon pulls to attract converts and keep them committed. QAnon has ruined families, it is increasing suicidality, and it is likely wrecking any hope of bipartisan governance. In Chapter

2, the book takes a closer look at how women are the unexpected powerhouse movers and shakers of QAnon. Chapter 3 delves into the psychology of conspiratorial beliefs, Chapter 4 offers some suggestions to help people escape the rabbit hole to get their family and friends out of QAnon and come back into the light. Chapter 5 explores the global spread of QAnon, and Chapter 6 debunks many of the QAnon myths and explains why QAnon has targeted specific individuals.

CHAPTER 2

JANUARY 6, 2021

Capitol Hill, the Failed Insurrection

Women made up a significant portion of the Capitol Hill rioters on January 6, 2021. The failed insurrection aiming to overturn the 2020 election results was preceded by dedicated rallies for female Trump supporters. Kylie Jane Kremer, who had cofounded the group Women for America First, organized the "Stop the Steal" rally in November and applied for the permit to hold the rally at the Capitol that day.[1] The FBI used social media posts and anonymous tips to track down the rioters, many of whom were arrested within a week or two after the attack. Almost two dozen women have been indicted following the assault on the Capitol building, and although this number only comprises 10 percent of the total present in the mob, women were nevertheless the driving force that day because of their pivotal role in bringing together an ad hoc network of far-right militants, Christian conservatives, and adherents of the QAnon conspiracy theory.[2]

Women are unlikely drivers for a movement that initially emerged inside the hyper-masculine virtual spaces of 4chan like

/pol/—the politically incorrect discussion board on 4chan. Young men, incels, and computer hackers typically dominated these message boards. Mobilization for the insurrection occurred across social media platforms, Subreddits like r/TheStorm, and the far-right message boards like TheDonald.win. Contributing to this disinformation environment were conservative news, Facebook discussion groups, and the right-wing extremist social media application Parler, all of which inspired female supporters of Donald Trump to gather in Washington to "stop the steal."

QAnon might have initially emerged from masculine spaces, but the movement only took off once it found fertile ground in feminine online spaces like women's Facebook groups and Instagram. This shift from the encrypted platforms and message boards through to the online ecosystem on the surface web explains how QAnon became a movement. The women in QAnon made the conspiracy appear palatable and perhaps even seem motivated by altruistic instincts to protect children.[3]

Certainly, QAnon's most visible perpetrators at the siege, like QAnon Shaman Jacob Chansley (Jake Angeli), captured the nation's imagination. With his painted face, wearing a Viking-horned helmet, Chansley looked like a cartoon Asterix come to life. A *New Yorker* video taken by Luke Mogelson inside the Capitol Rotunda on January 6 shows Chansley bellowing like a wounded animal.[4] CNN's Donie O'Sullivan attended a QAnon meeting in Arizona back in October 2020 before the election.[5] Chansley was present, face painted, wearing the horned helmet and again shirtless (no matter what the weather), exposing a chest branded with Norse tattoos. The representations have been coopted by the extremist right wing to validate their pure Nordic (read "white") origins.

The focal point for the media has been on the men who overran the Capitol, especially in light of threats made to specific female lawmakers like Alexandria Ocasio-Cortez and Nancy Pelosi. But it is the women who have been essential to sustaining the QAnon conspiracy as a movement. We know from studying terrorist groups that the vast majority, as many as 90 percent, fail within the first two years.[6] But groups that recruit women guarantee the entire family will be indoctrinated. To survive and thrive in such an environment where the likelihood of failure is high, militant groups must ensure their continuity and plans for succession. To do this, they prepare the "next generation." The best way to access the kids is to recruit the moms.

Women have been at the forefront of white racist movements for the past 100 years. Much of this has been forgotten as women's roles were whitewashed due to "a gender bias that shifts political seriousness away from 'nutty' (i.e., not dangerous) White women."[7] Seyward Darby's book, *Sisters in Hate: American Women on the Front Lines of White Nationalism,*[8]acknowledges "White supremacist [movements] would collapse without women's labor."[9] Furthermore, white women have been voting for Republicans since 1952 because "it is in their interest to protect the interests of white patriarchy."[10]

The coordination required for the January 6 protests occurred on right-wing extremist channels like Parler and on the messaging app Telegram. The discussions in the far-right closed information system argued that this election meddling was a secret plot hatched in China and Venezuela. In the eleventh hour, Facebook and Twitter attempted to prevent their sites from being used to organize the attempted coup but failed. Social media, MAGA channels like One America News and NewsMax all guaranteed the January 6, 2021, "Stop the Steal" rally would have a substantial turnout. Travel to Washington was reportedly funded by dark money loosely connected to the Trump administration or his wealthy enablers according to investigations by *BuzzFeed News* and the *Washington Post*.[11]

Looking at many of the images as they were broadcast live on January 6, one might have mistakenly assumed that only men had stormed the Capitol, but this was not the case. People noticed women only once they started getting arrested or killed. That day in DC, two women died, both of whom were QAnon believers. They became (temporarily) martyrs for the cause. QAnon women are symbols of the movement, and like martyrs across the political spectrum, they are able to motivate others to follow in their footsteps. QAnon propelled the events on January 6 just as much as the impeachment managers claimed that President Trump had done and as much as social media enabled the insurrection. At the Capitol playing out in real time on live TV, the country witnessed a pro-Trump mob overpowering U.S. Capitol Police officers, injuring dozens. One officer, Brian Sicknick, died as a result of his wounds. Two other officers committed suicide in the days after.

As we watched in horror, the news reported that a woman was fatally shot by police inside the Capitol, and three others died of medical emergencies.[12] The first casualty of the January 6 insurgency was Ashli Babbitt, shot as she attempted to enter through a window with a Trump flag draped around her shoulders like a cape.[13] Babbitt, an Air Force veteran of 14 years, had been scaling a barricade of furniture when a security officer shot her in the chest at point-blank range. The video of the shooting was aired for the first time during the impeachment hearings during Representative Stacey Plaskett's presentation of the evidence.

The case of women killed that day, and the wave of arrests afterwards, pose more questions than they answer about how and why women joined QAnon. Ashli Babbitt was in distress, and not just economically; she was having problems transitioning from the military to civilian life. Before the pandemic, Babbitt worked as a security guard for a nuclear power plant and struggled to keep her pool supply company afloat.[14] Babbitt's life after the military had proved more difficult than she expected, and she bounced from one job to the next until she found a new direction in QAnon, and then she jumped down the rabbit hole with both feet.

In a video she posted to social media, Babbitt railed against the general indifference she saw to the dangers posed by the secret cabal. "You guys refuse to choose America over your stupid political party, I am so tired of it."[15] The day before, on January 5, Ashli tweeted:

> Nothing will stop us . . . they can try and try and try but the storm is here and it is descending upon DC in less than 24 hours . . . dark to light![16]

Conspiracy theories like QAnon exploit vulnerable people during times of personal crisis, especially those who might lack social support networks. Preliminary research has suggested that one of the consequences of posttraumatic stress disorder (PTSD) is the feeling of not belonging. This may translate to members of the U.S. military being especially vulnerable to targeted recruitment. The death of Ashli Babbitt (a veteran of four tours) and the disturbing fact that 20 percent of those arrested for insurrection were veterans or active service soldiers offer a possible link between PTSD and belief in QAnon.

The other QAnon woman who died that day was Rosanne Boyland, a 34-year-old from Kennesaw, Georgia, who had come to DC "keep the fight alive." Boyland was trampled to death in the crowd.[17] Her family had begged her not to attend the rally, and she'd promised to stay out of the fray; but she wanted to show her support for the president, from whom she fervently believed that Democrats had stolen the election. Outside the Capitol steps she was caught up in the melee that narrowly converged into an entrance on the west promenade, the second level of the building. Boyland was pinned to the ground and trampled during the clashes between rioters and the police. After Boyland lost her footing in the crush, her friend Justin Winchell tried to pull her to safety.[18] "By the time that they decided to pick the person up and give them to the police officer, she had blue lips and blood was coming out her nose."[19] Despite administering CPR, by the time police finally reached her at 5 p.m. it was to no avail. Rosanne Boyland died at the scene.[20]

Like Ashli, Rosanne's family knew that she was troubled. Many women drawn to QAnon are vulnerable due to the circumstances in their lives. Rosanne had been a drug user who fought her addiction, cleaned up her life, and hoped to become a sobriety counselor.[21] She embraced Q mythology seemingly as a replacement drug. On her Facebook page, Rosanne disseminated QAnon content, reposted QAnon social media influencers, and praised President Trump.[22] One family member made a statement the following day, on January 7: "I've never tried to be a political person but it's my own personal belief that the president's words incited a riot that killed four of his biggest fans last night and I believe that we should invoke the 25th amendment at this time."[23]

It is important to note that QAnon grew exponentially in a very short time. Its spread is inextricably linked to the pandemic. In March 2020, QAnon Facebook groups increased by 120 percent, and posts with QAnon hashtags or content increased by a whopping 174 percent; one journalist tracking the impact of QAnon found that between January and August 2020, Instagram Q-supporting accounts "generated 63 million interactions and 133 million video views."[24] This was a massive amount, compared to other rival trending hashtags like #MeToo or #BlackLivesMatter.

A London think tank focused on QAnon's radicalization; the Institute for Strategic Dialogue recorded 69 million tweets, 487,000 Facebook posts, and 281,000 Instagram posts using Q hashtags or phrases from 2017 to 2020.[25] Twitter finally removed 7,000 accounts associated with QAnon in July 2020. Twitter explained that it had determined QAnon was an "online effort with the potential to lead to offline harm"—thus violating one of its terms of service. Facebook followed suit in August 2020, removing thousands more groups and accounts on their platform and on Instagram.[26]

Eventually most of the social media giants escalated anti-QAnon measures, including banning QAnon-promoting advertisements. Platforms like Etsy that previously sold Q-branded merchandise like T shirts, hats, and even onesies for babies banned the group and removed much of their goods. Like Tracy Beanz's use of Patreon and PayPal in her QAnon YouTube videos, the popularity of Etsy paraphernalia suggests one of the primary drivers for QAnon: that it was monetized. A handful of influencers and high-profile conspiracists (like General Michael Flynn) made a lot of money by selling Q-branded items. According to Vice News, many links with QAnon content on the right-wing Parler platform, QAnon Subreddits, or other Q-promoting posts led to General Flynn's legal defense fund website. Flynn's website contained Q merchandise until it was taken down after the failed January 6 insurrection.

Facebook determined that QAnon was dangerous relatively late in the game (for example, it was two years after Reddit had banned them), initially investigating how QAnon had hijacked the #SaveTheChildren hashtag to use as a recruiting and fundraising tool. In the fall of 2020, Facebook's dangerous organizations unit, led by a team of trained counterterrorism experts, announced that the platform would "remove any Facebook Pages, Groups and Instagram accounts representing QAnon, even if they contained no violent content."[27] While thousands of pages and groups were removed overnight, the platform wasn't able to eliminate all of the content—for example, posts by individuals that did not violate their terms of service.[28]

However, Facebook could not eliminate all of the conspiracy-laden groups and posts. In the lead up to January 6, 2021, social media had whipped up sentiment and outrage—encouraging thousands to flock to DC to "stop the steal." For Rosanne Boyland and Ashli Babbitt, it was too little too late.

Martyrs for the Cause

Ashli and Rosanne were mourned as martyrs to QAnon, with Babbitt described as a patriot whose "heart was pumping with fire and hope." Anonymous accounts hounded Republican politicians insisting that they "show support for our fallen MAGA patriots."[29] Posts on the far- right messaging app Parler honored Babbitt (in all caps in the original post):

> WOMAN MURDERED BY DC POLICE IDENTIFIED: ASHLI BABBIT WAS A WAR HERO, WHO SERVED 14 YEARS OVER FOUR TOURS OF IRAQHER LIFE WAS SENSELESSLY TAKEN TODAY WHEN SHE WAS GUNNED DOWN, DEFENDING OUR NATION'S FREEDOM TO HER LAST BREATHPRAY FOR HER FAMILY, AND MAY GOD WELCOME HER INTO HIS EVERLASTING KINGDOM.[30]

Babbitt's honorific, however, was short-lived. She was declared a QAnon martyr on January 6, but 24 hours later, supporters decided that she was actually an undercover Antifa deep state operative and a traitor to the cause. Although Ashli lost her martyr status among QAnon, other white nationalist movements—like White Power, National Socialists, Accelerationists, Boogaloo, and neo-Nazis—immediately adopted her as a symbol of "White America."[31]

Ashli's martyrdom seems to have "sprung from the Proud Boys ecosystem," the racist group President Trump instructed to "stand back and stand by." The Proud Boys emulated (plagiarized) the mantra repeated by Black Lives Matter supporters during the summer of 2020, insisting that their followers "say her name" and chanting "her name was Ashli Babbitt," echoing BLM's rallying cries about Breonna Taylor.[32]

Escalating Violence in the Name of Q

Ashli, Rosanne, and the insurrectionists at the Capitol on January 6, 2021, were not the first instances of QAnon violence. Since the conspiracy first emerged in 2017, people have been killed, and there have been numerous kidnapping attempts foiled by law enforcement. Many of the more violent incidents involved men, and so the media has focused on these acts of violence without mentioning the increase in QAnon women.

What is clear is that leading up to the failed insurrection, QAnon violence was on the rise. In the following list, we present the events leading up to the FBI designating QAnon as potentially a terrorist threat to the country and show the variety of crimes affiliated with the conspiracy even after the designation. Women were arrested for 5 of the 12 crimes from 2018–2020.[33] Most of the women were guilty of kidnapping or threats against politicians. Coincidentally, many of the women who were so concerned about saving the children were implicated in kidnapping attempts of their own children after having lost custody.

- One of the earliest incidents included a terrorist attempt against the Hoover Dam. On June 15, 2018, Matthew Wright blocked the bridge to the Hoover Dam using an armored vehicle with Q slogans (release the OIG Report). He was unhappy that President Trump had not yet made the mass arrests of the democratic Satan worshippers (predicted in the Q drops). Wright had two military-style rifles, two handguns and 900 rounds of ammunition in his vehicle, and eventually pled guilty to terrorism charges.[34]

- A man in California was arrested December 19, 2018, after law enforcement found bomb-making materials in his car, in a plot to blow up a display in Springfield, Illinois. "The man allegedly was planning to 'blow up a satanic temple monument' in the Capitol rotunda in Springfield, Illinois, to 'make Americans aware of Pizzagate and the New World Order.'"[35]

- In January 2019, Buckey Wolfe killed his brother James in Seattle by stabbing him in the head with a four-foot-long sword because he was certain that a lizard person had replaced his brother. Wolfe called 911 after he ran his brother through and told the dispatcher that he'd killed his brother because he thought his brother was a lizard. The recorded 911 call includes him saying, "Kill me, kill me, I can't live in this reality," and "God told me he was a lizard."[36]

- In March 13, 2019, Anthony Comello killed a mob boss from the Gambino crime family on Staten Island. The 24-year-old "ardently believed that Francesco (Franky Boy) Cali was a prominent member of the deep state and an appropriate target." Comello was certain President Trump would protect him and give him a full pardon.[37] Comello was found mentally unfit to stand trial; his lawyer Robert Gottlieb used his belief in the QAnon conspiracy as proof of his mental unfitness.

- In December 2019, Cynthia Abcug a 50-year-old woman from Parker, Colorado, was charged with conspiracy to commit kidnapping after becoming obsessed with "evil Satan worshipping pedophiles."[38] Her descent into the conspiracy theory was triggered by her son's removal from her custody. Cynthia suffered from a psychological disorder, Munchausen syndrome by proxy, where a parent fabricates their child's illness to garner sympathy and attention. Cynthia had stopped going to therapy and started meeting in person and online with other QAnon followers at all hours of the evening to discuss "evil Satan worshipers" and pedophiles.[39] Abcug kidnapped the child and traveled across the country, using an "underground railroad" network of QAnon supporters, before being arrested in Montana. In September 2020, Cynthia pled not guilty to second-degree kidnapping.[40]

- In April 2020, Eduardo Moreno, a train engineer from San Pedro, California, derailed a train because he believed the USNS *Mercy* hospital ship was part of suspicious plot to spread (and not cure) the coronavirus.[41]

- On April 30, 2020, Jessica Prim, a 37-year-old QAnon supporter from Illinois, was arrested after live streaming on Facebook her journey to New York City to "take out" Joe Biden and Hillary Clinton. A post on her Facebook page read: "Hillary Clinton and her assistant, Joe Biden and Tony [John's brother] Podesta need to be taken out in the name of Babylon! I can't be set free without them gone."[42] Prim, a stripper, was traveling with a dozen knives. She said she was driving to the USNS *Comfort*, a hospital ship docked in New York harbor, but accidentally ended up at the USS *Intrepid* aircraft carrier museum. Prim felt like "I was supposed to come to the *Comfort* and get some help because *I* was the coronavirus."[43] She claimed to have been inspired by President Trump: "I was watching the press conferences with Donald Trump on TV and felt like he was talking to me."[44]

- In July 2020, Canadian military reservist Corey Hurren rammed his truck through the gates of the Prime

Minister Justin Trudeau's residence in Ottawa. He was also "accused of uttering a threat to 'cause death or bodily harm' to Trudeau."[45] In March 2021 he was sentenced to six years in prison.

- In August 2020, Cecilia Fulbright rammed her vehicle into a crowd of civilians because she was under the impression they had kidnapped a girl for human trafficking. She was charged with driving while intoxicated and aggravated assault with a deadly weapon. Two of Fulbright's acquaintances claimed that she had become deeply absorbed in the QAnon conspiracy, including talking about how Trump was "literally taking down the cabal and the pedophile ring," and they said she continued to describe herself as a follower of QAnon even after her arrest.[46]

- In March 2020, Neely Petrie-Blanchard tried to kidnap her two daughters from their grandmother who had legal custody. Neely's Facebook wall was plastered with QAnon slogans and the hashtag #TheGreatAwakening. She posted pictures of herself wearing Q-branded clothing. She then hired a legal consultant to help her get her children back, and when her efforts failed, she shot him—believing he was working against her interests.[47]

- In October 2020, Emily Jolley fled with her 6-year-old son, whose father had sole legal custody. After a supervised visit, she took the child and disappeared and was later arrested in Oregon. Like Petrie-Blanchard, Jolley was a member of the Sovereign Citizens Movement,

> but her social media was full of references to Trump and QAnon. She had even posted an article claiming that Child Protective Services (CPS) stole children to drain them of adrenochrome, the special chemical that the evil cabal drank, a central tenet of the QAnon conspiracy.[48]

While the country has focused on the demographics of the insurrectionists, the role of women might be less obvious. Among the crimes listed above, between 2018 and 2020, women were involved in half. As of the time of this writing, there were 27 people who participated in the Capitol insurrection on January 6, 2021, who were connected to QAnon. The offenders for all QAnon attacks since 2018 come from 27 states, including 7 from California, 4 from Arizona, 3 from New Jersey, 3 from New York, 3 from Pennsylvania, and 3 from Virginia.

The media may have viewed what happened in DC on January 6 as largely male dominated, and in doing so inadvertently erased the role that QAnon women have played in the escalating violence. As with terrorist groups, women play important behind-the-scenes roles encouraging, supporting, and sustaining the violence. The QAnon Shaman Jacob Chansley left a note threatening Vice President Pence on the VP's chair. As with terrorist groups, Chansley's mother fully supported his actions; Martha Chansley defended her son as a great patriot, a veteran, and a person who loves this country.[49]

On January 6, 2021, there were many women in the crowd, egging the men on and even participating in the violence. To date, 20 women have been indicted, and every day the DC court files charges against more insurrectionists. Among one of the first to be indicted for her actions at the Capitol was Army veteran Jessica Watkins, who had recruited members for a local militia group and was affiliated with the Oath Keepers.[50]

Examining why QAnon is so popular among women and charting women's involvement with this dangerous conspiracy will help identify opportunities to help women exit from QAnon. We can draw on our experiences with women exiting violent extremist organizations to ascertain the best ways to help women find a pathway out.

A Brief History of Women and Extremism

Throughout the twentieth century, women have been active in violent insurgencies and conflicts that historically spawned terrorist groups, from the far left to the far right. Women's involvement has spanned the spectrum from disseminating propaganda, to planning operations, to carrying out the attacks themselves. Women were often active in groups that prioritized women's rights or made equality part of their political platform.

In Germany in the 1960s, the Baader-Meinhof gang's ideological leader Ulrike Meinhof, after whom the group was named, was a key organizer and ideologue. Women have historically formed the bulk of behind-the-scenes support networks for terror groups, maintaining safe houses, ferrying weapons, but also engaged in occasional frontline activities such as bank robbery and driving the getaway car (e.g., Astrid Proll). The Red Zora (Rote Zora), a breakaway faction of Baader-Meinhof, exclusively female, was responsible for 45 arson and bombing attacks from 1977 to 1988,[51] including an attack against the German supreme court to protest the country's abortion laws, the spread of sex shops, and the proliferation of multinational corporations; the group actively opposed genetic engineering, pornography, and the objectification of women.[52]

Elsewhere in Europe, women comprised about 17 percent of Euskadi Ta Askatasuna (ETA), the Basque separatist party, and often joined as part of family units. According to Carrie Hamilton, although men dominated the leadership in its first decade, in the 1960s a few women joined the movement. Some took up arms and engaged in frontline militant activities. By the end of that decade, "Yoyes" Dolores Gonzalez Katarain became part of the leadership, which, contrary to popular opinion, did not alleviate ETA's use of violence.[53] In 2009, ETA appointed Iratxe Sorzabal Diaz as its leader and four other women as commanders; one Spanish newspaper concluded:

> The five [women] are thought to have been closely involved in the decision to step up violence in a renewed attempt to force Madrid to grant the northwestern Basque region full independence from Spain.[54]

In Northern Ireland, women made up a critical part of the Provisional IRA (PIRA). Most of the women, like their sisters in Germany and Spain, provided much-needed support for the men. Republican women in Belfast and Derry became the not-so-secret weapon of PIRA—lookouts who raised a racket by banging garbage-can lids when British soldiers approached, shielded fugitive gunmen when squads of troops swooped into the Catholic ghettos or planted bombs. Over time women became more involved in frontline activities and in violence. Women began carrying weapons and taking part in armed encounters against British soldiers. Some of the women went on "active service," meaning that they took on military roles and engaged in frontline attacks.[55]

Among the Palestinian terrorist organizations, women filled a variety of roles—both supportive and operational. A handful of women were notorious hijackers or planted explosive ordinance. Perhaps the most notorious woman to engage in terrorism was Leila Khaled who became a poster child for Palestinian militancy in the 1970s after she participated in several hijackings against Israeli targets for the Popular Front for the Liberation of Palestine. Another militant, Dalal Mughrabi, a member of Fatah, became a source of inspiration after she organized a deadly roadside attack in March 1978 in which 37 Israelis died. These women helped inspire an entire generation of young girls in the refugee camps to follow in their footsteps. Poems, songs, and stories were written about Khaled in a dozen languages; a public square, soccer tournament, youth center, and girls' summer camp were named for Mughrabi.[56]

There was an observable shift in the Middle East—from secular organizations engaged in terrorism during the 1960s and 1970s to later groups advocating the use of violence based on religious justifications. These new groups, in part because of their religious (patriarchal) traditions, did not necessarily view women as potential recruits for the cause. Initially, some religious terrorist groups prevented women's participation and, on a few occasions, even sent would-be female recruits to rival (secular) groups.[57]

Women in extremist movements have stereotypically been portrayed as lacking agency. Lumped together with children, women are perceived as having been manipulated into believing extremist ideologies, and they are described as merely playing peripheral or supporting roles. This is despite the fact that 53 percent of Nigerian suicide bombers from Boko Haram and 30 percent of LTTE (Liberation Tigers of Tamil Eelam) and PKK (Kurdistan Workers' Party) suicide bombers in Sri Lanka and Turkey were women. Nevertheless, the trope has always been that "a man made her do it." Dangerous and misleading, it removes the responsibility from women—and dismisses a critical aspect of the emotional and behavioral aspects that are presenting in the vast majority of extremist organizations: the search for identity and belonging. The urge to belong, have purpose, and feel power is essential in successful radicalization, recruitment, and retention.

On the far right, women have been involved in terrorist groups like the KKK (Ku Klux Klan) for over 100 years, but they were often less visible as operatives, taking on a more traditional domestic role, even as they egged on the men or encouraged their children to follow in their father's footsteps. To this day women on the far right are presented with a regressive choice, according to Seyward Darby, since being a mother in the extremist far right is a revered status—having white babies to perpetuate the white race is their ultimate contribution.[58] In an op-ed in the *New York Times,* Annie Kelly explained that it was:

> something of a general rule that there are always more women involved than first meets the eye. It is generally men who grab the headlines, either because they are in leadership positions or commit acts of violence, while women are used for the behind-the-scenes work of recruitment and organizing.[59]

Pizzagate

Women have been a part of the QAnon conspiracy from its earliest days, before there was a Q. QAnon emerged in 2017, however Pizzagate—a conspiracy theory that evolved from John Podesta's hacked emails, published by Wikileaks—occurred the year before in December 2016. In Podesta's emails to friends and family, he often suggested "getting a pizza" at a popular local DC haunt, Comet Ping Pong Pizzeria. The conspiracy theory began on 4chan and speculated about links between Comet and the Democratic Party. It reached critical proportions as many became convinced that references to "cheese pizza" (CP) were actually code for "child pornography."

The conspiracy theory was popularized by women like Liz Crokin,[60] a self-declared follower of QAnon. She became infamous for targeting Chrissy Teigen and connecting her to Pizzagate.[61] Crokin is the original source for Roseanne Barr's tweet alleging that President Trump had released hundreds of children:

> President Trump has freed so many children held in bondage to pimps all over this world. Hundreds each month. He has broken up trafficking rings in high places everywhere.[62]

Crokin was also the inspiration for Marjorie Taylor Greene's conversion to QAnon, according to Greene's videos.[63]

Other prominent women that helped disseminate the baseless conspiracy theory include Ann Vandersteel, president of the far-right media outlet YourVoice America, who is firmly on the fringe.[64] The theory gelled further in a series of now banned alt-right Subreddit discussions in which women played a pivotal role and then spiraled out of control. The pizzeria owner, who had never met Hillary Clinton, began receiving phone and text messages threatening him and his staff. At the time, despite the clear and present danger, social media companies did virtually nothing to deescalate the danger.

Pizzagate culminated with Edgar Madison Welch, a father of two and volunteer firefighter from Salisbury, North Carolina, driving hundreds of miles to Washington, DC, in hopes of rescuing the children he believed were being held in the basement of the pizzeria and who were about to be trafficked. Welch entered Comet Ping Pong Pizzeria carrying a fully loaded AR-15 military-style rifle, a .38 revolver, a shotgun, and a knife, seeking to investigate the Pizzagate rumor. After a panicky evacuation by Comet's servers and customers, which included several children, he fired his rifle a few times at a locked closet door, hitting the computer equipment inside. There were no children in the basement—in fact, there was no basement. After a 45-minute standoff, Welch surrendered peacefully to the DC Metro Police, having found no evidence that underage children were being harbored in the restaurant.[65]

A mass casualty event had been narrowly averted.[66] Welch pled guilty and received four years imprisonment on federal charges of assault with a dangerous weapon and transporting a firearm over state lines. It is worth mentioning that despite Edgar Welch announcing that he had been wrong,[67] in April 2020 another QAnon supporter, Ryan Jaselskis, set fire to Comet Ping Pong pizzeria. Most QAnon devotees believe still that children were being trafficked inside the restaurant, and no amount of disconfirming evidence will shake their certainty.

Maternal Instinct and Domestic Terrorism in QAnon

Women constitute the softer side of QAnon, posting messages in pastel colors and capitalizing on women's maternal instinct to protect children. The participation of women in QAnon is not accidental. The women who flocked to QAnon often did so not because of violent radicalization but from the perspective of wanting to "save the children." This is fundamental to understanding why women are willing targets for QAnon. The conspiracy appealed to the "angels of their better nature" and traded on their innate altruism: Some accounts have referred to this group as the QAmoms.[68] Many of the images flooding their social media timelines include graphic content of children—bruised, beaten, and battered—precisely intended to instigate an immediate reaction and activate women's maternal instincts. "[T]here is something about the intense focus on harm being done to children and the graphic nature of the images and videos associated with Q . . . that is catered toward evoking shock and empathy."[69]

QAnon, like the terrorist group ISIS, understands that one of the *best* ways to appeal to women is by exploiting their altruism. Many far-right narratives appeal to their base to "save the white race" or "save individual liberties." These are popular with angry or disillusioned young men, whereas QAnon's narrative to "save the children" evokes a visceral—even maternal—reaction among women. The phrase "save the children" has been part of QAnon's successful pivot into mainstream culture and was taken from one of the oldest charities dedicated to child protection. QAnon believers spread false claims that Hillary Clinton trafficked and abused children and harvested adrenochrome from their blood. Both Jessica Watkins and Cecilia Fulbright were crying when they were arrested. Cecilia insisted that she was saving the children and that the target (i.e., the actual victims of the vehicle ramming) "were pedophiles and had kidnapped a girl for human trafficking."[70]

> Fulbright reportedly confessed to ramming the Dodge Caravan because she believed she was saving a child from a pedophile she had been following, but her account "did not match the timeline or any facts or evidence," according to the affidavit.[71]

A QAnon survivor, Lenka Perron, spent hours pouring over stories about the evil people in power. She all but ceased doing anything else like cooking, cleaning, or caring for her three children. Lenka was obsessed with tracking down the cabal. She told herself that all of it was worth it: "She was saving the country and the children would benefit."[72] Far-right conspiracy theorists and neo-Nazis often make claims about defending children.[73]

Annie Kelly notes that despite such sentiments arising from positive motivations, QAnon women can be very dangerous:

> Conspiracy theories are no less dangerous even when they claim to be driven by maternal love. At the heart of QAnon lies an undeniably frightening ethos that demands harsh punishment, even execution, for its ever-growing list of political enemies. History teaches us that sex panics do not end well for society's most vulnerable minorities; QAnon and its offshoots must be rejected in the strongest possible terms.[74]

Because QAnon was linked to all the crimes listed at the beginning of this chapter,[75] Christopher Wray, director of the FBI, warned that the conspiracy theory posed a domestic terrorism threat.[76] In 2019, Wray had explained why the country was predisposed for domestic extremism. At the time Wray was talking about the growth of the extremist right wing, but the same conditions that made radicalization possible made people vulnerable to dangerous conspiracy theories. There was an economic downturn, people felt the government was overreaching, and they were spending more time online. Lenka Perron described what had made her receptive to the conspiracy's messaging and could persist well after the Trump presidency: widespread distrust of authority, anger at powerful figures in politics and in the news media, and growing income inequality.[77]

The once-fringe conspiracy theory went mainstream under the conditions of the COVID-19 pandemic: Lockdowns, economic insecurity, and extended hours online became the norm for many. The surge in QAnon posts correlate to the stay-at-home orders issued as the pandemic raged across the country and the globe.

It should not be surprising that many of the QAnon-affiliated individuals arrested after the failed insurrection at the Capitol had a history of trauma or mental illness. According to the data collected by Michael Jensen, director of the PIRUS (Profiles of Individual Radicalization in the United States) project at the University of Maryland,

> More than 40% of the 31 QAnon offenders who committed crimes before and after the Capitol riot radicalized after experiencing a traumatic event. These experiences included the premature deaths of loved ones; physical, emotional, or sexual abuse; and post-traumatic stress disorder from military service.[78]

Women associated with QAnon had even higher rates of trauma.

> 83% of the female offenders in this [University of Maryland] sample experienced trauma prior to their radicalization that involved the physical and/or sexual abuse of their children by a romantic partner or family member. These women appear to have been drawn to the QAnon conspiracy theory due to a narrative that casts followers as key players in the fight against child exploitation and sex trafficking.[79]

Women's individual identity and sense of belonging play an essential role in how QAnon appeals to women. Up until recently, our understanding of extremism tended to be limited to religious-based movements or groups that were fighting over ethnicity, heritage, religious background, or disputed territory. Our ability to appreciate the danger posed by women has improved as more people study the phenomenon of female terrorism and as journalists stop assuming that women lack agency when they perpetrate acts of violence or terror. As the United States fractures, with political extremists on all sides turning to violent ideologies to address their grievances, women are playing a major role.

One of the primary reasons why conspiracy theories have seemingly metastasized in the last few years is that the people who believe in them tend to believe in more than one at a time. Like potato chips, people can't stop at just one. People who are vulnerable to one conspiracy theory are significantly more likely to believe in other related, adjacent, or overlapping conspiracy theories.

People who believe in QAnon also tend to be vaccine skeptics or anti-vaccine (anti-vaxxers). They are most likely to be anti-mask and assume either that COVID-19 is a hoax, exaggerated, or a deliberate plot from China to undermine the presidency of Donald Trump. Often they are also suspicious of 5G technology. As we show in Chapter 5, QAnon has managed to fold in local grievances when it moves from one location to the next. People who oppose 5G technologies worry that there is some malevolent plan behind the new technology. It is why on Christmas Day, December 25, 2020, Anthony Quinn Warner blew up a recreational vehicle outside the Nashville headquarters for AT&T. The pandemic and ensuing stay-at-home orders offered an intersection of beliefs: QAnon was able to overlap with all the other adjacent or complementary conspiracies like COVID-19 denial and vaccine skepticism. Parenting and anti-vaccine groups on Facebook blamed dark forces for the COVID-19 crisis, which spilled over into anti-mask, anti-lockdown sentiment.

QAnon includes people who layer anti-Semitic beliefs along with the QAnon conspiracy theory. A notable example was Mary Ann Mendoza, originally scheduled to speak on the second night of the 2020 Republican National Convention about her son's 2014 death at the hands of a drunk driver who was an undocumented alien. As the founder of Angel Families, whose children have died in an untimely fashion, she'd been selected to be a member of Donald Trump's campaign advisory board. While spouting QAnon conspiracies, she took to Twitter to recommend reading about the Rothschild family's plot to take over the world.[80] Mary Ann posted Twitter threads that claimed that the Federal Reserve had sunk the *Titanic* and that every president between John F. Kennedy and Donald Trump had been a "slave president" enthralled by the global cabal. The Twitter account she recommended, @WarNuse, promoted *The*

Protocols of the Elders of Zion.[81] At the eleventh hour, she was abruptly yanked off the RNC-scheduled program even after her prepared remarks had gone out to the assembled crowd.

People who post QAnon materials offer provocative and compelling narratives about how they *discovered* the truth. These stories might captivate the reader, but they offer little by way of evidence. In QAnon chatrooms and discussion boards, "Q proselytizers" impart their virtual pitch by encouraging others to "Do your own research" or to "*Find out what they're not telling you.*"[82] Thus, the proselytizers urge people to discover for themselves what is going on. As Lili Loofbourow, a journalist with *Slate,* puts it, "[This approach] expresses full faith in the reader's abilities to discover the truth, promises a light at the end of the tunnel, and appears to invite independent verification and free inquiry."[83] "Do your own research" can also be interpreted as: "Don't trust other people. Don't trust institutions. Listen to me."[84]

QAnon Jumps the Shark: Social Media Influencers and the Spread of the QCult

Once QAnon moved from encrypted pages and anonymous message boards to popular sites like Facebook and Instagram, it appealed to a completely new audience: soccer moms, yoga aficionados, and even vegans. Social media influencers in the United States but also in other countries played a crucial role in disseminating the QAnon message to a new demographic: QAmoms.[85]

Krystal Tini, a U.S. social media influencer, entrepreneur, and model has an Instagram page with 100,000 followers, believes in QAnon, and shares posts about the dangers of 5G technology causing COVID-19. She became interested in QAnon because she felt that it "gets people to think for themselves and not become a slave to the mainstream media."[86] Finding the clues and figuring out what all the Q-drops signified made Tini feel smart, special, and empowered.

Because you feel like you are solving a puzzle, it boosts your self-image. As people discover the answer, they feel like they are the only ones who can solve it. People derive a sense of accomplishment and even intellectual superiority over people who have not (yet) seen the light. *Gamifying* QAnon, as we explained in Chapter 1, has real physiological effects on the brain. Solving puzzles as a group creates the feeling of community and shared experiences:

> Everyone has something to focus on, a shared interest, and something to do. The puzzles are often just a way of getting together. If Q drops clues, then you have something to do and you have people to do it with. It's bonding. The same reason puzzles are used for corporate team building exercises or as party games.[87]

Solving a puzzle also encodes information in the brain in a different way than other types of learning. Puzzles and knowledge gained through our own efforts can feel incredibly rewarding and bring a hit of dopamine, the brain's pleasure drug, as a reward.[88] It is plausible that the way QAnon structures the release of information, in the form of Q-drops, sustains user engagement on the platform so that readers never leave.

CNN's Fareed Zakaria explains that this kind of variable schedule of reinforcement keeps people transfixed.[89] Furthermore, the addictive qualities of QAnon followed the development of apps to alert enthusiasts with push notifications the moment a new Q-drop posted to the message boards. But people who believe in QAnon are not figuring out these things for themselves because the Q-drops have pre-seeded conclusions. They point to unrelated events to imbue them with a secret meaning commensurate with the propaganda. Izabella Kaminska, an editor at the *Financial Times,* explains:

> The Q experience combines the thrill of discovery, the excitement of the rabbit hole, [with] the acceptance of a community that loves and respects you. Because you were convinced to "connect the dots yourself" you can see the absolute logic of it. Q does not want you to come to your own conclusions. Q is feeding you conclusions.[90]

The other common experience that happens to people who think they have figured out the puzzle is a proselytizing compulsion that takes hold of them. QAnon "influencer" Rebecca Pfeiffer started sharing information about Q when she felt that she had a moral obligation to her audience to share the content. "I truly believe I owed it to my audience to be more for them during this turning point in our culture."[91] Once a person figures out what is really going on, they feel as if they have a personal responsibility to share this knowledge, and in doing so, empower others. This is why people who fall down the rabbit hole seek to take friends and family along with them.

QAnon claims to have all the answers, but the reality of what is going on is the equivalent of taking the red pill. In the next chapter we explain the psychology of QAnon. Put simply, conspiracy theories elicit strong emotions among their followers, including outrage, fear, or anger that they can share and commiserate with likeminded individuals. Sharing these strong emotions satisfies a basic human need for connection. Many of the women who became ardent supporters of QAnon might also display a certain personality type that is more susceptible to conspiratorial beliefs. Ultimately conspiracy theories feel comforting against the backdrop of a complex and frightening world.

For some women, believing that there is worldwide evil conspiracy manipulating and controlling things is less stressful than believing that bad things happen to good people. In hindsight it is easy now to see how outlandish QAnon claims are, but at the time, for QAnon survivors like Lenka Perron, it was not so clear:

> Looking back, Lenka understands [now] how Q drew her in. Conspiracies were comforting, a way to get her bearings in a chaotic world that felt increasingly unequal and rigged against middle-class people like her. The stories offered agency: Evil cabals could be defeated. A sense that things were out of her control could not. While the theories were fiction, they hooked into an emotional vulnerability that sprang from something real.[92]

QAnon created a virtual community of people with shared values and goals; the price of admission to the club suggested exclusivity and conferred a feeling of pride to its members. This is salient for individuals who may feel socially isolated or lonely, especially during a global pandemic when we no longer socialize as we used to. Conspiracies offer social interactions in a virtual world. However this shared community can easily become an echo chamber. While Lenka stopped feeling isolated and alone, she was going further and further down the QAnon rabbit hole. "She was no longer a lonely victim of a force she did not understand, but now part of a bigger community of people seeking the truth. She loved the feeling of common purpose. They were learning together."[93]

The echo chamber is a result of the ways that social media algorithms suggest new pages or groups, but also if Q-curious people search using one of the well-known hashtags, they will immediately get QAnon materials and nothing else because the hashtag acts like a filter. This is the same phenomenon we have seen in other closed information systems used by neo-Nazi groups or cults (if they allow Internet access). There, algorithms drive people toward more and more extreme ways of thinking.[94] The intersection between women who subscribed to QAnon and were anti-mask or against stay-at-home orders begins to blur one into the other, as QAnon absorbs any adjacent or complementary conspiracy theory.

Facebook encourages likeminded individuals to cluster together, whether through a computer architecture structured to create "filter bubbles"[95] or through what Daniel Kahneman calls "cognitive ease"[96]—our willingness to more easily accept ideas that are familiar and comfortable. We also tend to avoid ideas that would take more effort to accept. Facebook's algorithms can be manipulated to generate an opinion. People who believe in QAnon exhibit a constellation of personality traits. There is some research on "schizotypy"—that is, personality type as a predictor to believing in conspiracies, including distrust, eccentricity, the need to feel special, as well as suspicion of others.[97] Lenka Perron articulated this feeling:

> Q managed to make us feel special, that we were being given very critical information that basically was

> going to save all that is good in the world and the United States. . . . We felt we were coming from a place of moral superiority. We were part of a special club.[98]

In 2020, QAnon appropriated the hashtag #SaveTheChildren from the charity of the same name, leveraging existing human rights and child protection campaigns against their primary inspiration: human trafficking. For a newly initiated QAnon-curious individual, searching for information on social media by using a hashtag refined the results the person would get. Combing through the Internet or social media by using a QAnon hashtag leads one to closed information ecosystems. It is an information bubble in which any disconfirming evidence is excluded; at the same time, it is an echo chamber in which conspiratorial beliefs are reinforced by group dynamics. This is no different than how jihadi groups operate. There are echo chambers and selective information bubbles:

> The bubble communities on Facebook shielded people from alternative views to our own, while also making it easier for views to be reinforced, enhanced—groomed even—towards more radical positions.[99]

QAnon's focus on #SaveTheChildren distracts from the work of nonprofits, like the actual Save the Children charity that has been engaged in child protection for decades. QAnon's obsession diverts resources that could be used to protect vulnerable children or causes law enforcement to waste their time on fictional cases of abuse at the expense of pursuing real cases. While it might seem harmless to post memes, some might escalate to ramming a vehicle into strangers, as was the case with Cecilia Fulbright in Waco, Texas.[100]

QAnon and the COVID-19 Pandemic

The COVID-19 pandemic offered the perfect storm for the QAnon conspiracy theory. A deadly invisible virus was spreading through the world leading to shutdowns, stay-at-home orders, and the opportunity to disseminate disinformation. This situation was further exacerbated by politicians who peddled disinformation that the virus was a hoax or possibly a deliberate bioweapon from China intended to undermine the Trump administration.

The year before, in July 2019, Christopher Wray, the director of the FBI, had explained that the United States was experiencing an uptick in right-wing extremism because of an economic downturn, the perception of government overreach, and sociopolitical conditions: racism, anti-Semitism, Islamophobia, misogyny, and negative reactions to legislation. Wray reiterated these conditions in 2020 to the House Homeland Security Committee—explaining that the pandemic had created an environment in which these preconditions were on steroids.[101]

Reactions to the pandemic from the QAnon community layered the conspiracies. Being anti-mask or insisting that the country reopen immediately went hand in hand with believing in a global conspiracy theory of blood-drinking elites.

Melissa Rein Lively became infamous when she was captured on video, losing her temper and destroying a mask display at Target. Lively had come to QAnon via natural wellness and spirituality websites. After Facebook algorithms suggested QAnon groups and pages, Lively spent her days searching for Q-drops as she drifted further from reality. In additional to consuming QAnon material, she also posted racist and anti-mask memes. One day she posted a burqa-clad woman with the caption, "Fine, I give up. I'll wear the damn mask."[102] Her newfound QAnon enthusiasm had a deleterious impact on her life. She lost her work clients when the Target video went viral, and while she apologized for the outburst, the damage was done.

After leaving QAnon, she explained that the narrative from QAnon, while horrible, offers some consolation. Feeling like there is a plan, even an evil one, is more comforting than thinking bad things happen to good people in a random way:

> The answers are horrifying and will scare you more than reality, but at least you feel oddly comforted, like, 'At least now I have the answer.' They tell you the institutions you're supposed to trust are lying to you. Anybody who tells you that QAnon is wrong [is] a bad guy, including your friends and family. It happens gradually, and you don't realize you're getting more and more deep in it.[103]

Facebook pages about herbal remedies, vaccine skepticism, home birth, and essential oils would suggest QAnon women's groups. There was even a QAnon connection to yoga. QAnon could also be found in the most unexpected platforms, including Nextdoor or Peloton.[104]

QAnon co-opted messages about natural living or health food—but eventually this led to indoctrination into white nationalism and xenophobia. QAnon plays into the concept of purity— the idea that you can "cleanse yourself and your life and your family's life of pollutants."[105] Messages about avoiding genetically modified foods (GMOs) can blur into messages about keeping non-white children out of schools.

QAnon was particularly effective on Instagram where image rather than text content dominates. Instagram's visual mode of communication has a more intense and more emotional appeal.[106] When it comes to disinformation on Instagram, QAnon targeted suburban women whose support could be decisive for Trump's future electoral success. It is a possible explanation for why the suburban soccer moms voted for QAnon-supporting candidates like Marjorie Taylor Greene or Lauren Boebert.[107] In recent years the Grand Old Party has engaged in outreach to suburban women by recruiting more female candidates, however many of the new GOP "stars on the right" are aligned with nativist, paranoid, and conspiracy theories like QAnon.[108] In 2020 there were 97 QAnon-affiliated candidates, over half were women.

The group of QAmoms—comprised of middle-class women interested in natural birth, parenting groups, yoga, or essential oils—explain why recent surveys cite 6 percent of Democrats believe in QAnon.[109] These women were already skeptical of expertise—like anti-vaxxers—and the pandemic confirmed their worst suspicions. Because this was a *novel* coronavirus, the CDC and the FDA appeared inconsistent and changed their recommendations almost weekly. This was partly because the original CDC models had been based on data from Wuhan, China. The models changed after the virus spread to Italy, and again once the United States had data. While some of the modifications occurred as new information came to light, other changes were the result of political pressure from the Trump administration.[110] The fact that recommendations shifted legitimized

QAnon suspicions that the virus was suspect, created in a lab, or altogether a hoax.

The increasing number of women in QAnon means that it is no longer just a right-wing movement; it transcends the political spectrum. Many women who supported Bernie over Hillary ended up in QAnon. It is equally true that women, whom we ordinarily assume are left wing, have also ended up supporting QAnon.

Downward Facing Dog, Upward Facing QAnon

We don't ordinarily associate yoga with extremism. QAnon turned peaceful chanting yogis into conspiracy theory peddling harum-scarum. Once the coronavirus arrived in the United States, the pandemic began to take hold in March 2020. Women who were into essential oils, or natural childbirth, noticed that their Instagram feeds had shifted. Yoga instructors tended to follow one another and famous yogis religiously. If the yogis on one feed began expressing doubts about COVID-19, challenging government lockdowns and mask-wearing requirements, this would spread through the yoga community like wildfire. These were people who were likely to suggest that natural medicine and meditation would offer better protection from the coronavirus than CDC recommendations. By April, Instagram was full of yogis disseminating conspiracy theories, including that 5G technology caused COVID-19 or that any future vaccine developed was really cover for a secret tracking device.[111]

Part of the reason that the pandemic saw the transformation of social media within the typically left wing, essential oil, and yoga crowd was because of the video *Plandemic. Plandemic* was a fake documentary fueling disinformation about the coronavirus. Most social media companies took down the video, but not before 8 million people had watched it within days.[112] The 26-minute video featured a discredited scientist, Dr. Judy Mikovits, describing a secret plot by global elites like Bill Gates and Dr. Anthony Fauci to use the pandemic to profit and seize political power.[113] Mikovits soon became a regular guest on far-right media channels, and she became the darling of far-right publications like *The Epoch Times* and *Gateway Pundit*.[114]

Dr. Christiane Northrup, a notable anti-vaxxer who became famous appearing on Oprah Winfrey's shows, aggressively promoted the video; it then circulated widely through the anti-vaxx community. From there the video was re-posted by a woman, Laura GK, connected to the "open protests," defying the government lockdown and stay-at-home regulations. The next day, Melissa Ackison, one of the 97 QAnon candidates who had lost her bid in the Ohio Republican primary, posted *Plandemic* on Facebook to 20,000 followers. Ackison's post brought the film to the Republican mainstream audience. By May 7, 2020, the movie was discovered by BuzzFeed News and came to the attention of the social media companies.[115]

Anti-vaxxers, Q-conspiracy theorists, and people who oppose government-mandated lockdowns all unified and seized upon the documentary. The video spread from YouTube to Facebook groups with tens of thousands of followers. For the yoga community, the documentary *Plandemic* was the gateway drug into QAnon. Many people who practiced yoga were already suspicious of vaccines. It was common to find that people who practiced yoga were vegetarians or vegans, and they eschewed GMOs (genetically modified food) or Western medicine. Journalist Rachel Greenspan interviewed yogis who subscribed to the QAnon conspiracy theory. They confided to her that "it was not super fringe for people [in yoga] to be doing a raw vegan diet, juice cleanses or fasts, or not 'believe' in Western medicine."[116]

Yoga-centered Instagram accounts went from posting inspirational messages adorned with serene images of light and love to being littered with posts about child exploitation, sex crimes, the devil, and an imminent war between good and evil. The shift was surprising. Most women who followed yoga had never seen a teacher talk about Satan before. Yogis were falling down the QAnon rabbit hole in large numbers.[117] Bizzie Gold, the founder of the very popular Buti Yoga, shared videos about the "Satanic agenda" and adrenochrome to his 56,000 Instagram followers. As we explained in Chapter 1, adrenochrome is the recreational drug of choice of Satan-worshipping elites who harvest it from terrified children, according to QAnon lore. It is the chemical that allows Hollywood elites to maintain their youthful appearance (rather than, say, plastic surgery) and, after Tom Hanks announced his COVID-19 diagnosis from Australia, QAnon insisted that adrenochrome was the cabal's cure for coronavirus.

For several years, Tom Hanks has been a frequent target of QAnon attacks. They accuse him of being part of the pedophile cabal. For many people, this might be surprising since Hanks's likability and contractual obligations make explicit that he can never play a villain in a film. QAnon antipathy toward the congenial Tom Hanks might be because he is a well-known supporter of Democratic candidates. Alternatively, it might be because of the character he played in *The Da Vinci Code*,[118] a film that mainstreamed conspiracies. Their hatred of Hanks is so strong that a QAnon member vandalized his star on the Hollywood Walk of Fame.

QAnon is obsessed with certain celebrities whom they accuse of trafficking in children or torturing them to harvest the much-prized adrenochrome. A series of Facebook posts by QAnon influencer Mama Wolf[119] linked Hillary Clinton, Oprah Winfrey, Bill Gates, Madonna, and Queen Elizabeth to Jeffrey Epstein's child trafficking, adrenochrome harvested from children's blood, and secret messages coded in Trump's tweets.[120] According to these diehard believers, Trump's notorious spelling errors (e.g., "Covfefe") were not actual typos but coded messages made to look like mistakes.

> Pay attention to the bigger picture. Trump has arrested and caught more pedophile and child trafficking rings in the world . . . but I bet you didn't know that because the mainstream (George Soros funded media) make out that he's a moron.[121]

Trump is their hero whose private conduct is more important than his public statements, which might contradict the savior narrative (e.g., Trump walking in on the contestants getting dressed at the Miss Teen USA pageant, bragging that he would date his daughter Ivanka, the hot mic comments about "grabbing women by the p#%&$," or the many allegations of sexual misconduct). To Trump's most devoted supporters, these public actions are nothing more than a cover—constituting what they believe is a 12-dimensional chess game in which Trump is a brilliant strategist.

In addition to social influencers and the yoga community, celebrities also played a role in advancing the QAnon conspiracy theory. They tend to be B-list celebrities like James Woods or Roseanne Barr, who might suffer backlash from fans but since they have already aligned themselves with Trump, the pushback would have minimal effect.

Many A-list celebrities have been the target of constant cyber harassment and allegations of perfidy—from Tom Hanks to Chrissy Teigen and even Ellen DeGeneres. DeGeneres was attacked for allegedly being involved in a scandal involving online furniture retailer Wayfair in the summer of 2020. Questions were raised in July when Reddit users in the "r/conspiracy" group claimed that Wayfair was trafficking children and posted screenshots of furniture with outrageously high price tags. QAnon followers accused Wayfair on Facebook and Instagram of trafficking children in their overpriced closets. Wayfair, like Ikea and many other furniture retailers, uses exotic-sounding names like Neriah, Samiyah, or Yaritza for their designs. The QAnon women found the prices of the closets to be unreasonably expensive (over $10,000) and deduced that they must have children inside them when they were able to match these names with names from the missing children's registry. In one case, Samiyah Mumin, who had gone missing briefly in 2019, took to Facebook live July 10, 2020, to confirm that she was not missing. The accusations persisted despite fact checkers from *USA Today* or Snopes finding zero evidence of any malfeasance.[122]

QAnon also finds opportunities to blame and castigate enemies in random situations of very bad luck. For example, QAnon blamed the explosions at the Beirut port on space lasers; QAnon also argues that "Jewish space lasers" are responsible for the 2020 California wildfires.[123]

QAnon, like all conspiracy theories, is more than just an *idea*. It manifests itself like a living organism and is capable of adapting to changes over time. QAnon has folded other conspiracies into its own master narrative.[124] QAnon integrated conspiracies as diverse as anti-5G, lizard people, and Dominion voting machines having stolen the election from Donald Trump. Like a black hole, it sucked in all the light from nearby galaxies. By incorporating all the different conspiracies, QAnon is a one-stop shop that offers something for everyone.

QAnon is thus able to draw in a diverse group of women. Some are highly educated and not ordinarily associated with ludicrous conspiracies; others are stay-at-home moms who only get their news from Facebook. They are certain that Q is real and protecting the children. Once QAnon shifted its primary social media platform to Instagram, a platform that is more attractive to middle- and upper-class women who would never affiliate with something as crass or trashy as an online conspiracy theory, QAnon expanded beyond the United States.[125]

On Inauguration Day, January 20, 2021, QAnon supporters eagerly waited for "the Storm" that the message boards had predicted for years. The reckoning would result in arrests for all the Democrats and Hollywood elites gathered in DC for Joseph R. Biden's inauguration; they would be marched down Pennsylvania Avenue and executed. QAnon supporters even built a gallows for the occasion. Watching their reactions in real time on the encrypted networks, like Telegram, they narrated the movements of President Trump as he climbed the stairs to Air Force One, expecting him to turn around and unleash "the Storm." When—instead of walking back down the steps—he entered the plane, shut the door, and took off for Florida, their reactions can only be described as apoplectic.

Once again, the oracle that was Q had gotten the prediction wrong. On January 20, 2021, they faced the crisis: What now?

In the wake of Joe Biden's inauguration, many women who were members of QAnon have started to leave the movement. However, according to a survey by the conservative American Enterprises Institute, belief in QAnon remains very high. Based on their survey published February 11, 2021, 29 percent of Republicans maintained a belief in QAnon as do 6 percent of Democrats.[126] QAnon's insertion into traditionally left-wing spaces and its ability to recruit women have afforded it a degree of resilience no matter how often the oracle of Q is wrong.

Some of the women who left QAnon bravely shared their stories with the media and are trying to piece their lives back together. In order to understand the challenges facing those who seek to exit, we need to appreciate how they became involved in the first place. We need to offer simple solutions to help them get out of this dangerous conspiracy theory. We cannot simply abandon friends and family who have become enthralled by the conspiracy theory. In many ways, they are victims of a predatory group who exploited fears for their financial benefit. Slowly pulling the thread allows us to plant a seed of doubt.

We liken it to the analogy of the pebble in the boot. Initially if a pebble gets into your boot, you might be able to ignore it. But eventually the pebble will cause you to limp. The tiny particle irritates, annoys, or even impairs. Finally, you will stop, untie your boot, and shake it out to get rid of the source of pain and discomfort.

In the next chapter, we explore the psychology of conspiracy theory and suggest some possible ways to help people leave QAnon behind.

CHAPTER 3

RED-PILLING, RIGHT-WING CONSPIRACIES, AND RADICALIZATION

Radical right-wing movements, from QAnon to Proud Boys, often talk about "red-pilling,"[1] referencing the Wachowski siblings' movie, *The Matrix* (1999). In the pivotal scene, Morpheus, a mysterious wise man, speaks to Neo, a disgruntled computer hacker who has sought him out:

> "It's that feeling you've had all your life. That feeling that something is wrong with the world. You don't know what it is, but it's there, like a splinter in your mind, driving you mad."

Morpheus explains that Neo lives inside the Matrix, a computer simulation of reality:

> "The Matrix is everywhere," Morpheus says. "It's all around us, even in this room. You can see it out your window, or

> on your television. You feel it when you go to work, or go to church, or pay your taxes. It is the world that has been pulled over your eyes to blind you from the truth."

"What truth?" asks Neo.

> "That you're a slave, Neo. That you, like everyone else, were born into bondage, kept inside a prison that you cannot smell, taste, or touch. A prison of your mind."

Morpheus offers Neo a choice:

> "You take the blue pill [and] . . . wake up in your bed and believe whatever you want to believe. You take the red pill, you stay in wonderland, and I show you how deep the rabbit hole goes."

"Remember that all I am offering is the truth. Nothing more," Morpheus adds.

The co-optation of the Matrix's metaphor by the radical right offers an important insight.

Like Neo, the people who seek out Q-conspiracy theories feel that "something is wrong with the world," that their lives are disconnected from some important truths. Like Neo, they feel that their quest might lead them into danger—yet they "take the red pill."

Conspiracy theories are neither new nor rare. What's different about QAnon is just how many conspiracy theories it accrues under its ideological umbrella, and how many people subscribe to the beliefs. The magnitude of the QAnon phenomenon poses unique threats. Just keeping up with the unfolding narratives is so time-consuming that followers might lose sleep, sever relationships, and lose their jobs, glued to their screens while they "connect the dots" day and night.[2] At the same time as enthusiasts become entangled in conspiratorial thinking, QAnon followers are further radicalized in a community of likeminded others. Most radicalize only in opinion, but a minority will materially support violence, plot attacks, or engage in political violence in real life.

Let's try first to understand the roots of feeling as though "something is wrong with the world" that fuels Q-conspiracy theories. What makes "red-pillers" risk alienating friends and family, or their lives and freedom, as did the insurrectionists who stormed the U.S. Capitol on January 6, 2021? What specific attraction does QAnon hold for women?

Unfreezing and the Tattering of the American Dream

A "cultural worldview" is a psychological term that describes a collection of normative systems that each of us holds. These sets of unwritten rules range from personal values (such as family values or religious beliefs) to social constructions (nations, governments, institutions and social norms). Many, if not all, of our actions are governed by our cultural worldview. We don't do bad things, like stealing, because of laws, morality, and/or religious beliefs. We seek good things, like education and career, because of cultural and social expectations. Altogether, normative systems serve as beacons that guide our life's journey, highlighting major milestones: respecting our elders, studying and training for a career, marrying, going to church, voting, paying taxes.

Sometimes one of these beacons can dim or die out. Maybe one's family is abusive, or maybe one fails out of school; a career may prove unfulfilling, or a political party may disappoint. These instances can be personally distressing. However, an isolated failure of a normative system to deliver on promised value is usually insufficient to send one looking for Morpheus and his red pill. Instead of falling down a rabbit hole, most pick themselves up, dust themselves off, and move on.

But sometimes several worldview tenets betray their value-giving purpose at once. This can happen, for example, if a war destroys families and possessions, weakens the government, and challenges survival. Or a personal crisis like mental illness or substance abuse may tear an individual away from family and friends, may cause the person to lose their job and to experience firsthand government inadequacies and the indifference of the community. In this situation, personal distress is compounded by an unraveling of social norms that tether us to reality. As a result, ideas of right and wrong, of life's goals and meaning, are all upended. This vulnerable state is what psychologists call "unfreezing."[3]

Being unfrozen is unsettling. Humans are social creatures, and communities are built around norms and values. Without them, people feel lost and isolated. Unfrozen individuals are motivated to connect, to find a new system of norms and values, to feel their life moving in a meaningful direction again.

In the state of unfreezing, individuals become easy marks for recruitment by radical groups, including religious cults or terrorist organizations. To an unfrozen individual, a group's ideology is less important than the newfound community. Gratitude for support from a radical group mixes with resentment against those who caused the unfreezing, and, with time, the individual can embrace both the group's radical ideology and its radical agenda. Analysis of terrorist case histories found unfreezing to be a potent mechanism of individual radicalization.

For many QAnon followers, as their cultural worldview fractured and normative systems eroded, they felt lonely and lost, fearful for their future, and angry at those they saw as responsible. This cultural unfreezing was what pushed them down the rabbit hole of right-wing conspiracy theories.

Since the 1990s, the American Dream that many QAnon followers grew up with has been upended by a cruel reality. Ideas they learned to hold dear have been violated before their eyes. Benevolent government, truthful science, moral religion, traditional gender roles—the very people who were supposed to uphold these values have betrayed public trust. Weakening social values contributed to the feeling that "there's something wrong with the world," leading many to seek the "truth" of the red pill—conspiracy theories—and paving the way for QAnon.

The most prevalent Q conspiracies build on genuine facts that reference failures of the current value system. They then supply an explanation for the betrayal ("the conspiracy") and propose the cure ("the plan").

The conspiracies' factual foundation addresses the grievances that brought people to QAnon in the first place. But facts are limiting. Maybe your doctor is dismissive of you, but mine is actually nice. Your grievance with the government is different from mine, and as I listen to you tell the facts, they may sound like you were part of the problem. Facts anchor an individual's experience and keep it from joining the swelling wave of similar experiences. An individual is left alone with their own anger, fear, and doubt. Fiction, on the other hand, can amplify and explain the emotions stirred by facts. "Doctors make our children sick by injecting them with vaccines to profit off the suffering." The facts of individual experiences that kept us rooted to our private fears and anger are replaced by communal fiction. Fanning the flames of strong emotions, lies can validate painful individual experiences and build a community around a shared emotional truth.

The Lie's Emotional Truth

Imagine being cheated by a car mechanic. You feel violated, even made a fool of. The financial injury is multiplied by moral outrage and by fear of future violations. You tell your friends, in person or on Facebook, about your experience.

One of them says, "Car mechanics are always out to cheat you. They're all like that."

This is probably an exaggeration, if you stop and think. But do you want to? Because another option provided by your friend's statement is to feel better about having been cheated. Discernment takes effort and gets you nothing but conflict. By contrast, nodding along to the lie bolsters the social connection and gets you out of the unpleasant feelings. Now it's not just you who suffered at a mechanic's dishonest hands: It's millions of people, and they can't all be fools, so neither are you.

Another friend says, "Do you know how much mechanics scam off people like us? My friend's neighbor is a mechanic, and he has a boat and a huge house, wears a Rolex watch, and he takes sailing vacations in Europe!"

You may wonder if there's more to the story than the friend is revealing, if perhaps the friend's neighbor is more than just a mechanic, or perhaps it's not actually his house, or maybe the Rolex is fake. But a more inviting choice is to indulge in the outrage suggested by this statement, an outrage that so well resonates with your own. Now you're justified in your feeling. Instead of cowering in personal embarrassment over having been cheated, you swell up in collective anger.

A third friend chimes in, "I've read there's an agreement between car manufacturers and mechanics to keep secret information about catastrophic design flaws that kill thousands of drivers every year. The mechanics get bonuses for covering up, so the manufacturers don't have to face public outrage or invest in redesign."

You think back to something you read somewhere (or maybe you heard?) about cases where there really were design flaws that car manufacturers kept hidden to minimize cost, and people actually died as a result. Chills run down your spine. You're scared. But this kind of distant and diffused danger is better than the personal disappointment you started with: Now you have someone other than yourself to blame. What's better, the fear you now feel about evil mechanics and greedy car manufacturers is shared by friends, and a problem shared is a problem halved! You feel seen and supported instead of insignificant and isolated. If someone pointed out the "facts"—that there are conscientious mechanics, that most don't get rich off customers, and that there is no secret deal between car manufacturers and mechanics—this would challenge all that you've gained by accepting the fiction and drag you right back into feeling bad about yourself and fearful of the future.

The fiction allows a current of shared emotion to flood the minutiae of facts. Shared emotions create a community, washing away the moral injury. While we cannot be certain about secret cabals or evil mechanics, we *can* be certain of how we feel. In the time of challenged certitudes, that emotional truth is within our grasp. For some, it becomes the only truth worth reaching for.

An emotional truth or tenet lies beneath every lie of QAnon. Unearthing these will help us understand QAnon followers. This chapter will consider four major truths that gave rise to

QAnon lies. For each, we will suggest a psychological link to the unfreezing (worldview-tenet cracking) that likely contributed to far-right radicalization and pinpoint the unique features that make women especially vulnerable to this conspiracy theory. Finally, we will connect these truths to the QAnon lies, tracing narrative elements of the their fiction to their psychological origins.

True Lies

Disgust with Government and Hollywood Elites

Perhaps the most obvious major truth that has led to an explosion of QAnon followers has been the public's growing revulsion at the moral failings of powerful people. The U.S. government has been marred by embarrassing sex scandals for over two decades. In 1998, President Clinton famously (and falsely) claimed, "I did not have sexual relations with that woman" about an affair he had with a staffer 27 years his junior. In 2016, New York congressman and New York City mayoral candidate Anthony Weiner denied "with certitude" explicit communications with a 15-year-old, only to later admit the truth. As the Weiner scandal unfolded, his wife Huma Abedin—an aide to the former secretary of state and then-presidential candidate Hillary Clinton—had her laptop seized by the authorities. The laptop contained some of Hillary Clinton's emails relevant to the controversy about her illegally using a personal server to send official communications, an issue that affected the presidential election that soon followed.[4]

While the transgressions by these two men were disgusting, it was their denials that may have done the most damage to the credibility of the government, especially to the Democratic Party to which both belonged. The violations were shameful; the denials followed by reluctant admissions of guilt were embarrassing.

Research shows that shame arises from violating *moral* norms, while embarrassment comes from violating *social* norms.[5] Shame is reserved for more serious transgressions and is mostly internalized. Embarrassment may occur over a relatively lesser failing, but it requires outside observers to witness it. One can be ashamed of stealing something whether or not one is caught. On the other hand, being falsely accused of stealing is embarrassing, though not shameful. Therefore, while the shame of the extramarital affairs was incumbent upon the men responsible, the subsequent embarrassment resulting from repeated public lies and eventual confessions was something the public shared. We, the U.S. citizens, were made to witness and to feel embarrassed in real time, and so the political became personal.

The manner in which the government dispatched Clinton's and Weiner's failings left many observers dissatisfied. By violating social norms through sexual misconduct, and by their bad faith denials, high-ranking politicians left citizens disillusioned with them and with the party that failed to properly sanction them. For many QAnons, the political elites lost moral authority and credibility. As a result, they rejected the Democratic Party, if not the entire government. One of the worldview tenets was cracked.

Oddly, there was no parallel outrage when sex scandals erupted over Republicans— South Carolina's Mark Sanford or Iowa's Larry Craig, for example. One reason for less notoriety in these sex scandals may be because Republican politicians didn't feel the need to go on a media tour to explain themselves or because the media devoted less attention to them. Another possibility is that, being more conservative, Republican voters were more outraged about sex scandals than Democrats, and Republican bias against Democratic politicians made them see Clinton and Weiner as more disgusting than Sanford and Craig.

The fact that these scandals were related to *sexual* misconduct means that women were disproportionally affected. Women tend to be more sexually conservative than men[6] and less comfortable with violations of sexual norms. In fact, women, rather than men, are the guardians of sexual standards for behavior and attitudes: Changes in women's, not men's, standards of acceptable sexual practices and opinions can shift societal norms.[7] Studies of mock jurors have found that women are more emotionally moved by victims of sexual misconduct; women also tend to be more punitive toward the violators and more empathetic with the victims.[8] In other words, the widely publicized sexual escapades of Bill Clinton and Anthony Weiner have left women more disgusted and outraged with the government than they did men.

Both Clinton and Weiner were married at the time of their affairs. This fact likewise impacted women's opinions disproportionately. Women react more negatively than men to adulterous political scandals and are more likely to demand the immediate resignation from the guilty party. This is especially true for Republican women who hold traditional gender stereotypes.[9] It's probably not a coincidence that the initial wave of QAnon women were Republican and tended to believe in traditional gender roles.

The sex scandals involved women either "young enough to be his daughter," in the case of Bill Clinton, or an underage girl, in the case of Anthony Weiner. Women are more emotionally affected by the age of victims. Research using mock juries found that women are more prone to believe young victims of sexual assault, find them to have suffered more harm, and blame the perpetrators more, whereas men are more likely to question the victim's testimony, find them to be less harmed, and feel that the victim might share some of the responsibility for the assault.[10]

In short, the sexual misconduct of high-profile politicians—their embarrassing denials and their failure to redeem themselves, magnified by the political system's ineffective reactions—likely resulted in many people's distrust of the U.S. government, especially of the Democratic Party. Women were most likely to be affected, as they tended to react stronger to violators of sexual norms, are more likely to blame perpetrators, and generally side with the victims of sexual misconduct.

With the outrage sparked by real news stories, Q-conspiracy theories are focused on the sexual violation of children by high-profile predators. These started with Pizzagate, as we discussed in Chapter 2. Though completely fabricated and since disproved, the conspiracy theory likely cost Hillary Clinton votes in the 2016 presidential election.[11] The narrative tradition of child victims of sexual and physical abuse perpetrated by depraved global elites and Hollywood celebrities from a secret cabal continued in the more recent Q-conspiracy theories.

The reference to Hollywood elites in QAnon narratives likely stems from actual sex scandals involving powerful men taking advantage of much younger women. The #MeToo movement emerged alongside QAnon and the highly publicized trial of Bill Cosby, "America's Dad," famous for playing a patriarch *The Cosby Show* in the 1980s. By 2005, Bill Cosby had become the center of a sex scandal when he was accused of drugging and raping more than 50 women.[12] Most of the victims were much younger than Cosby, who was in his 40s and 50s when the assaults took place. Six of the victims were under 18 at the time of assault, and one was 15 years old.[13] Between 2005, when the initial accusations against Cosby surfaced, and 2014, when one of his victims succeeded in suing him, he vehemently denied all accusations, calling them "preposterous" and questioning the accusers' credibility.

At the same time as Cosby denied allegations against him, sex scandals entangled another Hollywood titan: Harvey Weinstein. Like Cosby, Weinstein's accusers numbered in the dozens, and were all considerably younger than he, including one 16-year-old.[14] Like Cosby, Weinstein denied any wrongdoing. And like Cosby, he ended up convicted in court and sentenced to prison. Both Cosby and Weinstein were married at the time of their assaults.

Like the political elites, these members of the Hollywood elites violated public trust. Their repeated denials contributed to the breakdown of the worldview tenet that held Hollywood in high esteem. As with Washington, DC, Hollywood sex scandals resonated strongly with women, especially Republican women who believe in traditional gender roles.

What connected the dots into a full-blown conspiracy theory for Ceally Smith was a news story about Jeffrey Epstein. Epstein had been photographed and filmed with a number of high-profile political figures, including politicians, academics, entertainers, and even members of the British royal family (Prince Andrew). While in federal custody on charges of trafficking and sexual exploitation of minors, Epstein was found dead in his prison cell. When Smith read that Epstein's death had been ruled a suicide, it didn't ring true. She went online, searching for alternative explanations to the official story. Soon, she found Q lore about powerful pedophiles running extensive networks of sexually and physically abused children. Smith became a convert to QAnon.[15]

Conveying their concerns over abused children, QAnons display slogans such as "save the children" and "stop child trafficking" on their clothes, social media pages, and on the signs they carry at protests and rallies.[16] QAnons believe that Donald J. Trump (whom they refer to as Q+) is the only person who can put an end to the ongoing atrocities. The irony of Trump's documented association with Jeffrey Epstein—a convicted trafficker and sexual abuser—as well as a number of lawsuits filed against Trump by women and girls—accusing him of harassment, misconduct, or rape—is lost on the QAnon followers. QAnons dismiss all criticism of Trump. We address this paradox later in the chapter.

Thus, when Donald Trump repeatedly claimed that the 2020 presidential election was stolen from him, many QAnon followers were willing to do whatever it took to save their leader, the man they viewed as the only hope for the abused children. One such believer was 49-year-old Christine Priola, a former occupational therapist for the Cleveland Metropolitan School District, now indicted on federal charges for storming the Capitol building on January 6. On January 8, two days after her participation in the violent insurrection that left five dead and dozens injured, Priola quit her job. In her resignation letter, she wrote: " . . . I will be switching paths to expose the global evil of human trafficking and pedophilia, including in our government and children's services agencies."[17]

Distrust in Science

Although progress has been made toward gender equality in the United States, women are still doing much more than men where it comes to buying food and cooking,[18] raising children,[19] and taking care of the sick.[20] In each of these domains, science used to have the final word on what was right and wrong. However, in recent years, the role of science in women's lives changed from the arbiter of truth to an ambivalent, even dangerous force.

Buying healthy food has become a challenge that requires keeping up with an ever-growing amount of information, including whistleblower reports about the food industry, changing government food standards, news stories about food-borne sickness and recalls, and creative ways in which food manufacturers obscure the truth about their products. Pesticides, hormones, GMOs (genetically modified organisms), added chemicals—stabilizers, colorings, and preservatives—all products of science, have made finding wholesome, healthy food an uphill battle. And women are mostly the ones waging this battle against tricky and deceitful science.

Mothers feel pressured to keep up with news of which chemicals to avoid to keep their children safe and healthy. BPA (Bisphenol A) in baby bottles, deaths from wrongly labeled baby medicine, toys that leach brain-damaging lead—news stories like these abound. Conflicting scientific advice on what's best for babies and children is also common. Scientists previously advised formula for babies but then insisted that formula made babies less intelligent, and less healthy. Scientists said to avoid all allergens for the first two years of life, but then they found that avoidance actually causes allergies. In the United

States, with very little help from community or government, the burden (and the guilt) for anything going wrong with a child is almost entirely on the mother. With the stakes sky high, it's easy for mothers to become overwhelmed with fear and anxiety about conflicting and insidious science in their children's lives.

Healthcare is another domain where science enters women's daily lives. Medical misogyny (a tendency of doctors to overlook or dismiss women's symptoms as psychosomatic) leaves many women physically harmed and feeling neglected and stupid.[21]The rising costs of prescription drugs and medical care have put basic care out of reach for many people in the United States. The prescription painkiller scandal exposed actual conspiracies by pharmacy executives, scientists, and physicians to get people addicted to their products, and then profit off them again, by offering treatments for the addiction.[22] This has left many bitterly disappointed in the science and practice of medicine. When drugs that cost a fortune actually harm rather than heal, trust in science erodes, while suspicions of medical pain-for-profit schemes grow.

Where science made women feel dumb, QAnon makes them feel clever for "connecting the dots" of an all-encompassing conspiracy theory. The choice between trusting the scientists or trusting Q is a no-brainer for QAnon women.

As a former employee of a pharmaceutical company and a recovering painkiller addict, Lauren Witzke experienced firsthand the depravity of bad scientists responsible for the opioid crisis.[23] Witzke supported anti-scientific Q-conspiracy theories, including the "flat earth" theory. On her social media, she repeatedly posted the QAnon pledge WWG1WGA (where we go one, we go all) and was photographed wearing a Q-branded T shirt.[24]

With the brunt of discredited medical science borne disproportionately by women, their personal experiences, amplified by lack of control over important domains of their lives, led many to seek the "truth" of QAnon's red pill about vaccines. Some of the most popular QAnon conspiracies revolve around nefarious vaccine manufacturing: microchip trackers that Bill Gates would put into "vaccines" and other vaccines causing autism and diseases that Big Pharma creates to get rich off the kids' suffering. They believe that COVID-19 was manufactured in order for the elites to get rich off the pandemic. When vaccines for COVID-19 became available, more women than men were distrustful about their safety, and refused to take them. The gender difference in rejection of the COVID-19 vaccine (45% versus 33%) is believed to be due to more women (than men) who believe conspiracy theories.[25]

One such woman is Rachel Powell, a 40-year-old mother of eight who was on an FBI "Wanted" poster for her involvement in the January 6 storming of the Capitol before she was indicted. Powell's online activity suggests her dive into the rabbit hole of conspiracy theories was precipitated by the COVID-19 pandemic and the resulting lockdowns.[26]

Before the pandemic, Powell seemed content to raise her eight children (all homeschooled), tend her garden, care for her chickens, and occasionally sell surplus produce at a local farmer's market. Online, she expressed concerns about Trump as a presidential candidate and her amazement that so many people supported him. But after the onset of the pandemic, Powell began attending anti-lockdown protests, driving as far as 40 miles to join them. She got her information primarily from Alex Jones and Rudy Giuliani. Her views on Trump changed, and in the 2020 presidential election she cast her ballot for him. Powell's vocal advocacy against mask wearing resulted in her expulsion from the farmer's market. That didn't dampen her fervor. "I'm unashamedly a super spreader," she posted on her Facebook timeline, along with a video of a mask-less dinner party. In another Facebook posting, Powell wrote, "I won't get a vaccine either. I hear what you're saying about the whole world being in on the conspiracy as far as the corona virus goes."[27]

Powell's radicalization culminated in her breaking the windows of the Capitol building:

> Videos show her, wearing a pink hat and sunglasses, using a battering ram to smash a window and a bullhorn to issue orders. "People should probably coördinate together if you're going to take this building," she called out, leaning through a shattered window and addressing a group of rioters already inside. "We got another window to break to make in-and-out easy."[28]

Powell was protesting against an election that Trump falsely claimed had been stolen from him, a lie that both Rudy Giuliani and Alex Jones repeated. The emotional truth of this single mother of eight toiling every day to feed them healthy food and keep them safe was shaken by the deadly virus she could not comprehend or control. Her fears were soothed by QAnon's elaborate denials of COVID-19. There is no danger, QAnon posts proved: It's all a lie, no need to wear a mask or worry about it. Having found social and emotional support in the QAnon community, Powell also embraced their radical ideology about the "stolen" election and the radical action to "stop the steal."

Religion's Moral Failures

The Catholic clergy sex abuse scandal began unfolding before public eyes in the 1980s. By 2020, over 3,000 priests from around the world had been credibly implicated in systemically abusing children as young as 3 years old.[29] Like politicians and Hollywood elites, the Catholic Church denied any wrongdoing. Church leaders dismissed, silenced, or settled individual cases, keeping offending priests out of trouble by transferring them to different parishes and maintaining the façade of moral authority. But the narrative spun out of control when newspapers like the *Boston Globe* spread the horror of the abuse beyond the Church's ability to keep it quiet.

The abuse violated children. It violated public trust—if you can't leave your children alone with a priest, with whom can you leave them? And it debased the church's moral authority.

Perhaps because of the resonance of the Catholic Church scandal, stories about child sex abuse in other religious traditions began coming out. Social media, especially the #MeToo movement, encouraged victims to speak out, and in doing so to find a community and strength to seek justice, such as #ChurchToo.

Reports of children sexually abused by rabbis in the Orthodox Jewish community have been denied and suppressed for decades, before being exposed.[30] Similarly, although the Dalai Lama knew about sexual abuse by Buddhist teachers, it wasn't until a whistleblower conducted her own investigation, amassing the testimonies of dozens of victims from decades of abuse, that the Dalai Lama made any public mention of it.[31] In the Protestant community, too, it wasn't until female bloggers began digging through court and police records, sermons and emails, and publishing about the widespread sexual abuse of children that the

Protestant church made any effort to reconcile with the issue.[32] Likewise, Islamic religious leaders were implicated in the Middle East, Europe, and North America.[33]Even outside of organized religions, spiritual leaders of mainstream yogic traditions (e.g., Ashtanga,[34] Bikram,[35] Anusara[36]) have been credibly accused of sexual abuse.

Across the board, those who claimed moral authority refused to abide by their own rules. Their respective religious traditions disregarded the victims entrusted in their care. The result was another worldview tenet cracking.

Disgust and outrage at this systemic failure led some to abandon their religion. Ten percent of young Protestants have left the church because they found the clerical sexual misconduct was not taken seriously.[37] Likewise, 11 percent of Catholics said they were considering leaving their religion because of how the Church handled the sex scandal.[38] Less obvious, but no less significant, was the broader effect of this mass unfreezing: disconnection from norms that spiritual traditions used to provide.[39] Seventy percent of Catholics surveyed said they felt the Church was in a crisis that "demanded immediate attention."[40] For the majority, their religious tradition was no longer the cornerstone of their worldview upon which they could seek refuge from life's uncertainties. There was no sanctuary to be found in religion, no moral clarity. The religious community, shaken by the trauma of the abuse and the embarrassment of the system's failure, fractured as well.

With loss of moral clarity, those who turned to QAnon for answers and comfort found all that they could no longer believe religion was fit to offer: ideas about good and evil; a spiritual community in other followers; a spiritual practice in connecting the dots and opening their minds to the "truth";

and a savior in Donald J. Trump. In fact, QAnon could be a kind of religion.[41]

Addressing one of the root causes of radicalization among its followers, QAnon narratives satisfy their outrage against religious authorities. One such story is about Pope Francis being arrested and charged with 80 counts of child sexual abuse.[42]

QAnon narratives—featuring sexually abused children and powerful, secretive perps, including Oprah, Tom Hanks, Bill and Hillary Clinton, George Soros, and the Rothschild family[43]—stem from factual stories of children sexually abused by powerful people. The fear and outrage mothers feel when contemplating something like that happening to their own child can be overwhelming and disorienting. But a community of similarly worried others creates a buffer against the anxiety. In Q lore, real stories about people who were supposed to represent "good" doing evil things evolve into stories about the cabal of powerful and famous people who are known as "good" (i.e., Tom Hanks, Oprah) but are actually eating children in their spare time.

The fear and uncertainty that drove people to QAnon are assuaged by vague plots against the bad guys (the cabal) and faith in the good guys (Trump and the QAnon community). From feeling isolated and out of control, a QAnon follower high on Q lore begins to feel that, although things are perilous, the QAnon community is in this together. They will do something to protect the children. They have powerful allies fighting on their behalf. A little fiction can turn fear and uncertainty into belonging and agency.

Shifting Gender Roles

Traditional gender roles have been changing in the United States since the sexual revolution of the 1960s. People in their 70s remember a time when a woman's place was in the kitchen, and the husband was the sole breadwinner. For many in the United States, those were the good old days, a paradise lost: a Great America, which Trump promised to return in his campaign slogan, "Make America Great Again." Partly because of this appeal, Trump won the majority of white women's votes in both the 2016[44] and 2020[45] presidential elections.

Traditional gender roles, missed by many white women, limited their abilities to pursue dreams outside of home and family. But as U.S. laws opened up these opportunities, and the expectations of women changed to include a college degree and a paying job, the responsibilities for keeping the home and raising children continued to rest overwhelmingly on women's shoulders. Working women still do more of the cooking, cleaning, shopping, and childrearing, only now they have to do all those things after work.[46]

In the workplace, women are not paid as much as men for the same job[47]—that is, if women can even get the same job, because men get more than twice as many promotions as women.[48]On a daily basis, women face discrimination in the workplace in the form of microaggressions, hostilities, and work–life balance, adding up to a stressful environment fraught with anxiety and frustration.[49] In other words, women who aspire to more than the traditional gender roles still have to carry their burdens at home, and pay a high price for their ambitions at work.

For women who do not wish to have a career, an idyllic Little House on the Prairie is often out of reach, as few families can live comfortably on a single income anymore. Especially for white, suburban women, who were raised with the expectations of having their mothers' life one day, the evolution of the social construction of gender is not a welcome change. They often find themselves between a rock and a hard place, feeling inadequate for not achieving the career goals society imposes on them and wistful for the lifestyle they can't afford without achieving those goals. It seems women in the United States have been served a kind of Pyrrhic victory, where they are damned if they strive for more traditionally male roles and damned if they don't.

For women who cherished traditional gender roles, the expanding definitions of gender and marriage have added insult to their already injured self-identity. If their idea of self has been constructed around being "a good girl," smiling, and serving homemade food, then people like Congresswoman Alexandria Ocasio-Cortez, who openly challenge authority, threaten their foundational beliefs. If marriage has been their life's highest aspiration, then the fact that now marriage could be between two men besmirches their dream. If their ability to have children has been their greatest ambition, and their self-identification is primarily as a mother, then recognition of transgender women as their equals insults their values.

The shifting gender roles have cracked a worldview tenet for many women, especially white Republican women. In QAnon, they seek a respite from this unfreezing. The idea of Donald Trump as the ultimate masculine hero who would rescue abused children, smite the cannibals and pedophiles, and Make America Great Again became irresistible.

Tall, blonde, and rich, Trump embodied the Prince Charming they envisioned. He was neither of the government nor of Hollywood and thus was immune to the shadow cast over them. Instead, Trump represented business, perhaps the only monolith of the American Dream that still towered above the raging storms of crumbling authorities, shifting norms, and diminishing values.

Money still has value. People who have it are still better off than those who don't. And people who have A LOT of it, well—they must have something extra special about them, like a superpower. It certainly seemed to be the case with Trump, given how often his name popped up in their daily lives. He was on TV. Landmark buildings bore his name. He owned casinos, the magical places where anyone could get rich. Trump Steaks, Trump Ties, and Trump University showcased Trump's reach. He seemed omnipresent, and, after he became president, omnipotent.

Trump's open contempt for the establishment only proved he railed against the discredited institutions and was on QAnon's side. His disdain for outspoken women proved he respected traditional gender roles. Trump's campaign chant "Lock her up!" reassured QAnons that the cabal member Hillary Clinton would get what she deserved.

Trump praised QAnon followers as people who "love our country" and "are very strongly against pedophilia." "I understand they like me very much," he said about QAnon, "Which I appreciate."[50] Trump amplified QAnon-promoting accounts on Twitter.[51] Nobody else offered any solace to these people's broken dreams and shattered worldviews. Trump alone seemed to have tuned into their desperation and their need for inspiration. His speeches and tweets, as untethered to reality as QAnon's collective psyche, didn't provide details, plans, or names. They sounded as vague as QAnon conspiracies. He told nightmarish stories of women being tortured by foreign gangs and promised to build a great big wall to keep Americans safe. The virus would disappear like magic, he prophesized.

Trump's repetition of phrases low on information but high on emotion resonated with QAnon followers: "many people said" and "we're going to get them" and "tremendous" and "huge" and "*believe* me." They wanted to believe. That's why they came to QAnon in the first place: to find new things to believe in after the old beliefs crumbled.

Ashley Vanderbilt, a 27-year-old mother, began to spend a lot of time online after she was laid off from her job at a construction company. On TikTok, she watched video after video suggested by the app's algorithms. Her belief in QAnon grew, and with it, her faith in Donald Trump. In Ms. Vanderbilt's mind, Trump became a messianic figure who could do no wrong. At one point, she recalls asking herself, "Am I putting Trump above God?"[52]

And so, with their belief in Trump as their savior, QAnon women twisted facts to accommodate fiction: Accusations against Trump were attempts to frame him by the evil cabal and his powerful enemies. The mass media were owned by Soros, so naturally they were lying to bring Trump down. COVID-19 was a hoax. The lockdowns were intended to undermine Trump's presidency. The election was being stolen by the cabal, aided by the mainstream media. Only Trump could save the children. Only Trump could bring down the cabal. And so QAnon had to "stop the steal."[53]

Gina Bisignano, a California beauty salon owner, wore a red Trump 2020 sweatshirt to an anti-lockdown rally where she screamed homophobic slurs at a passing woman. As the woman recorded, Bisignano doubled down, demanding "Are you a boy or a girl?" "You probably had an abortion this morning," she said. After the video went viral,[54] Bisignano's salon's online ratings took a nosedive. So did her fortunes. When she was filmed again, at the January 6 riot in Washington, DC, Bisignano said that she had lost her business. "I love my country, and I love my president, and I'm a single mother, and I love our Lord, and they can't take that away from me," she said tearfully. "[Jesus] is our king, and Trump is our president," she said. Bisignano was indicted on seven counts for her role in the January 6 riots.[55]

The four major worldview tenets presented here—government and elites, science, religion, and gender roles—have each been undermined; belief in them has been shaken in recent decades. The resulting mass unfreezing has left many feeling anxious, lost, powerless, and out of control. Each of these emotions contributes to an increase in the conspiratorial mindset.[56] The anger against the systems that betrayed them inspired many to quest for a red pill and a rabbit hole of "alternative facts." With the convenience of social media at their fingertips, QAnon followers found much more than that.

FolQlore

Storytelling is as old as humanity itself. Narrating difficult experiences helps make sense of individual emotions—that's why talk therapy can be so helpful.[57] Collective myth-making also helps communities to process shared trauma.[58] From this perspective, QAnon offered a way to cope with disappointments and frustrations by collectively narrating around shared experiences.

FolQlore satisfies four important needs for QAnon followers: a need to feel smart (cognitive utility); a need to feel connected (social utility); a need to feel positive emotions (emotional utility); and a need to feel like one's life has a purpose (personal utility). Figure 3.1 illustrates these needs and how they relate to the four major truths we've been discussing.

As much as QAnon narratives are about children, children are not what motivates QAnons. Mind-warping stories illustrate this paradox. Josh Jennings, for example, was an avid QAnon devotee. His Facebook timeline was peppered with the #SaveTheChildren hashtag and multiple postings condemning physical and sexual abuse of children. In real life, however, Jennings was charged with physically abusing and eventually murdering his girlfriend's 10-month-old daughter.[59]

Then there's Cynthia Abcug, whose son was removed from her home by Child Protective Services as a victim of Munchausen by proxy, a psychological disorder where the mother intentionally sickens the child to get attention for herself.[60] Lenka Perron, the QAnon follower who later left the movement, was less violent but no less hypocritical. She found herself spending so much time on QAnon forums about saving (theoretical) children that her three (actual) children—11, 15, and 19—were largely left to fend for themselves and eat takeout.[61] Similarly, Lauren Witzke, the #SaveTheChildren-posting QAnon follower and (failed) Republican senatorial candidate, proposed cutting welfare benefits from poor families and supported Trump's immigration policy that separated children as young as nursing infants from their mothers, with no plans to reunite them.

For QAnons like Jennings, the "children" are unrelated to any real child. Rather, they are a symbol, a disembodied idea of innocence and goodness. The needs satisfied through QAnon

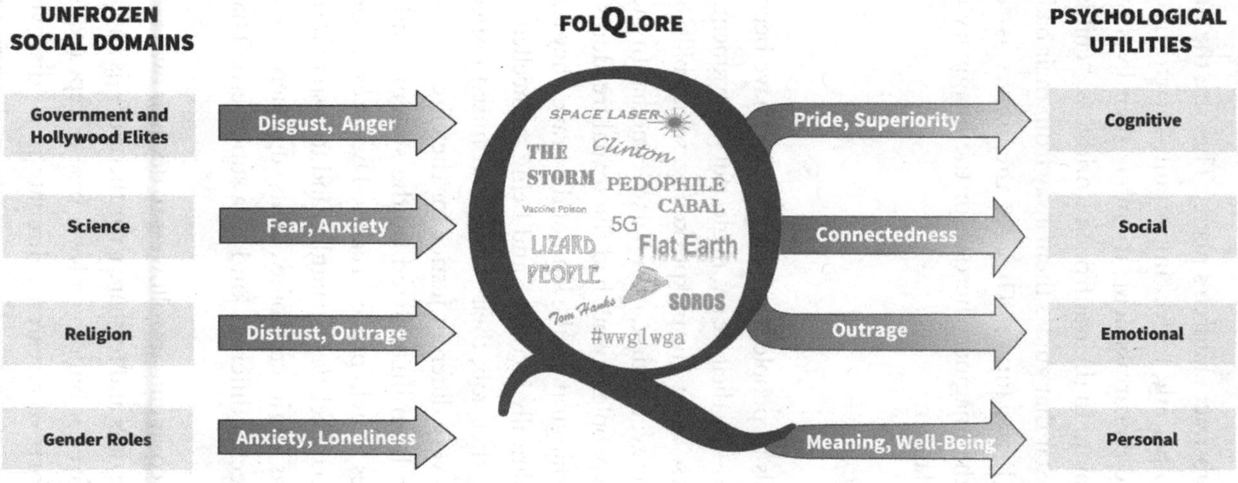

Figure 3.1. Psychology of QAnonization. Source: Sophia Moskalenko and Kristian Warpinski.

are not some abstract children's needs. They are the followers' own needs: to belong; to feel important, smart, superior; to escape fear and embarrassment; to imbue their lives with purpose and meaning. In their unfrozen worldview, "children" is a distant North Star that guides them away from their bad present and toward a better future. They see themselves as "catchers in the rye"—the imaginary heroes for the imaginary children in imaginary danger.

Cognitive Utility

QAnon appeals to people who, for decades, have been feeling talked-down to—by their sleazy, neglectful government; by cunning, arrogant scientists; by pickpocketing, selfish billionaires; by hypocritical clergy; by lying, manipulative media. In the land of the free, these people haven't had the sexual freedoms of Hollywood or Washington. In the land of the brave, they fear saying something politically incorrect and being "cancelled"—losing their business, their job, their friends. Promised justice for all, they've seen a very different justice for the elites.

They have been infantilized by the system. And so they crave fairy tales to help process reality. They seek a story to tell *their* stories, to reflect *their* struggles, and to inspire *their* hopes. Hollywood has lost its credibility, all its superheroes worthless, and so they seek a different kind of a superhero. That's what Q offers.

QAnon encouraging its followers to do their own research—to connect the dots and to share their theories—is an ingenious marketing move for building a loyal base of repeat customers. When the efforts of research culminate in a "discovery," the experience becomes rewarding, activating pleasure centers in the brain.[62] It certainly helps that there are no wrong answers in the folQlore: Any "dot" can be connected with any other. The more fantastical the resulting story, the more of a "Whoa" moment for the seeker. The dopamine hit of making narrative connections can easily become addictive.[63] People find themselves spending more and more time online, digging deeper and deeper into folQlore.

In solving QAnon puzzles, people feel proud for discovering "the Truth" that the powerful wanted to keep secret. They feel smart for putting the puzzle together. And they feel superior to those still in the dark. These feelings of pride and intellectual superiority add up to QAnon's *cognitive utility*.

Social Utility

Even before the pandemic, Americans were leading relatively isolated lives. The average population density in the United States is 92 residents per square mile[64] (versus about 143 residents per square mile in Europe).[65] Most U.S. residents (70%) live in detached houses[66] in small towns and suburbs where they have to drive to get to work, school, or the grocery store.[67] Americans also work more hours and take fewer vacation days than Europeans.[68]American preferences for personal cars, detached homes, and more income result in long and lonely commutes, with less time and fewer venues for socialization. Taken together, these factors contribute to the stark difference in feelings of loneliness between Americans (46%)[69] and Europeans (6%).[70]

COVID-19 lockdowns made an already dire situation worse.

More physically isolated, more overwhelmed by additional demands placed on them by homebound children, and more stressed about the threat of the deadly virus, women disproportionately suffered from increased loneliness during the pandemic.[71] Social media offered a much-desired respite.

Psychological studies have discovered that social isolation increases conspiratorial thinking.[72] It's no wonder, then, that lonely women found QAnon an inviting social milieu.

Exploring QAnon's alternative reality, QAnon followers encourage one another's efforts, assuage their doubts. and support their discoveries. Their online hive always buzzes, never sleeps, and is reachable at the stroke of a finger. In the real world, many QAnons experience hostility and rejection by what they call the cancel culture. Some, like Gina Bisignano, have lost their livelihoods for expressing their beliefs. Others have lost connections with friends and family. But in the online QAnon bubble, they encounter people who "get them." Here, they feel understood and appreciated.

Deep inside, QAnon followers might suspect the folQlore stories are untrue. But they suspend disbelief, because the stories stand for something that IS true: the shared idea that there's "something wrong with the world" and that they are part of an elite group—red-pillers— who know "the Truth" and will do something about it together. "Where we go one, we go all" (WWG1WGA) QAnons claim. Nobody is alone, the slogan implies, as long as they are part of QAnon. This *social utility* is far more important than facts.

There's a caveat, however.

Just as Q-conspiracy theories are only vaguely related to reality, so, too, the QAnon online community is only vaguely real. Other members don't truly know you or care about your life; you can't count on them to help you shovel the driveway after a snowstorm or to sit with you through a crying spell.

The more time they spend on social media, the lonelier people feel.[73] QAnon creates a vicious cycle, with followers withdrawing from real-life social circles, feeling lonely, resorting to QAnon community on social media, and in the end feeling even lonelier. The cost of building online connections is alienation from real-life ones.

Emotional Utility

Within the QAnon community, facts are beside the point. What matters instead are shared emotions. QAnons are scared of the same things, be they COVID-19, vaccines, or California forest fires. When made to feel anxious, people tend to seek the company of those who are anxious about the same threat.[74] They're right to do so, because being in the company of similarly anxious others does in fact reduce anxiety.

Not only companionship, but also the content of QAnon helps to deal with difficult emotions. Conspiracy theories that deny the horrific reality of school shootings like Sandy Hook or Parkland offer an escape from the dread that one's own children could be shot. Fear of COVID-19 can be overwhelming . . . unless there's actually no COVID-19, just a seasonal flu and a sinister cabal trying to grift public funds while people are in lockdown. The adrenaline released in response to fear is repurposed for outrage: Someone is making out like a bandit off our suffering!

From feeling bad about oneself for not being able to protect one's children from shootings, or one's loved ones from COVID-19, QAnons go to feeling good about having figured out the conspiracy theory and being in on "the plan" to stop it. Blaming the cabal, Bill Gates, or George Soros relieves the pain of blaming oneself. As folQlore transforms helplessness, fear, and anxiety into outrage, QAnon serves an *emotional utility*.

But here, too, there's a caveat.

All the pleasant feelings—pride, belonging, righteous anger—come at a price. The cost of embracing feel-good narratives divorced from reality is the shock of having to face reality from time to time. When facts defy folQlore's predictions (as they did when Biden won the 2020 presidential election), QAnon members experience high anxiety, as well as thoughts of self-harm and suicide.[75]The outrage that feels so much better than helplessness and fear can occasionally spill into radical action that lands one in jail, or leaves one dead on the steps of the Capitol building. Like drugs of addiction, conspiracy theories provide a quick emotional fix, but over time, they can destroy users' lives.

Personal Utility

Some QAnons seem to have stumbled into the conspiracy theory world as a result of losing their footing in the real one. Ashli Babbitt, the woman who was shot and killed during the mob breach of the Capitol on January 6, had trouble transitioning to civilian life after she left the military. In QAnon, she found the purpose her civilian life lacked. A similar path characterized the QAnonization of 51-year-old Lt. Col. Ret. Larry Brock[76] of Texas. Brock was photographed inside the breached Capitol building carrying plastic zip-tie handcuffs, presumably meant to restrain kidnapped lawmakers. After a highly successful military career, Brock couldn't find the same thrill and fulfillment until he discovered QAnon. Another "zip-tie man," Eric Munchel,[77] came to storm the Capitol with his mother, Lisa Eisenhart, with whom he was still living. An unemployed bartender, Munchel had a criminal arrest record for violent assault. His social media featured pictures of him sporting military gear, a tentative association to the high-risk, high-status life he wanted but couldn't have—until QAnon. Rosanne Boyland, trampled to death by the mob storming the Capitol, was a recovering drug addict with a history of drug-related arrests. Her QAnonization was an attempt to fill her life, devastated by years of substance abuse, with meaning and purpose.

But for many QAnons, it wasn't unemployment, addiction, or trouble with the law that sent them searching for the red pill. Neither economic anxiety nor teenage rebellion drove their radicalization: Two thirds of those arrested for participation in the January 6 riot were 35 or older, and 40 percent owned a business or held white-collar jobs.[78] One surprising finding, however, points to the importance of threatened worldviews and shifting value systems. Most who came to "the Storm" did not come from deep-red pro-Trump states. Rather, they came from battleground states where Biden won close to half the votes.[79]

While social norms can be deeply entrenched in established Democratic or deeply Republican states, in battleground states the battles rage not only over votes, but also over all the things the votes represent: marriage laws, gender norms, the role of religion and science in school curriculum and daily lives. It is in the battleground states that the shifting of worldview's tectonic plates is most salient and mass unfreezing most prevalent.

Research on radicalization has consistently found that the subjective matters more than the objective when predicting violent trajectories.[80] Relative deprivation is more predictive of anger and resentment than objective deprivation.[81]Their bank accounts may not have been in distress, but that didn't help the psychological distress of changing culture and eroding social norms. Highly subjective "life meaning" is a better predictor of overall well-being than objective economic measures.[82]

One of the predictors of meaning in life is awe, the experience of "perceptually vast stimuli that transcend one's ordinary reference frame"[83]—like the "Whoa" moment QAnon followers experience when, escaping their relative deprivation, they connect the dots into a pattern. Their pain and anger transcend ordinary reference frames, filling their lives with meaning.

To those searching for meaning in the devastated sociocultural landscape, QAnon promises to make everything better. Personally discovering "the Truth," followers experience awe, and their lives become more fulfilling as a result. Contemplating "the plan" and carrying out "the Storm" filled them with the significance they so desperately sought. In this, QAnon provided a ***personal utility.***

The caveat here is obvious. If life's meaning is based on a conspiracy theory, it's as strong as the conspiracy theory's weakest link. When Trump left DC instead of assuming the presidency and proceeding with the promised arrests of the cabal, when "the plan" failed and the forecasted "Storm" was barely a drizzle, those who invested their well-being into the lie felt betrayed. "Trump just used us and our fear," said a disgruntled Lenka Perron.[84] "It's obvious now we've been had. No plan, no Q, nothing,"[85] said a post on a QAnon forum. Another post said, "It's like being a kid and seeing the big gift under the tree thinking it is exactly what you want only to open it and realize it was a lump of coal."[86]

CHAPTER 4

LIFE AFTER Q

"The Storm" blew over. January 6, 2021, came and went without any of the cabal being arrested as Q had prophesized. There were no televised trials or executions of powerful pedophiles. No high-flying cannibals were taken to the Guantanamo prison. On January 20th, Joe Biden was sworn in as the president of the United States, instead of Trump beginning his second term as "the plan" had promised.

Disappointment and disbelief rippled over the QAnon-based Internet forums. Predictably, reactions fell into one of three categories. The Diehards doubled down on their belief system. The Doubters tried to reconcile the reality they couldn't deny with the ideas they couldn't abandon. And the Defectors dropped out, disillusioned with QAnon.

The Diehards

Faced with the failure of Q prophecies, the Diehards dug deeper into the folQlore, claiming everything—the certification of the election, the failed insurrection, and the inauguration—was part of "the plan." On Gab, a social network known for its far-right userbase, a QAnon account with 130,000 followers posted, "Does it make sense that Trump would 'give up' like this? What if it had to be this way, what if this actually ends up being the best way? . . . Call me crazy, but I don't think this movie is done."[1] Another Diehard wrote, "Like many of you, I am in shock by today's [events] and then I realized why it had to happen and that Q told us it would happen and, why this NEEDED to happen."[2]

Joe Biden didn't actually become president, Diehards said. Rather, the televised inauguration was another hoax, a ruse to distract the uninitiated. Some claimed that Biden's inauguration was actually taped 11 hours earlier, while on January 20th, in a secret ceremony, Trump was sworn in as president. Others rolled with the idea that the inauguration was indeed held in Washington, DC, and Biden was sworn in, but that it was part of an entrapment plan set up by Trump to incriminate Biden and the deep state. "Things have just started," explained Tiffany, a Diehard QAnon: "They had to 'commit' the crime to fully lock the deal."[3]

Among the "clues" Diehards counted as evidence for their freshly baked conspiracy theory was the number of flags on the dais at Trump's farewell address before he departed Washington, DC, for Florida. There were 17 flags, they observed. Guess what the 17th letter of the alphabet is? It's Q! Clearly, this was a hidden message from Trump that "the plan" was still working. Another clue was that the Bible on which Biden swore was wrapped in a leather binding, which meant that he didn't actually swear on the Bible and so wasn't a legitimate president.

"Be prepared, and stay cool," Diehard Valerie Gilbert wrote to her Facebook friends. "Slow and steady wins the race. We're in the home stretch now."[4]

The Doubters

For many QAnons, the public failure of Q prophecies stirred *cognitive dissonance*, an anxiety-ridden state that arises when facts can't be easily reconciled with one's self-image.[5] Q was not helping, having gone eerily quiet. Since November 2020, Q posted only four times, leaving the followers to deal with their disappointments on their own. Some feared they had been misled or betrayed.

"I am so scared right now, I really feel nothing is going to happen now," wrote one Doubter on a Telegram channel frequented by QAnons. "I'm just devastated."[6]

The Doubters weren't ready to concoct another conspiracy theory to explain the glaring mismatch between the reality and Q's predictions. Something went wrong, that much was clear to them. At the same time, however, they weren't ready to give up on the ideas of saving abused children or finding and punishing the pedophiles and cannibals responsible for their suffering. "I will continue speaking truth. I have not given up. I still have faith. I still know that God Wins," a Gab account posted.[7]

After Twitter banned Donald Trump, and Facebook shut down accounts that were posting disinformation, QAnon traffic on these social media declined precipitously.[8] Some of the most radical hashtags related to the "stolen election" conspiracy theory (#FightForTrump, #HoldTheLine, and "#MarchForTrump") declined by 95 percent across Twitter, Facebook, and Instagram.[9]

Tens of thousands of QAnons migrated to unmoderated social media, such as Gab, 4chan, and 8chan. These more permissive Internet forums already hosted hate groups and radical movements that had been kicked off of Twitter, Facebook, Instagram, and Reddit for violations of their terms of conditions. They cheered the influx of QAnon Doubters as a unique recruitment opportunity. On 4chan, an anonymous account posted,

> This would be the perfect time to start posting Nat Soc [Nazism] propaganda in Q anon groups. Clearly, this is a very low point for Q believers, and once people have been broken, they will look for ways to cling back to hope again.[10]

The Proud Boys were similarly abuzz on Telegram,

> Parler being shut down has sent tens of thousands (or more) of people to telegram. All of them are seeking refuge and looking for answers since their Q-bullshit lied to them. Now is our opportunity to grab them by the hand and lead them toward ideological truth. Join their normie chats and show them love and unity.[11]

Strategies for bringing QAnon Doubters into alt-right proper included pushing on them "the most extreme talking points that they already have in their head thanks to Trump."[12]

The Defectors

Some QAnons had seen enough—Trump's failure to lead them in the insurrection that he allegedly incited, Q's failure to guide them after the November election, and the eventual transfer of power to President Biden. They connected the dots into a bigger picture: QAnon was full of lies.

"Power has changed hands and that is the end. In the time we needed Trump and Q the most . . . [they] both shut up and left,"[13] someone posted on a QAnon-related forum.

In the aftermath of the January 6 insurrection, law enforcement began identifying people who stormed the Capitol building—and rolling out arrest warrants. This was another jarring reality check—not only because they didn't expect any negative consequences of their actions, but also because the community they've come to see as their family abandoned them when they needed it most. "Not one patriot is standing up for me," said Jenna Ryan, a real estate agent who became infamous for flying to the January 6 insurrection by private jet. "I'm a complete villain. I was down there based on what my president said. 'Stop the steal.' Now I see that it was all over nothing. He was just having us down there for an ego boost. I was there for him."[14]

While QAnons were being indicted for trying to deliver the presidency to Trump, their hero and leader did not seem to care about them. In the final days of his presidency, Trump was issuing dozens of pardons. But not a single presidential pardon named a QAnon follower who stormed the Capitol building for him.

"So just to recap: Trump will pardon Lil Wayne, Kodak Black, high profile Jewish fraudsters . . . No pardons for middle class whites who risked their livelihoods by going to 'war' for Trump,"[15] summarized one post on a white supremacist channel on Telegram. Gut-wrenching feelings of abandonment and betrayal led many QAnons to leave.

For others, defection came from the head, not the heart. Jitarth Jadeja was a true believer in QAnon, until one Q clue, designed to cement followers' beliefs in Q legitimacy, did the opposite for him. The Q-drop said President Trump would use the phrase "tip top" in one of his speeches to send a coded signal of support for QAnon. Amazingly, soon thereafter, Trump did use that phrase. But when Jadeja did some online research, he found many other instances in the past when Trump had said "tip top." It was clear to Jadeja that Q had used the same trick that is often used by horoscopes and fortunetellers: pointing out something that seems unique but is in fact quite common. Q's "tip top" drop was a version of "Your heart has been broken by someone you deeply trusted" or "There's someone important in your life whose name begins with a J."

Jadeja was crushed by his discovery. "It was the worst feeling I had in my life," he said. He discovered a Subreddit called r/Qult_Headquarters, "dedicated to documenting, critiquing, and debunking the chan poster known as 'Q' and his devotees." On the Subreddit, Jadeja posted a 659-word essay that began, "Q fooled me."[16] To Jadeja's great surprise, instead of the ridicule he feared, he found a welcoming and supportive community on the forum. This newfound connection with other Defectors helped him to leave QAnon for good.

Melissa Rein Lively's defection came, not from the heart, not from the head, but from her husband calling the police on her. The Scottsdale, Arizona, businesswoman's life became consumed by her addiction to QAnon. Her husband staged an intervention and gave her an ultimatum: the family or QAnon.

Lively, as we discussed in Chapter 2, is the QAnon follower who became infamous for live streaming herself as she destroyed a facemask display at Target and yelled at store employees. As a result of her public outburst, the PR business she had built from the ground up was destroyed: Her clients didn't want to have anything to do with her. Lively, her husband, and even his business partner were getting death threats. She didn't feel safe anymore. "I was all consumed with doom-scrolling on the Internet. I was living in these conspiracy theories. All of this fear porn that I was consuming online was just feeding my depression and anxiety."[17] Lively's husband tried to get through to her, to convince her to leave QAnon, but failed. That's when he called the police.

Lively live streamed the intervention, too. She told the police that she was a "QAnon spokesperson" and that she was on the phone with President Trump "all the time." After the police detained her to take her to a nearby mental health facility, she screamed, "You're doing this to me because I'm Jewish!"

In retrospect, Lively sees her husband's intervention as an act of kindness to someone whose psychological disorder took over her life. At the mental health facility, she was diagnosed with bipolar disorder and with posttraumatic stress disorder stemming from losing both her parents at a young age. Intensive therapy she has been receiving helped her to leave the world of QAnon behind. As a PR professional, she has made it her business to publicly apologize to Target and the employees she had mistreated. She has signed new clients and has reconciled with her husband. Like Jadeja, Lively was moved to find that people were willing to give her a second chance.

Diehards, Doubters, and Defectors present unique challenges to policymakers and to security services. In this chapter, we will consider what could aid QAnon Defectors in reintegrating into "normal" life, what could draw QAnon Doubters out of the conspiracy theory world, and what could minimize the danger from QAnon Diehards.

But QAnon's damage is not limited to its followers. A recent poll found that 6 out of 10 Americans couldn't correctly identify four or more conspiracy theories as false.[18] That number represents about 125 million Americans whose beliefs were upended by QAnon disinformation. This group includes QAnon Doubters, but it also includes a vastly larger group of people who have not yet fallen into the rabbit hole of conspiracy theory. They seem to teeter on the edge of it. These millions of Americans are uncertain about their reality. They likely experience anxiety and fear because of this uncertainty. The interventions proposed in the following discussion would benefit them as well as former QAnons.

The same NPR/Ipsos poll found that one in five Americans believed the following statement is true: "A group of Satan-worshipping elites who run a child sex ring are trying to control our politics and media."[19] One in five Americans projects to roughly 36 million adults who are Diehards. This staggering number suggests that most of us know someone—a family member, a friend, a colleague, or a neighbor—who is deep into the QAnon rabbit hole. In the weeks following the January 6 insurrection, news stories featured devastating firsthand accounts of adult children losing their parents to QAnon[20] and of parents whose adult children become QAnonized and severed contact with them.[21] Siblings stopped speaking, and long-term romantic partnerships broke up when one person in the relationship followed the white rabbit into QAnon.[22]

QAnon leaves behind a trail of broken families and friendships, with millions of people left to pick up the pieces. They, too, need help. The interventions proposed here are designed to address the needs of those who themselves have never believed any of Q's lies, but whose lives have nonetheless been shaken by them.

Four-Pronged Approach

QAnon arose from a perfect storm of social norms crumbling amidst the fear and loneliness of a global pandemic. Like a rising tide lifts all boats, this perfect storm pushed different people into QAnon for different reasons. To get them out, similarly diverse methods will be needed. Here, we will present four approaches to de-QAnonization.

The first set of counter-QAnon measures would increase psychological resilience to a conspiracy-theory phenomenon like QAnon. We imagine these measures as *building immunity* to disinformation, fear mongering, and false prophecies. It would include teaching critical thinking and social media literacy and offering "psychological inoculation" against conspiratorial thinking. This intervention prong would especially benefit Doubters.

The second set of measures aims to decrease the danger of QAnon-type disinformation to the general public, reducing the virulence of conspiracy theories. *Limiting exposure* to dangerous rhetoric online would curb radicalization by enforcing social media terms of conduct and de-platforming or otherwise limiting accounts that spew disinformation. Here, we suggest improvement of social media filter algorithms, airing out troll-infested forums, and flooding the unregulated online space with narratives that would undermine conspiracy theories. Limiting exposure would benefit Diehards, Doubters, and Defectors, as well as other non-QAnon Internet users.

A third set of measures proposes professional treatments for mental health issues that brought people into QAnon, or that arose from following it. Included in this intervention prong would be individual cognitive psychotherapy, support groups, and volunteering. *Offering treatment* would be of greatest use to those Defectors who are ready to admit they have a psychological problem and are willing to seek help for it. It would also benefit non-QAnons whose psychological well-being has suffered because of QAnonized loved ones.

Finally, the fourth approach recommends *adjusting expectations.* Those of us outside of QAnon may feel scared, confused, or angry with people falling for blatant lies. We may want the craziness to stop, immediately. Adjusting our expectations would moderate our stress levels. For the Defectors who had left QAnon, it's equally important to set realistic goals about their re-entering "normal" life and rebuilding broken relationships. Adjusting expectations would help former QAnons and non-QAnons alike. Here, we propose comprehensive mindfulness training. Figure 4.1 illustrates the measures that can be helpful in saving people from the impact of QAnon.

Building Immunity

Critical Thinking and Social Media Literacy

Q may be one person or a few different people, but they had a lot of help getting the message out. Less than two weeks after the first Q post appeared on 4chan, Russian Internet trolls began amplifying the post. In 2019, accounts suspected of being controlled by Russia's government- based Internet Research Agency sent out a large number of tweets tagged with #QAnon and #WWGQWGA.[23] After Twitter removed the offending accounts, the Kremlin-controlled news agency Russia Today (RT) devoted more and more coverage to QAnon, condemning Twitter's "censorship" and posting Q-conspiracy

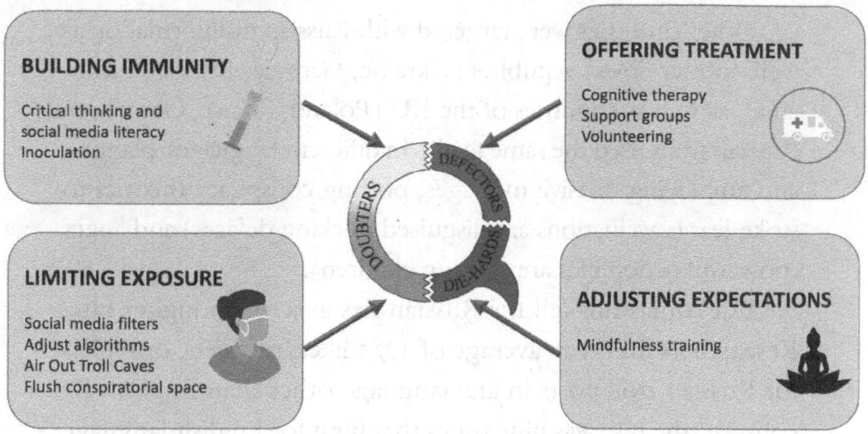

Figure 4.1. Counter-Q measures. Source: Sophia Moskalenko and Kristian Warpinski.

theories. RT issued a similar slew of QAnon-supporting content after Facebook removed accounts that spread disinformation. Heartened by RT's support for their cause, QAnon followers began sharing more content from Russian outlets, including RT and Graphika.[24]

Russian propaganda has targeted not just QAnon supporters but all Americans. In the months before the 2016 presidential election, an estimated 126 million U.S. Facebook users had seen posts, stories, or other content created by accounts backed by the Russian government,[25] and an additional 20 million have been exposed to this Russian content on Facebook-owned Instagram.[26] A similar picture emerges from Twitter and YouTube. Russia has weaponized social media to spread rumors, conspiracy theories, and emotion-stirring images in a coordinated effort to radicalize the United States from within.[27]

Other countries were targeted with Russian disinformation as well: former Soviet republics (Ukraine, Georgia, Estonia, Lithuania), as well as countries of the EU (Poland, France, Germany). Russian trolls used the same tactics in different languages: planting and amplifying divisive messages, posting conspiracy theories to stoke fear (vaccinations are disguised tracking devices) and anger (powerful pedophiles are abusing children).

But Americans fell for Russian lies at a much higher rate. Researchers found an average of 1.73 likes, retweets, or replies for Russian troll posts in any language other than English. By contrast, the rate was nine times that high for English-language posts (15.25).[28] Americans, it turned out, were easy targets for the Russian propaganda, including Q-conspiracy theories.

One cause of this American vulnerability is that U.S. education lags behind Europe in teaching critical thinking and social media literacy. The First Amendment to the U.S. Constitution guarantees freedom of speech, no matter how vile. Perhaps because of this country's foundational principle, Americans don't appreciate the danger of some speech in quite the same way as do Germans, who have experienced the power of Nazi propaganda, or as do former Soviet countries, which have lived through propaganda-driven communist regimes.

QAnon's rise shows how important it is to build up psychological defenses against malevolent actors who use false narratives to radicalize. A recent study found that believing in COVID-19 conspiracy theories correlates with inability to follow scientific reasoning.[29] Another study discovered that people who had trouble performing complex mental tasks were more likely to hold radical views.[30] These two findings speak to the same fact: Inability to think critically predicts a radical and conspiratorial mindset. Americans should follow the European example in teaching critical thinking and social media literacy from an early age and through adulthood.

European countries teach critical thinking as part of their school curriculum, paying special attention to disinformation online. For example, Finland's schoolchildren learn to identify fake news by studying examples of fake stories, altered photos, and divisive content designed to foment group conflict.[31] From elementary school onward, Finnish children practice sorting online content into truth or fiction, assessing media bias and deciphering how clickbait content preys on users' emotions. This approach has a track record of success. A variety of media literacy courses and initiatives implemented across European schools have shown to be effective at building students' ability to defend against disinformation.[32]

Similar courses should be integrated into U.S. school curriculums. Many American parents worry about their children's online exposure to bad influences of all kinds, including to sexual predators. Introducing educational initiatives to teach children to identify and resist online dangers would do wonders not only for the children's psychological resilience, but also for their parents' peace of mind. Knowing children are learning how to protect themselves against online predators would relieve the pressure on parents to seek out and fight a global pedophilic cabal.

In addition, to build immunity against online disinformation in adults, media literacy programs should be available in public libraries. Many stay-at-home moms do not have the knowledge to discern one source of Internet information from another and may have only a vague idea about Internet trolls or bots. Free courses on basic concepts of social media's power and pitfalls would help these women to become better-informed consumers of information. This would make them less vulnerable to online radicalization. As a bonus, community-based media literacy programs would open a new social milieu and possibilities for new real-life friendships.

Finally, social media companies would do well to integrate social media literacy exercises within individual user experiences. A person opening their Facebook or Instagram should occasionally be nudged to take a quick test of their ability to "tell a fake profile from a real one" or to "spot seven signs a post is fake news." Through interactive and engaging content like this, users would improve their media literacy and boost their psychological resistance to QAnon-style disinformation.

Inoculation

It's easy to get inoculation wrong, with biological viruses as well as with viral ideas. If someone tells you "Don't think about a pink elephant," this attempt at thought inoculation is likely to do the opposite. Even if you weren't inclined to think of a pink elephant before, you will after the warning.

This may seem like common sense. However, politicians often get this truism wrong. For example, Nancy Reagan's inoculation advice against drug use ("Just say no") has been adopted as the official slogan of D.A.R.E.—a drug-prevention program that spent millions of government dollars popularizing it. Following in her footsteps, Bob Dole, a one-time Republican presidential candidate, offered a new variation the 1990s: "Just don't do it." Research showed that these anti-drug slogans just didn't do it for teenagers at risk, whom they primarily targeted.[33] Those exposed to the anti-drug slogans were no less likely to try drugs than those who weren't. While "Just say no" didn't help inoculate against drug use, at least it didn't harm people's chances to stay away from drugs.

Real danger lies with ham-handed attempts at inoculation that have the opposite of the desired effect. Presenting people with weak arguments against their beliefs can do exactly that. For instance, telling teenagers to exclusively practice abstinence because it's morally superior to sex (a weak argument) actually results in more teenagers having sex and more teens becoming pregnant.[34] When an individual can mentally or verbally defend their position against weak arguments, they feel more certain that they were right. Having won a fight against an alternative view, they are less likely to entertain it. Thus, instead of undermining original beliefs, weak arguments can make them stronger.[35]

For this reason, it is a bad idea to argue with QAnon followers. Conspiracy theorists are adept at dismissing or explaining away any evidence that contradicts their views. Arguing with nonbelievers is likely to entrench QAnons even deeper in their beliefs.

By the same token, simply labeling disinformation, as Twitter did to Donald Trump's tweets before banning him, is likely to be counterproductive. The labels affirm conspiracy theory supporters' paranoia about the "deep state" censoring their leaders. At the same time, the labels effectively signal to them which content to pay attention to, "pink elephant" style.

One type of inoculation, however, offers great promise in fighting against the spread of conspiracy theory. This technique makes people's defensiveness work to their benefit, a little like jujitsu. It goes something like this: Imagine you're about to meet someone. But before they walk up to you, I whisper into your ear, "This is a scam artist, and you are their ideal target.

Just FYI." I haven't given you any facts, but I have made you suspicious. Anything this new person says to you after my warning is bound to be scrutinized. If they do something bad, they confirm your suspicions. If they do something nice, you suspect there's a catch. If they are, in fact, a scam artist, it would be mighty hard for them to fool you now.

Researchers used this cunning technique to inoculate teenage boys against the appeal of junk food.[36] Some boys were told about the dangers of junk food—a straightforward message similar to the "Just say no" of anti-drug campaigns. Other boys, however, were told about the devious ways the food industry manipulates adolescents into buying junk food. The second message emphasized how adults were controlling teenagers—a sentiment that would resonate with teens, triggering their defenses. In the three months that followed, researchers tracked what food the boys' chose at their school cafeteria. For the first group, which was told to stay away from unhealthy food, there was no difference. They consumed as much junk food after the researchers' intervention as before. But in the second group, researchers saw a strong and lasting effect of their message. Teens who were forewarned about deception aimed at them made better food choices. The inoculation worked.

Expanding this finding, a recent study tried attitude inoculation against political messaging.[37] Participants in the study were presented with a slightly reworded manifesto from a 1960s terrorist group, Weather Underground. But some of them were inoculated in advance: They were told that they might encounter a political message from an extremist group that recruits "people just like you." These inoculated participants were much more likely to argue against the radical political message and be suspicious about the group behind it than participants who didn't receive an inoculation.

An effective counter-conspiracy theory campaign would include inoculating messages on social media. These would micro-target people vulnerable to disinformation, warning them about nefarious groups seeking to recruit "people just like them." For example, a white, suburban woman browsing pastel-colored Instagram posts might see a banner alerting her that "some of this content was created by Russian trolls to manipulate opinions of American white, suburban women." Or a mother, watching YouTube videos about child abuse, might see one reporting on the high volume of fake online content about pedophiles that seeks to exploit mothers' protective instincts in order to milk them for donations to fake charities. We need more research to calibrate both the micro-targeting and the messaging. What is already clear is that attitude inoculation would be a great step toward building psychological resilience to QAnon.

Limiting Exposure

Social Media Filters

The tech giants—Twitter, Facebook, Instagram, and YouTube—have begun clamping down on disinformation after the January 6 insurrection brought QAnon into focus for the U.S. public. A number of conspiracy-spewing accounts have been shut down, including those of Donald J. Trump, General Michael Flynn, and Alex Jones, as well as over 70,000 Twitter QAnon accounts. This was a long-overdue and much-needed action. The results were immediate and impressive. In just one week, the amount of misinformation on these platforms went down by 73 percent.[38]

With the super spreader accounts gone, the momentum to rile support and recruit new people into the QAnon movement also died down. Mentions of election fraud and the stolen election dropped from 2.5 million to just 688,000. Likewise, the use of hashtags #FightForTrump, #HoldTheLine, and #MarchForTrump declined by 95 percent. Facebook users also became a lot less likely to click on or "like" right-leaning content in the days after Facebook banned Trump. It turns out that social distancing works not only with biological viruses but also with viral information.

Although successful, this effort was reactive rather than proactive. By the time QAnon followers stormed the Capitol, social media had already allowed conspiracy theories to proliferate. Influential individuals—super spreaders—had lent them credibility by reposting, liking, or engaging with their content. As a result, the number of people exposed to the radical rhetoric ballooned. Even when the social media companies eventually shut down conspiracy-posting accounts, there was no apparent coordination among the platforms. Users kicked off one platform transitioned to another, taking followers with them.

To curtail the spread of conspiracy theories, there must be a centralized and coordinated contingency plan for all social media platforms. Social media companies must take responsibility for addressing problematic content in real time—preventatively—before it has a chance to spread.

Adjust Algorithms

Part of what made QAnon into a giant social movement were the social media algorithms that recommended content to users. A woman worried about COVID-19 infecting her family would go online seeking information about the virus, and the algorithms would lead her down a "garden path" toward videos and posts about a Chinese bioweapons laboratory designing COVID-19 to control the world or about COVID-19 vaccines turning her children into homosexuals. Searching for information about Trump's re-election, another woman would see recommendations about a secret cabal of pedophiles that Trump was fighting. As with the 6 o'clock news on TV, fear mongering and cliffhangers assured that the users would stay glued to their screens. Post by post, click by click, they ended up in the rabbit hole without even trying.

The algorithms are proprietary: Internet companies keep secret how they decide which recommendations users see. Researchers can't get access to user data that Facebook, YouTube, Twitter, and others collect. But these restrictions are not applied equally. Thus, Cambridge Analytica, a private political consulting company, was implicated in a 2018 scandalous data breach, in which it had reportedly obtained private data from over 87 million Facebook users. Cambridge Analytica then used these highly detailed personal data to micro-target vulnerable users—for example, by discouraging them from voting.[39]

Going forward, social media companies must implement more oversight and offer more transparency. They should also consistently enforce their own terms of conduct, banning violators. This will cripple the capacity of malicious actors (such as Cambridge Analytica or Russian bots or trolls) from spreading conspiracy theories.

But that's not enough.

Another problem QAnon exploited was that "alternative" social media platforms—such as Parler, Telegram, 4chan, and 8chan—do not abide by even the limited number of regulatory guidelines currently enforced by Twitter and Facebook. These alternative platforms remain a digital Wild West, providing a refuge to the most radical, and thus most dangerous, individuals and groups. Lawmakers must consider the implications of this unregulated Internet space and design some system of accountability. In the meantime, the following strategies work on the dark web just as well as on mainstream platforms.

Air Out Troll Caves

Russian psyops (psychological operations) have systematized and weaponized online trolling. Reportedly, thousands of Russian citizens are employed full-time as Internet trolls, clicking and commenting day and night to champion the Motherland's interests.[40] A post with thousands of likes tends to be recommended by social media algorithms more than one with just a few likes. Trolls trick the algorithms into prioritizing the content that they rally behind. And when the algorithms bring up troll-ridden posts on users' timelines, users more often click on them and believe the content, because they think many other people liked it. Thus, trolls have perfected the art of tricking both computer programs and people on social media. But what if this art can be used for good instead of evil?

What if, instead of trolls (or perhaps in addition to them), there were "elves"—individuals whose job would be to add reality checks and counterarguments to discussion boards and forums? Elves would challenge anyone who posts disinformation to "bring receipts" or admit they were full of hot, stinky troll air. With elves airing out troll caves, an average user would get a clearer perspective than they would with only trolls skewing their view.

Psychologists studying group discussions discovered that the more arguments for a radical position a person encounters, the more probable it is that they shift their opinion, becoming more radical themselves.[41] If you hear two people mention a crazy rumor, you're more likely to question it than if a hundred people mention it. And if you see thousands of people agreeing with the crazy rumor, you are more apt to think that maybe it's not so crazy after all. You're a lot more likely to believe the crazy rumor yourself. A discussion board with active trolls running rampant is a radicalization minefield.

This is especially so with the kind of content that characterizes QAnon posts. In the classical series of experiments, Solomon Asch demonstrated that a unanimous majority stating an obvious falsehood can make a person accept and repeat the falsehood to avoid looking (and feeling) ridiculous.[42] When asked to compare the lengths of three lines, for example, three quarters of participants would disregard the evidence of their own eyes and say that the short line was the long one—because the majority said so. (The majority, as you may have guessed, were experimenter's accomplices, instructed to lie.) Asch called this tendency *conformity*. The larger the group, the less likely a person was to disagree with the group's clearly wrong opinions, and the more likely they were to conform to the majority. But Asch discovered a cure for conformity. When one member of the group (also an accomplice of the experimenter) voiced disagreement with the majority, participants' conformity evaporated. Like in Hans Christian Andersen's fairy tale, when a little kid cried out "The emperor is naked," others chimed in and supported this view. So, too, in online discussion, a dissenting voice is a powerful reality check that can break the spell of conformity.

An elf entering a forum buzzing about vaccines that turn children into homosexuals might ask the most active users for evidence. "Can you give me a link to a study that shows that?" They can also challenge the assertion that the story is true: "I googled, but I can't find any facts about this. Sounds like fake news to me." If sources are posted, an elf might question the sources' legitimacy: "Dude, that's not, like, a real report. It's just some guy speaking into his camera phone."

Planting elves would undermine the influence of the majority on troll-driven forums. Seeing trolls' ridiculous or factually wrong statements challenged would empower users to resist trolls' disinformation. Thus, introducing elves who would add counterarguments against radical opinions and would make users less likely to embrace radical rhetoric.

Flush Conspiratorial Space

QAnon offered users the joy of connecting the dots and figuring out for themselves "the Truth" and "the plan." This activity seemed like creative discovery to them, when in fact the "dots" were arranged with a particular sinister purpose, and most QAnons would end up with the same conspiracy theories after connecting them. This is akin to what psychologists call *groupthink*—a tendency of individuals in groups to fall in line, adopting the same ideas, no matter how flawed those ideas might be.[43] Groupthink is going along to get along, at the expense of facts and sometimes common sense.

One way to disrupt groupthink in the digital space is to flood the social interactions with appealing alternatives. As a result, people are more likely to question, and less likely to follow, the garden path prepared for them.

One study demonstrated how this could be accomplished with the help of bots—computer programs posing as human Internet users. Instead of connecting the dots into conspiracy theories, the study focused on inkblot interpretations, the kind used in Rorschach personality test.[44] As with conspiracy theories, when Internet forums interpreted inkblots, they tended to converge on a single, most popular version. "It's a butterfly," the group would decide, ignoring other suggestions (crab, bunny, couch). And the larger the group, the more likely it was to embrace a single interpretation. Groupthink made people suppress their own dissenting opinion and embrace the most popular opinion instead.

But then study authors did something to disrupt this process. Knowing that "butterfly" was the most likely interpretation to emerge, they introduced bots into group discussion and made them suggest an unlikely and unpopular vision of the inkblot: "sumo wrestler." Sure enough, as bots flooded the field, their interpretation gained followers. Fewer people were now agreeing that the inkblot looked like a butterfly. Once the bots comprised over 37 percent of the group, sumo wrestler became the dominant interpretation in the group. What's more, this interpretation stuck with participants. Even after they were no longer in the same forum, even when they were shown a new inkblot that looked like a crab, not a butterfly, participants "brainwashed" by the bots were likely to see a sumo wrestler in it.

Translating these findings into the conspiracy theory world, by flooding Internet discussions with alternatives to conspiracy theories, bots can make people less likely to connect the dots into the pattern pushed on them by malicious actors or by groups like QAnon. This technique would work on mainstream media as well as on the dark web. Flooding the conspiratorial space would limit exposure to dangerous rhetoric for Diehards and Doubters, as well as for those teetering on the edge of the rabbit hole.

To disrupt the spread of conspiracy theories, flooding would require two steps. In the first step, focus groups would explore conspiratorial "crumbs." These focus groups would then be instructed to connect the dots in a way that differed from the prevailing interpretation. In step two, bots would inject these alternative interpretations into the conspiratorial space on the dark web or on mainstream social media. With bots flooding forums, users would be pulled away from conspiracy theories.

Offering Treatment

QAnon's rise coincided with the onset of the COVID-19 pandemic and the lockdowns that followed. This was also the time of a developing mental health crisis in the United States: The rates of depression and anxiety among Americans went up by a factor of 4, from 1 in 10 people reporting symptoms before the pandemic to 4 in 10 reporting them after.[45] QAnon appealed to people already feeling anxious and depressed, and following QAnon exacerbated these feelings.

People who dove into the depths of conspiracy theory world often lost social connections outside of it. Some lost their businesses because of their beliefs. Isolation and financial troubles added strain on mental health, causing people to seek comfort in the QAnon community and pushing them even deeper into the radical belief system. The vicious circle continually chipped away at psychological well-being.

In this book, we presented several cases of ex-QAnon women. Even within this thin slice of the movement, there was a high prevalence and a great diversity of psychological disorder: Munchausen by proxy, substance abuse, depression, anxiety, PTSD, and bipolar disorder. Each of these is a devastating disease that can render those suffering from it incapable of handling the demands of daily life.

Consider the severity of psychopathology it would take for a mother to say, "If Biden wins, the world is over, basically . . . I would probably take my children and sit in the garage and turn my car on, and it would be over."[46] Tina Arthur, owner of a small business, made this statement in the context of sharing her belief that Democrats are part of the world-ruling cabal and that they rape children and drink their blood. But the context is less important than the fact that Arthur's statement is a credible threat, with a detailed and accessible plan to harm herself and her minor children. Conspiracy theories aside, someone like Tina Arthur would benefit from psychological help.

A report mining criminal records of QAnon followers who were arrested for storming the U.S. Capitol on January 6 found an exorbitant number of them (68%) with documented psychiatric problems. These mental disorders ranged from depression and anxiety to paranoid schizophrenia, bipolar disorder, and PTSD.[47] For comparison, only 21 percent of Americans had a diagnosed psychological disorder in 2019[48]—a rate less than one third of that among QAnon insurrectionists. The same report found that seven out of eight women who committed violence at the Capitol riot had experienced a psychological trauma that led to their radicalization. The trauma was typically around their children being physically and/or sexually abused by their partners or by family members. The rates of psychopathology and reported psychological trauma among QAnons charged with crimes related to the January 6 insurrection are magnitudes higher than average. The overwhelming majority of these people are psychologically unwell and in dire need of comprehensive mental health treatment.

In fact, QAnon's rise can be viewed as a symptom of a mass mental health crisis. Individuals who embrace Q-conspiracy theories may be inadvertently expressing deeper psychological problems, in the same way that self-harming behaviors or psychosomatic complaints flag deeper psychological issues. The American Psychological Association must direct resources toward studying beliefs in conspiracy theories as a symptom of other mental health problems, or as a separate diagnosis.

Presently, mental health services are out of reach for many Americans who don't have health insurance, or whose health insurance doesn't cover therapy. Even primary healthcare is in short supply in the United States, which means many people who suffer from psychological problems never receive a diagnosis or treatment. A comprehensive approach to rehabilitating former QAnon members would include psychological assessment, and, where needed, professional psychological services such as individual or group therapy.

Cognitive Therapy

Cognitive therapy, designed by Aaron Beck, is a highly successful treatment for a variety of psychological disorders.[49] Its methods include guiding patients through the process of questioning their implicit assumptions ("nobody cares about me" or "doctors are only ever looking to get rich off of people's suffering") and recognizing their knee-jerk emotional reactions (shutting down at the prospect of a social interaction, or anger at medical professionals). Once patients learn to recognize their problematic patterns of thought and emotion, they can begin to counter them.

By repeatedly reinforcing this process of discernment, in therapy sessions and in "homework" assignment that patients complete between appointments, they develop a more mindful, less reactive cognitive style. This cognitive style helps to guard against falling into faulty thought patterns that lead to harmful behaviors. Before, a person might watch an Internet video about abused children and become overwhelmed with anxiety and guilt. Escaping these emotions, they might get onto Internet forums discussing the video, where their guilt would be redirected toward scapegoats like Soros and Clinton, and their anxiety might be repurposed into anger and plans for retaliation. After cognitive therapy, however, a patient would learn to recognize their emotions, including unpleasant ones. Instead of seeking to escape them in online forums, they would follow psychological techniques to reduce anxiety and guilt. Instead of adopting problematic beliefs (pedophiles and cannibals are running the world), they would question them.

For QAnon followers, cognitive therapy would help not only their beliefs in conspiracy theories, but also the cognitive and emotional needs that brought them to QAnon in the first place. Maybe the thought of COVID-19 made a woman feel like a bad mother for not being able to protect her children from the virus. Or maybe it was the thought of pedophile priests and politicians preying on young kids. This anxiety then pushed her into the rabbit hole of QAnon conspiracies. Cognitive therapy would help such a patient work through her cognition: What does it mean to be a "good mother"? Can any mother protect her children from EVERY danger? If not, how could one still be a good mother? What are some things that make a good mother? A homework assignment for that week might be to observe and note the actions the patient performs routinely that she would recognize as good parenting (i.e., feeding, helping, hugging the child) and maybe to add one new "good mother" behavior that she wouldn't normally do (i.e., reading to the child before bed). In the subsequent sessions, the patient would reassess her belief about parenting in general, and about her own parenting.

For those whose QAnon descent was precipitated by loneliness and isolation, cognitive therapy could address their social needs. In this case, therapy goals could include learning and practicing social skills required to shore up a social network outside of QAnon. Homework assignments could be making small talk with a neighbor, saying hello to a stranger, or making a phone call to a friend or a family member. With the therapist's help, the patient would review these experiences, noting problematic cognitions as well as what helped to overcome these.

To summarize, cognitive therapy can address the needs that give rise to conspiratorial beliefs. It can also offer the tools to rebuild the patient's social, emotional, and personal life.

Support Groups

Loneliness, exacerbated by the COVID-19 pandemic shutdowns, was one of the major forces that drove people into QAnon. Once they were deep in QAnon, social isolation only got worse. This is how QAnon Defector Jitarth Jadeja described it:

> "I think superficially it did seem like [QAnon] gave me comfort," Jadeja said. "I didn't realize the nefarious kind of impact it was having on me because it was very insidious how it slowly disconnected me from reality."

> "No one believes you. No one wants to talk to you about it. . . . You get all angsty and crabby and whatnot. [S]uch shouting, irrational, you sound like the homeless guy on the street yelling about Judgment Day."[50]

Online QAnon community provided an illusion of instant, omnipresent connection, which is hard to find in the real world. Especially for former QAnons, who have often lost contact with family and friends over their beliefs, leaving QAnon puts them right back where they started: feeling lonely. Therefore, decreasing social exclusion must be a priority to prevent former QAnons from relapsing into their old ways. Support groups can help.

There are already a growing number of online forums that offer a safe space for Defectors to commiserate and to support one another. Popular Subreddits such as r/QAnonCasualties and r/ReQuovery invite both former Q and people affected by QAnonized loved ones to share their experience and tips for life after Q.

Additionally, former cult members, like Steven Hassan, founder of the Freedom of Mind Resource Center, are spearheading efforts to help Q followers re-enter the world outside of QAnon.[51] Hassan himself had been recruited into the Reverend Moon cult at the age 19. After years in the cult, he left, and has since turned his defection into a career of helping other victims of mind control. Hassan says that the process of indoctrination and radicalization into a cult is identical whether it's the Moonies, Scientology, or QAnon,[52] and the process of de-radicalization is also similar. Former members of cults (like Scientology) or of radical groups (like neo-Nazis) might be invaluable to recovering QAnons, Doubters and Defectors alike, by sharing the challenges they had faced after defection, as well as success stories in overcoming these challenges.

Another useful model of social support for those trying to break a harmful habit has been perfected by Alcoholics Anonymous. Regular meetings with others (QAnons Anonymous, perhaps) who wouldn't judge because they have been through the same lows would provide the face-to-face contact so many QAnons crave. Former QAnons might also benefit from having a sponsor they could count on when they need support and guidance, someone who would answer their calls and not turn their back on them no matter what their beliefs. By having a specific person to turn to in moments of crisis, who would support without judging, QAnon Defectors would fulfill both social and emotional needs.

Volunteering

Volunteering is a somewhat counterintuitive source of psychological and physical well-being for women and men, young and old.[53] People who volunteer, whether with official charities or simply by helping their friends and neighbors without expecting anything in return, enjoy a variety of benefits: more happiness, higher self-esteem, and more self-confidence, as well as greater physical health and longer lifespans. One explanation for this surprising effect is that volunteering allows people to interact with less fortunate others, which makes volunteers feel more grateful for what they have and happier as a result. Another is that volunteering channels stress and anxiety into productive action, relieving the negative effects that stress biochemicals have on the body and on the mind. Both of these mechanisms would be especially beneficial to former QAnon members.

Instead of surfing the Internet, sick with worry for imaginary abused children, why not spend time and energy volunteering at a local children's hospital, or at the local library's story hour? Seeing actual children, and actually helping them, would bring incomparable moral and emotional rewards, rendering the appeal of QAnon moot. Women can help other women care for children, or volunteer to take over cooking one night a week, so a struggling single mother next door can have a break. Women whose gender identity feels threatened can reaffirm it through these traditionally feminine actions, while at the same time building social connections. Volunteering is a feel-good fest where everybody wins, like on an Oprah show: You get a benefit, you get a benefit, *everybody* gets a benefit.

Volunteering can also focus on helping other former QAnon followers. Defectors are best equipped to help Doubters get out of QAnon's grip. With the wealth of their own experiences, Defectors can serve as sponsors/mentors in the AA-type support programs. They can also become elves in online forums, fighting trolls and disinformation. They can volunteer to serve on focus groups to work out alternatives to conspiracy theories that would then be used by bots to flood the conspiratorial space. Finally, former QAnon members would be of great help in programs to educate people on media literacy and teach them critical thinking. Outreach programs at schools and among vulnerable populations could use Defectors' expertise and firsthand knowledge to educate the general public on the dangers of disinformation.

These volunteering activities would help people transcend the trauma and disappointment of their QAnon membership. By giving their lives purpose and meaning, volunteering could serve a personal utility far better than Qanon ever could. As a bonus, former Qanon volunteers would reap all the science-proven rewards of meaningful sacrifice: better quality of life, better health, and more happiness.

Through rebuilding social connections and volunteering, former Qanon followers would be less susceptible to being manipulated into feeling outrage, fear, or anger. They would therefore be more resilient to attempts at weaponizing their reactions through social media. And investing personal time and efforts into fellow Americans would help bridge the social divisions that carry potential for QAnon-style mass radicalization.

Adjusting Expectations

With so many people in the United States believing conspiracy theories, those of us who do not are not immune to QAnon's damage. Whereas the three previous counter-QAnon approaches (building immunity, limiting exposure, and offering treatment) primarily targeted QAnons, the fourth prong, adjusting expectations, focuses on those of us outside QAnon.

A well-established finding of radicalization research is that radicalization on one side begets radicalization on the opposing side.[54] When someone attacks us, we want to attack back. When someone questions our way of life and our social norms, we feel anger toward them that can boil into aggression. The terrorist attacks of 9/11, for example, resulted in the American public's support for unnecessary wars abroad and for violations of constitutional rights at home. We became mass radicalized. The costs of that mass radicalization are still haunting us 20 years later. Adjusting expectations about conspiracy theories can help us avoid similarly costly mass radicalization in response to the threat of QAnon.

Conspiracy theories have been part of human civilization since its beginning. Even the major tropes of QAnon conspiracy lore have remained consistent over hundreds of years: evil Jews, child abuse, harmful substances that the powerful use to their advantage, a secret cabal that runs the world. These falsehoods have survived world wars, pandemics, natural disasters, and regime changes. Their popularity waxes and wanes—up in times of uncertainty and shifting social norms and down when the society is functioning like a well-oiled mechanism, with the government and social institutions fulfilling people's expectations. It would be nice if conspiracy theories disappeared forever, and everyone was rational and reasonable. But it's not very likely. Conspiracy theories will probably stick around—whatever becomes of QAnon.

With this in mind, measures to counter QAnon's messaging and images are no more important than measures to counter our own psychological reactions to QAnon. Here, we recommend comprehensive mindfulness training.

Mindfulness Training

Mindfulness-based stress reduction (MBSR) is a clinical program that was developed and systematized by John Kabat-Zinn,[55] a molecular biologist whose interest in Buddhism inspired him to study how some Buddhist practices affect physiological stress response. MBSR combines meditation, breathing exercises, and mindful movement (yoga, tai chi, or chi gong) with practicing awareness. Clinical studies have documented beneficial effects of MBSR on clinical disorders, including depression and anxiety, but also on general well-being. Blood chemistry analyses confirm MBSR's positive effects on stress hormones. MRI scans of individuals trained in MBSR show changes in their brain structures consistent with reduced stress response and less reactive psychological style. In short, MBSR helps fortify psychological defenses and reduce stress by training people to connect with the present moment rather than worry about the future or regret the past.

For those of us whose loved ones have been swept up in QAnon conspiracies, MBSR could offer a much-needed sanctuary from stress caused by frustration and helplessness. Like airlines' instructions to passengers, first priority in dealing with crises should be taking care of oneself. Only after our own psychological needs are met can we be of help to others. Especially if your loved one is a Diehard QAnon, mindfulness would help to adjust expectations and to guard against soul-crushing disappointments.

A typical MBSR course brings together a group of people once a week, for eight weeks. Unlike therapy, MBSR students are not expected to talk about themselves. Unlike a therapist, an MBSR teacher won't ask, "What brings you here today?" The assumption is that everyone's life has stress and struggle, and everyone can use mindfulness to help deal with it. Whatever brings people into MBSR, they learn to be fully present in the moment. By focusing on immediate physical sensations, emotional experiences, and arising thoughts, MBSR students learn to recognize that all of these are transient. Sensations, feelings, and thoughts come and go—none are permanent. Learning to let go of persistent thoughts that can otherwise become obsessions or ruminations reduces stress. Mindful movement connects people with bodily sensations, helping them to recognize the physiological markers of stress. Meditation and breathing exercises offer an avenue to distance oneself from nagging worries and self-defeating patterns.

Without mindfulness practice, we are reactive to the vagaries of being. A bad phone call or a negative online post can push us into a downward spiral. Our shoulders hunch, breath becomes shallow, we grind our teeth. All of this feeds the body's stress response, sending stress hormones throughout tissues and organs, and releasing anxiety-producing chemicals in the brain. An hour later, we find ourselves still obsessing, only now our entire life—past, present, and future—is somehow tied in with that damned phone call or stupid post. We feel not good enough, defective, defeated.

With mindfulness, life's vagaries would still be there, but we would learn to catch our reaction to them before they become overwhelming. We would notice our posture—and straighten the spine. We would take a deep breath—and then another. And another one after that. We would get up and stretch or take a walk outside. The negative thoughts would still come, but we would know not to engage with them. Like clouds, they would pass over our mental horizon. Instead of being at the mercy of life's challenges, mindfulness allows us to practice being in charge of our reactions to them.

Positive effects of MBSR last long after the eight-week course is over. For many, mindfulness they learn in an MBSR course becomes an important part of their life. With the positive effects of mindfulness well established in research findings, many health insurance plans now cover the cost of the eight-week course.

MBSR is a systematized and well-studied way to learn and practice mindfulness, but it is not the only way. Books that teach mindfulness techniques can be picked up at your local library for free. There are online videos on YouTube that can demonstrate yoga and breathing exercises. Many apps available for smartphones and tablets teach and help you practice meditation, awareness, and mindful movement.

While QAnon followers may be on the extreme end, the Internet and social media can be addictive for all of us. Content that stirs fears, anxiety, and anger is most engaging, and therefore most prevalent. The illusion is that we are controlling it, by clicking on the app icon, by reading when and what we choose. But the fact is, the Internet can be a medium for controlling us: Our attention, our emotions, our opinions and behaviors. What's worse, Internet companies are only too eager to encourage our unhealthy dependence on them. Awareness is the first step toward maintaining agency and avoiding manipulation. Cultivating mindfulness about our online exposure would do wonders for our psychological health.

CHAPTER 5

QONTAGION

On August 22, 2020, 200 street rallies were held across the United States, Canada, and European countries, as well as in eleven cities and towns in the UK, under the slogan "Save Our Children." #SaveTheChildren was a fundraising campaign for the UK-based charity Save the Children, but the hashtag was hijacked by QAnon believers in July 2020, leading Facebook to temporarily disable it after it became awash with misinformation.[1] In "band-wagoning" onto the charity's hashtag, QAnon took root in the social media timelines of middle- and upper-class women who would never consider affiliating with an online conspiracy theory except for one that appealed to their maternal instinct.[2] What is noteworthy is that the visuals used as part of the QAnon hashtag #SaveTheChildren featured battered and bruised children, almost all of whom were white. Long past are the days of Sally Struthers's entreaties for donations to Christian Children's Fund, which showed mostly non-white children with distended bellies and covered in flies. In contrast to the graphic images posted by QAnon, the *actual* Save the Children charity features smiling children from Africa, Latin America, and Southeast Asia.

In Chapter 1 we explored how the COVID-19 pandemic supercharged conspiracy theories—but none so much as QAnon. As the pandemic is a global phenomenon, so too have the conspiracies gone global. With QAnon's growing popularity in the United States, it has likewise metastasized to dozens of other countries from Brazil to Germany, France, the Balkans, the UK and Indonesia.[3] In June 2020, the Institute for Strategic Dialogue counted 450,000 members of QAnon on the European continent.[4] However, this figure is probably only the tip of the iceberg. The conspiracy theory has managed to attach itself to local grievances in countries around the world, and in doing so it successfully blends anti-government, anti-lockdown, and anti-Semitic rhetoric with its beliefs about the global pedophile ring.

QAnon has grown internationally in two ways: By embracing local grievances and coopting local interests, QAnon resonates with an international audience; and by embedding itself with particular strains in Christianity, it communicates a degree of legitimacy. Two countries have amplified QAnon disinformation with the goal of undermining people's trust in institutions: Russia and China.

The Gospel of Q

In the United States, QAnon has infiltrated several religious denominations: Catholicism, Protestantism, and the evangelical church. Evangelical Christians elevated Trump to godlike status in 2016 when they put their full support behind then-candidate Trump. In the United States, AEI conducted a survey after the January 6, 2021, failed insurrection at the Capitol. The results of the survey defy logic; they found that 29 percent of Republicans and 27 percent of white evangelicals—the most of any religious group—believe the widely debunked collection of Q-conspiracy theories is completely or mostly accurate.[5]

QAnon infiltrated several Christian denominations besides evangelicals, including 15 percent of white Protestants, 18 percent of white Catholics, 11 percent of Hispanic Catholics, 7 percent of Black Protestants, 22 percent nonaffiliated, and 12 percent of non-Christians.[6] As the conspiracy belief seeped into the religious fabric of U.S. life, it merged with the proselytizing zeal of some of these groups. Left unfettered, it is equally likely that traditional missionary work by Christian groups will become imbued with Q ideology.

As it has absorbed local grievances abroad, among evangelicals, QAnon blended its beliefs with religious dogma, cherry-picking verses from religious texts to substantiate its most outlandish claims. Despite so many of the QAnon predictions failing to manifest, evangelicals proselytize the conspiracy theory with the same religious zeal they bring to their missionary work. Adrienne LaFrance, editor for *The Atlantic*, has suggested that QAnon is not an everyday conspiracy but it is becoming a religion in its own right.[7]

QAnon spread among evangelicals for the same reasons that conspiracy theories increased multiple times over: as a result of the pandemic and quarantine. Instead of attending Sunday services in person, people were forced to worship at home without the benefits of group cohesion, comfort, and community. Without this succor, they experienced loneliness and isolation. Like the rest of the world, they spent additional hours on Facebook and the Internet. What made evangelicals especially vulnerable to QAnon was that the language and terminology that QAnon used sounded explicitly Christian, debating the existence of good and evil. The primacy of prophecy and the concept of the "Great Awakening" resonate with evangelical Christians because for many believers this describes how they experienced their own path to finding Christ or their prophecies about the Rapture.

QAnon has coopted Christian-sounding ideas to promote their false claims. The movement is imbued with Christian theology and language, with Q regularly quoting from the Bible and urging his followers to "put on the armor of God."[8] This language and these references resonate positively precisely because they are familiar and ingrained. The clearly defined gulf between good and evil in which the other side is completely vilified (as blood-drinking pedophiles) promotes a type of dehumanization and intense *othering*.[9]

Katelyn Beaty, a writer for the Religion News Services, interviewed evangelical pastors whose worshippers were falling down the QAnon rabbit hole. One pastor from Missouri—Mark Fugitt of the Round Grove Baptist Church—recounted all the conspiracy theories that his parishioners had been sharing on social media. The list included claims that 5G is an evil plot for mind control; that George Floyd's murder is a hoax; that Bill Gates is related to the devil; that wearing masks might kill you; that the pandemic isn't real; and that there might be something to Pizzagate after all.[10] On the TV news show *60 Minutes*, Leslie Stahl interviewed Derek Kabilis, a pastor from Ohio, who has been more aggressive in calling QAnon a heresy.[11] However, the vast majority of Christian pastors have been reticent to take a stand against QAnon for fear of losing parishioners from their ministry to the conspiracy theory.

The leaders of the evangelical church are witnessing a crisis of authority in institutions—the government, the press, and even their own church—a crisis that is leading people to QAnon. Some pastors attributed the spread of QAnon to the so-called "death of expertise"—a distrust of authority that leads some people to undervalue competency and wisdom and where ignorance is considered a virtue.[12]

According to researcher Marc-André Argentino, one church in Indiana—the Omega Kingdom Ministry (OKM), led by Russ Wagner—hosts a two-hour Sunday service showing how Bible prophecies confirm QAnon's messages. OKM's leadership includes Kevin Bushey, a retired colonel who ran for election to the Maine House of Representatives in District 151. Wagner and Bushey advise their congregation to avoid the mainstream media (even Fox News and NewsMax are Luciferian in their estimation) in favor of QAnon YouTube channels or tracing Q-drops using the Qmap site developed by Jason Gelinas.[13]When evangelical Christians shun mainstream media, this exacerbates the problem of misinformation:

> The distrust in mainstream media and that willingness to write off mainstream media information as fake news opens the door for evangelicals to turn to alternative and fringe news sources, including those that traffic in conspiracy theories.[14]

Beginning in 2011, Trump actively courted evangelical support and appeared on the Christian Broadcasting Network, having been coached by Paula White to appeal to a religious Christian audience. As someone who could not cite even one biblical verse, Trump seemingly pandered to evangelical priorities (opposing abortion and same-sex marriage). When Trump finally launched his campaign in 2015, the evangelical base was surprisingly enthralled. Many evangelicals till this day claim that Trump was the most pro-life president ever to grace the office.[15] Trump's shared grievance with evangelicals—that the political, legal, and social changes in the country robbed Christian America of what they considered to be God's intention for the United States.

Support for Trump among evangelicals has been consistently high despite their dwindling numbers as their children migrate from the church's beliefs. Many evangelicals believe that God has chosen Trump, an unlikely leader, to lead the country in challenging times and to restore it to greatness.[16] In surveys, over 6 out of 10 (63%) evangelical Christian Republicans believed that an unelected group of government officials, known as the deep state, were trying to undermine the Trump administration. Despite pastors ignoring it or a handful opposing it, between 27 and 30 percent of evangelicals continued to believe in the conspiracy theory.[17]

> One possible explanation for why evangelical Christian Republicans are more likely to embrace conspiracy theories is their affinity to Trump. Trump played an active role in promoting misinformation.[18]

One of the major evangelical QAnon influencers is Dave Hayes, who uses the pen name "Praying Medic." The Praying Medic persona has amassed more than 750,000 followers across Twitter and YouTube. This Arizona-based evangelical faith healer has become a popular and influential interpreter of QAnon writings, and he is one of the most influential QAnons in the world. Hayes often meets with international QAnon supporters.[19]

Eighty percent of evangelical church members support Trump, and 29 percent also support QAnon. By embracing adjacent conspiracy theories—for example, the anti-vaxx movement—QAnon has filtered into other religious organizations that are likewise anti-vaxx, including (most shockingly), Orthodox Jews. One would have assumed that the anti-Semitic content of QAnon's beliefs would appall Jews. However, the Orthodox community in the United States overwhelmingly supports two elements consistent with QAnon beliefs: support for Trump and vaccine skepticism.[20]

While Silicon Valley began shutting down Q Facebook pages and Etsy and Twitter accounts in the summer of 2020, some new groups emerged to entice new followers. They migrated to new platforms like Parler and Gab and a few unexpected ones (like Peleton or Nextdoor).[21] Even after aggressive de-platforming of the biggest QAnon Twitter influencers in October 2020, in the month leading up to the election, as many as 93,000 channels remained.[22] Users also found a variety of ways to fool the moderators and the automatic enforcement systems by changing their hashtags or using the number 17 instead of the letter Q—for example, #Q17, #17Anon, or #CueAnon. Facebook has taken down thousands of pages but could not take down individual accounts that did not violate its terms of service. A British report from the group Hope Not Hate summarized the de-platforming whack-a-mole problem succinctly: "[A]ny action against them will therefore require endless vigilance against rebranded replacements repopulating the platforms."[23]

However, by this point, the conspiracy theory had crossed the Rubicon. QAnon had gone global.

Global Q

As social media companies were pulling down QAnon Facebook pages in the United States, new social media pages appeared in "Austria, Denmark, Hungary, Poland, the Czech Republic, Russia, and Israel."[24] In July 2020, Vice News began to document the global scope of QAnon, with thousands of followers in 25 different countries from the UK, Canada, Finland, France, Germany, Russia, and even Japan and Iran.[25] One QAnon researcher tracked the conspiracy through Facebook pages in 71 countries around the world (Table 5.1).[26] Figure 5.1 shows the global spread of QAnon followers.

> This internationalization presents an uphill battle for social media companies already facing increased pressure from governments to combat disinformation on their platforms in English, let alone a myriad other languages.[27]

In the international chapters of QAnon, the role that former President Trump plays varies. According to Melanie Smith of Graphika, QAnon subsidiaries in Japan and Brazil rely less on Trump as the focal point and are self-sustaining as an ideology.[28] In Japan, General Michael Flynn is QAnon's focal point more than former President Trump. Japan is a receptive milieu to conspiratorial thinking in part because *Mü* magazine has peddled various conspiracies for 40 years, and 2chan originated in Japan.[29] Based on Graphika's research, General Flynn is aware of his influence in Japan and follows several QAnon influencers in the Far East, including one woman whose Twitter handle was @okabaeri9111 (Twitter deleted the account as part of the crackdown on QAnon-promoting accounts). Eri Okabayashi ran

Table 5.1. List of countries with dedicated QAnon Facebook pages.

Algeria	France	Portugal
Andorra	Germany	Republic of Ireland
Angola	Greece	Romania
Argentina	Honduras	Russia
Australia	Hungary	Scotland
Austria	India	Senegal
Bahrain	Iraq	Serbia
Belgium	Israel	Singapore
Bolivia	Italy	Slovakia
Bosnia and Herzegovina	Japan	Slovenia
	Lithuania	South Africa
Brazil	Luxembourg	South Korea
Bulgaria	Macedonia	Spain
Canada	Mauritania	Sweden
Chile	Mexico	Switzerland
China	Moldova	Tanzania
Columbia	Netherlands	Thailand
Costa Rica	New Zealand	Ukraine
Croatia	Northern Ireland	United Kingdom
Cyprus	Norway	United States
Czech Republic	Pakistan	Uruguay
Denmark	Paraguay	Venezuela
Ecuador	Peru	Wales
England	Philippines	
Finland	Poland	

Source: Marc-André Argentino, "Twitter / @_MAArgentino: Lets Talk About QAnon Worldwide . . . " (August 8, 2020).

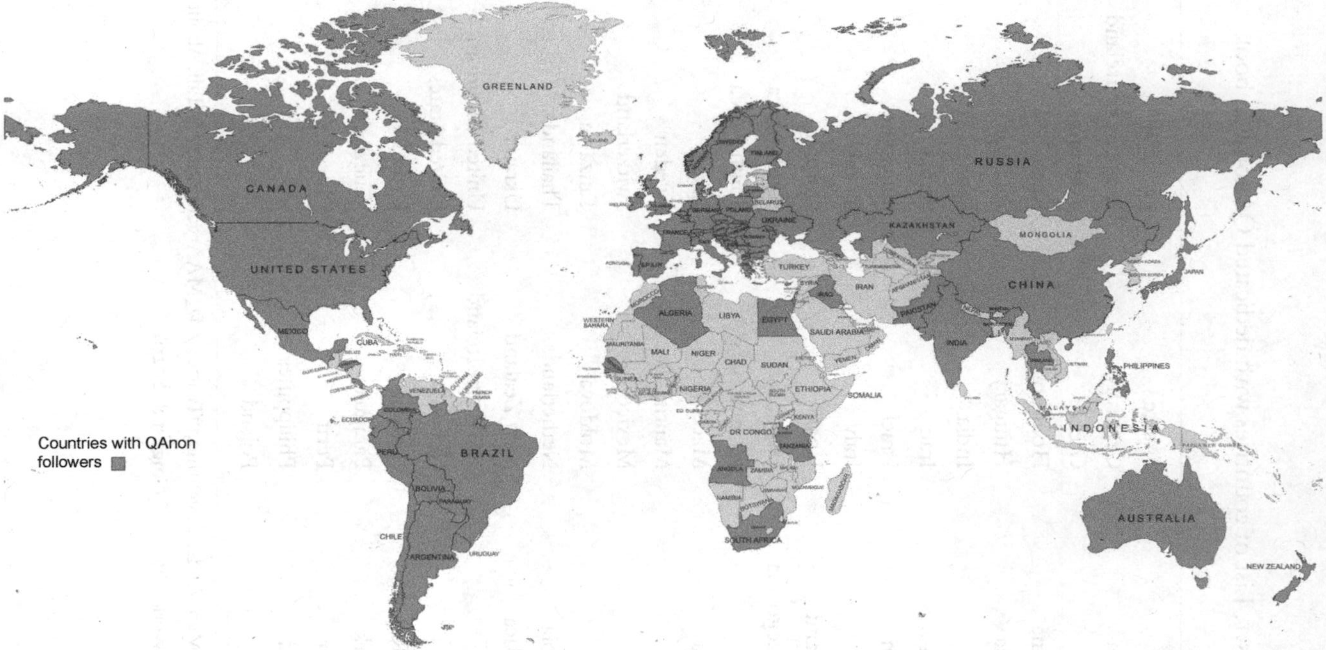

Figure 5.1. Qontagion: Countries with QAnon followers. Source: Sophia Moskalenko.

the Japanese QAnon community (sometimes called "J-Anons"), which reportedly had more than 80,000 followers and claims she is both the founder of QArmyJapanFlynn (Qmap Japan) and the official translator of Q content into Japanese. Okabayashi's interest in QAnon stems from her deep-seated qualms about Japan's treatment of women and motherhood.[30]

According to the *New York Times*, however, most Japanese do not subscribe to J-Anon's eccentric theories—including that the imperial family has been replaced by body doubles or that the bombings of Hiroshima and Nagasaki were cover for a jobs-creation program for the interior.[31] Japan is largely resistant to disinformation, partly because of its laws regarding fair media practices, partly because its newspapers have substantial circulations, and partly because of its high levels of literacy. Such mitigation strategies might be useful for countries trying to inoculate against dangerous conspiracies.

In most of the European QAnon chapters, Trump maintains his prominent place as the *chosen one* to save the children. In countries like Germany, Trump is the savior who will rescue the people from Angela Merkel's corruption.[32] QAnon has made deep inroads in Germany with hundreds of thousands of supporters (200,000 in October 2020) and increasing every month. The German-language Qlobal Change network has 106,000 subscribers to its YouTube channel and 122,000 subscribers to its Telegram channel.[33]

Like the United States, the German far right has latched onto Q. The conspiracy theory in Germany coalesced around a NATO joint military exercise. Josef Holnburger, cited in the *New York Times*, insists that there is an overlap between far-right influencers and groups aggressively pushing QAnon.[34] In Germany, QAnon brings together an ideologically incoherent mix of anti-vaxxers, fringe thinkers, and citizens who believe that the pandemic is overblown. The earliest QAnon evangelists were members of the Reichsbürger or "citizens of the Reich" movement, a blend of groups bonded by their common rejection of the German state. Their apocalyptic, anti-Semitic conspiracy theories dovetail with QAnon narratives. They believed that Trump would restore the Reich.[35] A report by Network Contagion, a think tank run by former Republican Congressman Denver Riggleman, explains the contagion of QAnon in Germany:

> Conspiracy theories about underground bunkers, aliens, and mind-control microchips already proliferated in the far right through 4chan's sister site, Kohlchan and other sites. However, the COVID-19 pandemic and ensuing restrictions provided the impetus for a widespread illiberal resistance movement tied to the populist radical right party.[36]

German celebrities and influencers like R&B singer Xavier Naidoo and Libertarian politician Oliver Janich encouraged people to follow them down the rabbit hole. QAnon has managed to thrive in the country despite the fact that much of its materials is anti-Semitic. By German law, disseminating this type of material can result in five years in jail. The German right-wing opposition to Merkel uses Q slogans like "WWG1WGA," and Jürgen Elsässer's far-right publication *Compact* has featured a giant Q on its cover and since 2019 has dedicated several issues to the conspiracy theory.[37]

One German Facebook page AUGEN AUF ("eyes open") has over 61,000 followers and posts conspiracy theory content, including memes that are shared over and over again. The

German content mirrors the U.S. memes of following the rabbit and choosing the red pill. In one post, an image of a white rabbit includes the text "leave the matrix, time is up," linking to one of the German-language Telegram channels, seemingly intended to avoid Facebook's prying eyes (or AI used to locate the content).[38]

Attila Hildmann, a vegan chef, amplified QAnon propaganda on Telegram for months. He took Trump's defeat hard and posted his "resignation" from QAnon to his 114,000 Telegram followers, calling Q a CIA "psychological operation." While some supporters like Hildmann became disillusioned by Trump's defeat, others remained hopeful. "As the Americans say, in God we trust," one poster on a German Telegram group wrote. "Now is the time to trust."[39]

QAnon Facebook accounts indicate even more global interest from the Philippines to Finland, Chile to New Zealand. QAnon in Brazil focuses on the close relationship between former President Trump and Jair Bolsonaro. In Brazil, second only to the United States in terms of COVID-19 casualties, Bolsonaro echoed Trump's conspiratorial behavior and amplified Trump's claims about the utility of hydroxychloroquine, the anti-malaria drug QAnon influencers believed could cure coronavirus.

QAnon absorbs local grievances and concerns—this is the secret to its success and growth. Anna Merlan has likened it to a "conspiracy singularity," where multiple conspiracies merge into a melting pot of unimaginable density. She describes Q absorbing adjacent conspiracies such that all the conspiracy theories come together and overlap, drawing each other's constituents.[40] For other researchers, QAnon is an amorphous blob that changes based on the situation. "When things change, the story changes, too."[41] *Elle* magazine's Anne Helen Petersen considers it to be an adaptable organism.[42]

We consider QAnon to be like a sticky ball, rolling down a hill; as it rolls, faster and faster, it picks up other conspiracies and their supporters along the way—growing ever larger over time. QAnon is a meta conspiracy theory offering something different for everyone and thus able to accommodate a large constituency that has little in common except for a shared belief in QAnon.

In Britain QAnon appeals to Brexit supporters; in Italy, it appeals to anti-vaxxers.[43] In most of the European countries, the conspiracy theory is tinged with an antagonism toward immigrants and refugees. In the UK, QAnon Facebook groups debate whether Trump's ally, Boris Johnson, is advancing "the plan" according to schedule. QAnon in the UK also merges antagonism about 5G. Prime Minister Johnson's decision to ban Huawei from the 5G networks is proof of Johnson's allegiance to Q. Like in the United States, UK celebrities play a role in disseminating the conspiracy theory. For example, pop singer Robbie Williams endorsed Pizzagate on Twitter.[44]

Merging with local issues, QAnon in the UK has been focused on Prince Andrew's relationship to Jeffrey Epstein and the disappearance of three-year-old Madeleine McCann in Portugal in May 2007.

The long history of conspiratorial thinking in the UK has resulted in fertile ground for QAnon. Q-conspiracy theorists like Martin Geddes have hundreds of thousands of followers and can convey the conspiracy theory's most absurd details using quasi-scientific thinking. In the Netherlands, social media accounts that align themselves with Geert Wilders, the Dutch far-right politician, merge QAnon elements with anti-lockdown measures.[45]

The number of posts and demonstrations can measure manifestations of QAnon activity in Canada, the UK, Germany, Romania, Poland, Australia, and Indonesia; we can also study a failed attack against Canadian Prime Minister Justin Trudeau. The very same structural conditions that impacted the United States during the pandemic increased the appeal of QAnon internationally. Trudeau closed the Canadian border on March 21, 2020, to control the spread of COVID-19. However, this failed to stop the U.S. export of QAnon from traveling northward. QAnon surged in Canada just as it did everywhere else with the rise of Internet usage at home. As with everywhere else, Canadian QAnon followers drew together an amalgamation of yoga moms, yellow vests (*gilets jaunes*), anti-vaxxers, pedophilia obsessives, and white nationalists.[46]

The Canadian QAnon attempt against Trudeau (briefly mentioned in Chapter 2) occurred in July 2020 when a heavily armed reservist named Corey Hurren drove 2,600 kilometers (over 1,600 miles) from Bowsman, Manitoba, to Ottawa to ram his vehicle through the gates of Rideau Hall. Before the attack, Hurren posted Q-inspired content to his company's Instagram account. After the attack, Hurren changed his story and claimed that he was actually motivated by financial problems caused by the pandemic. He had grievances against the government and was concerned about the prospect of losing his gun rights.[47] Hurren pled guilty in February 2021 to seven counts of weapons possession and one charge of mischief from causing $100,000 worth of damage to the Rideau Hall gate.[48] In another instance, a Canadian influencer, Amazing Polly, was implicated in the Wayfair allegations—disseminating QAnon propaganda before YouTube purged her account in October 2021. Another Canadian influencer,

Danielle LaPorte, used her Instagram account to publicize the #SaveTheChildren hashtag that was hijacked by QAnon in the summer of 2020.

Hijacking the charity's hashtag hurt children more than it helped the work of child protection. QAnon exaggerates trafficking statistics in order to communicate the enormity of the problem. *Elle* magazine explains that it is a distraction from agencies and nonprofits that have actually been doing this work for decades, "diverting resources that could be used to actually protect vulnerable children."[49] QAnon followers' near obsession with child trafficking might have influenced the Trump administration to announce its campaign to "save the children." A budget of $35 million announced by the State Department earmarked for trafficking turned out to be no more than an illusion. The money that former President Trump and Ivanka Trump publicized[50] was never actually spent on trafficking initiatives[51] despite reports to the contrary.[52] Rather, the focus on child trafficking was part of the Trump administration's wink toward a growing QAnon voting bloc of QAmoms.

While some U.S. QAnon supporters were starting to lose hope after the 2020 election, the Canadian QAnon channels continued to organize protests in several Canadian cities and circulated the (false) claim that Justin Trudeau planned an "immediate military intervention on American soil" if Trump refused to concede.[53]

In France, the DéQodeurs website is the entry point into the French QAnon galaxy. The French version mixes philosophical esotericism with disinformation and extremist rhetoric. The local connection is with the yellow jackets protest movement.[54] As is the case throughout Europe, French QAnon melds local issues while highlighting QAnon's usual priorities. French President Emmanuel Macron is part of the cabal. The French QAnon movement describes itself as

> [a] group of French, anti-globalization patriots, who campaign to wake up Nations . . . to inform the French people, and more generally, all Francophones that are manipulated by traditional media on today's worldly stakes.[55]

French QAnon has posted news clips from Russian Television (RT) and repeated disinformation about the U.S. Democratic Party being filled with pedophiles alongside thinly veiled racist articles about George Floyd. The French government is understandably concerned. Macron ordered a multi-agency inquiry into conspiracy theory movements, while French security agencies have been investigating the intersection of QAnon with neo-Nazism.[56] The individual credited with QAnon's popularity in France is Léonard Sojili, an Albanian 9/11 "truther" who began posting online disinformation in 2011 and started disseminating the QAnon conspiracy theory on a YouTube channel called Thinkerview, which boasts 800,000 French subscribers.[57]

QAnon is a hoax, but it has likely even exceeded its creators' expectations. The online movement about a supposed conspiracy theory controlled by the U.S. deep state has become a global ideology with representation all over the planet. While we might call QAnon a conspiracy theory, some of its adherents consider it to be a movement, whereas others are increasingly calling it a "cult"[58] because of its adaptability and how it distorts people's reality and relationship with their families and society.

There appears to be some debate about the centrality of Trump in some of the international versions of QAnon. For

Tristan Mendes, of the University of Paris, "[QAnon] lost its American attachment when it went global, it adapted to the natural context in all the countries where it landed."[59] Yet in French, British, and even Finnish QAnon circles, former President Trump remains the chosen one selected to bring down the global cabal. Graphika "understands" that QAnon offers malicious foreign actors the "ideal delivery mechanism for the seeding of conspiratorial content and blatant disinformation into the politically-engaged US mainstream."[60] Accounts tweeting #WWG1WGA were often pro-Russian accounts. According to the Graphika study, there were only three users responsible for 17,000 tweets; Twitter removed the users as part of their crackdown against suspected Kremlin disinformation operations. Accounts promoting the hashtag #PizzaGate were also affiliated with the (now infamous) Russian Internet Research Agency.[61]

Russia's efforts in amplifying QAnon have promoted Vladimir Putin's primary interest in "Making Russia Great Again" as well as his master plan of undermining democracy in the United States and abroad.[62] To be expected, Russian disinformation related to QAnon is replete with anti-Semitism, in particular attacks against philanthropist George Soros. In many ways, Russia's role in popularizing QAnon in other countries brings our story full circle. Recall, the basis of QAnon myths are anti-Semitic stereotypes from *The Protocols of the Elders of Zion*, originating in Russia 120 years prior, with little change in the tenor or tone in its vilification of Jews.

Hatred of Jews and anti-Semitism connect the European racist political parties with the U.S. far right and their belief about "replacement theory." From the marchers in Charlottesville in August 2017 to the January 6 insurrection at the

Capitol, the fear of replacement brings together the strangest bedfellows. *New Yorker* war correspondent Luke Mogelson explains what is meant by the "Great Replacement":

> The contention is that Europe and the United States are under siege from nonwhites and non-Christians, and that these groups are incompatible with Western culture, identity, and prosperity. Many white supremacists maintain that the ultimate outcome of the Great Replacement is "white genocide." In Charlottesville, neo-Nazis chanted, "Jews will not replace us!" . . . and both the New Zealand mosque and El Paso Walmart massacres cited the Great Replacement in their manifestos.[63]

QAnon is unique compared to many other conspiracy theories or terrorist movements, which we have studied for three decades. This is not simply because of QAnon's superior ability to absorb and adapt itself to local conditions—Al Qaeda and ISIS were also able to do that. But like apocalyptic terrorist movements, QAnon's religious zeal and eschatology contend that it is purifying the world of evil. QAnon will redeem a corrupt world and usher in a new golden age. QAnon is like a millenarian sect—a "syncretic political cult, with a basic millenarian structure."[64]

One of the more surprising consequences of QAnon has been an unintended backlash against Russia, one of the countries that amplified QAnon content on social media in an attempt to weaken U.S. institutions and erode people's trust in government and the media. Russian government-backed social media accounts nurtured the QAnon conspiracy theory in its infancy, using bots and sock accounts. "From November 2017 on, QAnon was the single most frequent hashtag tweeted by accounts that Twitter has since identified as Russian-backed, with the term used some 17,000 times."[65]

Russian accounts amplified and promoted Pizzagate. Then Russia turned to promoting Tracy Beanz (Diaz) tweeting instructional videos about how to locate Q-drops and posted to her YouTube channel about deciphering the breadcrumb Q-drops with Trump's tweets or speeches. Russia and China used a variety of contrivances as part of their misinformation toolkit. Russian bots boosted the hashtag #ReleaseTheMemo on Twitter within three months of the birth of QAnon in 2017.[66]

But Russia now has a QAnon problem of its own. As Silicon Valley de-platformed many QAnon accounts, QAnon shifted to semi-encrypted platforms like Telegram—as had ISIS when it was de-platformed in December 2015. By moving to Telegram, owned by Pavel Durov, it opened the floodgates to a Russian constituency. On both Telegram and Russia's version of Facebook, VKontakte, QAnon social media posts began flooding account timelines. Groups dedicated to spreading the conspiracy theory in Russian have grown to include tens of thousands of members.[67] Like the rest of the globe, Russia is suffering from the COVID-19 pandemic, and economic crises have caused unemployment to reach an eight-year high. Many Russian QAnon members opposed mask mandates and other public health measures while Putin (like Trump) has downplayed the virus but stayed out of public sight for months at a time.[68]

Russia's QAnon movement is divided over whether Vladimir Putin is part of the global cabal manipulating world events or, because of his proximity to Trump, an ally behind the scenes. Other QAnon supporters have a hard time believing that Trump has been uniquely chosen to save the children, and as a result Trump's pivotal role in QAnon narratives is downplayed in Russia.

QAnon Politik

With ample evidence of Russia supporting and amplifying QAnon social media content, it is important to identify the man behind the curtain. Q may not have been directly controlled by Russia, but Russia has been using QAnon to advance its interests. Vladimir Putin has ruled Russia for over 20 years, ever since he was hand-picked by Russia's first democratically elected president, Boris Yeltsin. In 2020, the Russian constitution was changed to enable Putin to rule for two more consecutive terms (another 16 years), until 2036.[69] In April 2021, Putin signed the amendments into law.

Putin's reign has become famous for the way he constructed a "vertical of power," with him at the top, and anyone below either heeding his command or suffering the consequences. Twenty years into this effort, it is safe to assume that Russian foreign policy efforts are Putin's foreign policy efforts. In this sense, QAnon's spread is a well-executed psyop—a psychological operation to influence "hearts and minds"—a specialty of Putin's KGB training.

When he became the Russian president, Putin was a political dark horse, barely known to the public. There was a good reason for this anonymity. Putin had been a spy, an officer of the KGB, the Комитет государственной безопасности (Committee for State Security), the notoriously secretive Russian intelligence agency tasked with tracking and tackling both internal and external threats to the ruling system.[70] The KGB specialized in psyops to keep tabs on critics of the Soviet ideology.

Rumors designed to discredit dangerous opponents and direct the public to actions desired by the Soviet government were a trademark of these psyops.[71] With the advent of digital communications, the former KGB, now FSB,[72] invested heavily in reorganizing to leverage the informational warfare capabilities provided by the high-speed networks. As part of this effort, Russia established the Internet Research Agency, the troll factory in St. Petersburg.[73] Putin's attempts to destabilize Western democracies and Western-leaning former Soviet republics range from funding divisive political figures (i.e., Marine Le Pen in France[74] and Viktor Yanukovych in Ukraine[75]), to sending Agent Provocateurs to foment protests in Germany[76] and France,[77] to informational warfare such as QAnon.

One study analyzed narratives transmitted by different media backed by the Russian government.[78] These included news media officially affiliated with the Russian government (TASS, Russia Today) and with Russia's presidential administration, but also those radical left- and right-wing resources linked with the "vertical of power" and "patriotic" accounts indirectly connected to Putin—such as the media holdings of Yevgeny Prigozhin (Putin's friend[79] wanted by the FBI for conspiracy to defraud the United States[80]). The study found all of these diverse sources releasing the same or similar narratives in a highly coordinated manner. The narratives included QAnon content, adapted for the former Soviet or European audiences targeted by these media.

Thus, the "manufactured virus"—that in the American QAnon version originated in a Chinese biolab in Wuhan—in the Russian version originated in a U.S. lab and was brought to China by NATO soldiers. The NATO soldiers are carrying the virus around the world, the narrative explains, because it serves the deep state's purpose to get rich off the mandated masks and the lockdowns. This story was followed up in the Russian-controlled informational space by fear-mongering stories about the dangers of collaborating with the United States in the area of biochemistry. These follow-up stories supplied a list of "dangerous" laboratories in Ukraine, Georgia, and Kazakhstan—post-Soviet countries that Russia has attempted to bring back under its influence. The nature of the folQlore is the same: Use the real threat of the virus, add to it a sinister component of plotting governments, and point the finger at potential targets of public anger. Only the main characters are recast to better fit the audience's mindset. The Russian version of QAnon folQlore blames NATO, an organization Putin detests, and directs public fear and outrage at countries that reject Russian control.

Another analysis traced the origins of the Russified QAnon story about the World Health Organization (WHO).[81] This narrative claimed the WHO was created by the multi-millionaire Rockefeller, who had survived seven (or eight) heart transplants, for the purpose of running the world, including vaccinations designed to control population growth and destroy people's individuality. This conspiracy theory—pushed by Russia-backed accounts on Russian-language social media VKontakte, Telegram, and Odnoklassniki, as well as on Facebook and on YouTube—is shrouded in fear-inducing commentary about COVID-19 vaccines and treatments offered through WHO (but, really, by the "world government").

Clear parallels can be drawn to the U.S. version of the same conspiracy theory. Both narratives fan public distrust in science and fear of vaccines. In marketing this story to Russian-speaking audiences in Europe and in the former Soviet states, Russian "narrative writers" rebranded Wuhan/China (a Russian ally) into WHO (an organization Russia undermines). Instead of Hillary Clinton (a figure of little significance to most Russian speakers) playing a vampire, it is Rockefeller who is painted as barely human, after he had used up seven other people's hearts, not to mention "Rockefeller" sounds Jewish in Russian, feeding into the anti-Semitic narratives.

The added benefit of manipulating people into distrusting the enemies of the Motherland like NATO and WHO is that conspiracy theories provide a distraction. While the crowd is busy worrying about imaginary dangers and blaming convenient scapegoats, experienced crowd masters are free to reign as they please.

Trained in secrecy and espionage, Putin is rumored to never himself use the Internet, getting his information in *papochki*—paper folders. He must know better than anyone the dangers lurking online, having masterminded the spinning of a web of lies and reaped its benefits.

Qonclusions

As the many predictions from Q have not seen fruition, there have been diverse reactions from constituents in the United States. We have seen continuously that QAnon keeps moving the goal posts. First Trump was supposed to win the 2020 election. That is why so many QAnon supporters were active in the "Stop the Steal" protests. Then "the Storm" was supposed to be January 6. In some ways the failed insurrection was just that: 1 in 10 people arrested at the Capitol were connected to the QAnon conspiracy theory. The inauguration on January 20, 2021, was supposed to generate "the Storm," when the cabal would be publicly outed, arrested, and executed. Yet the date passed without any of the predictions coming true. Then March 4, 2021, came and went. March 4 has a complicated explanation, drawing from some of the anti-government militia mythology about the gold standard.

QAnon supporters see the repeated failures of accurately predicting events as less of a deficiency and more of "the sands keep shifting." They interpret the failed prophecies either by doubling down or assuming, since they did the research themselves, that they got the date wrong. QAnon supporters reiterate: "Trust the plan" and so they continue to support the conspiracy theory even as each prophecy or date goes by without the expected "Storm."

Part of the problem is that child trafficking is a problem, and certain elements of QAnon myths resonate as being true. In the United States, the arrest and mysterious death of Jeffrey Epstein, and in the UK, the arrest of Jimmy Saville, "demonstrate that elite pedophile rings do exist, and that they do sometimes enjoy protection from powerful political and cultural figures."[82] For true believers, it's a divine plan. For others it is a social movement. For the people at the top, it is a money grab, and they've been getting rich off of selling the conspiracy and exploiting lonely and unhappy people. For evangelicals to continue to believe despite the many disappointments, they need something evangelicals have in great supply: faith. Evangelical pastor and Wheaton College professor Ed Stetzer explains:

> People of faith believe there is a divine plan—that there are forces of good and forces of evil at work in the world. . . . QAnon is a train that runs on the tracks that religion has already put in place.[83]

When Q stopped posting drops in the aftermath of the 2020 election (December 2020), some of the better-known Q influencers stepped in to take control. Recall, these are the influencers who have benefited the most from the financial support of QAnon believers or from selling merchandise or profiting from increased traffic to their websites.

Whatever happens to QAnon in the United States, as long as the Republican Party does not disavow it, it will not completely disappear. QAnon has seeped into the religious sphere, the political sphere, and the international sphere; we will be dealing with the challenges associated with QAnon for years to come.

CHAPTER 6

FAQS

Q: Why Does QAnon Appeal to Women?

QAnon's focus on pedophiles' abducting and abusing children, and hashtags like #SaveTheChildren, resonate especially strongly with women, tugging on their protective, motherly instincts. Even before the pandemic, news stories about Jeffrey Epstein's "Lolita Island" and related rumors about powerful elites engaging in sexual exploitation of minors led many mothers to worry about sex slavery and human trafficking in a way they hadn't before.

With the COVID-19 pandemic, suburban white women were cut off from their usual social networks, be it the PTA or soccer mom groups, leaving them missing the sense of purpose and active involvement. Online forums dedicated to "saving the children" offered a replacement for that loss. Many women felt as though they were part of an important mission when they searched for clues and identified pedophiles. Often, these women didn't realize they were entering the QAnon rabbit hole as they were clicking deeper and deeper into conspiracy theories.

In the time of political turmoil, many white suburban women felt uneasy about discussing politics online. But there is very little controversy about caring for abused children. Women who did not feel comfortable with "political" topics like Black Lives Matter could engage with strangers online without triggering uncomfortable exchanges. Who would object to saving the children? It was a perfectly agreeable subject to be worried about together. "Think about children loaded up into the back of trucks like cargo to be bought and sold like property, for their tiny bodies to be used and abused,"[1] posted one pastel-colored Instagram account with over 120,000 followers. The QAnon "save the children"-themed memes seem innocuous. You might have one in your feed and not even realize it is a gateway to QAnon. #SaveTheChildren is the softest of dog whistles whose call is strongest for women.

Q: If Conspiracies Aren't New, Then What's So Special About QAnon?

One novelty of QAnon is how diverse the folQlore is. It combines stories about a pedophile cabal and lizard people, about microchip vaccines and Osama bin Laden still being alive. Q lore includes lasers setting California on fire from space so that Jews can build a superhighway, COVID-19 being invented as a hoax to undermine the Trump presidency, and Hillary Clinton wearing a baby's cut-off face, Hannibal Lecter-style. It's a meta conspiracy theory. Like Amazon.com of the conspiracy world, Q has something for every customer, only a few clicks away.

The Internet is another novelty that makes QAnon especially problematic. With algorithms offering a never-ending stream of conspiracy theories, a vulnerable individual can get sucked into the Q alternative reality in the comfort of their own home. QAnon forums create a community of like-minded people, feeding their hunger for connection and understanding. As we witnessed at the January 6 insurrection, this Internet community can easily be mobilized for radical real-world action. More people brought together by conspiracy theories, more easily connected through the Internet, and more radicalized for violent action—these can add up to a perfect storm.

Q: Why All the Sex in the Conspiracy Theories?

Sex in folQlore echoes real sex scandals from the news and fuels genuine outrage at the misconduct and impunity of political and cultural elites. As in marketing, sex sells in politics, too. It attracts attention and keeps audiences engaged. And it does something else: It builds anger. Research has discovered that watching a sexual video can translate to even greater aggression at the slightest provocation than watching a violent video.[2] This tendency is called "excitation transfer." Sexual thoughts build up excitement that is then transferred into anger and aggression. Sexual content is part of how QAnon radicalizes its followers.

Q: Why Do Hollywood Elites Feature in Conspiracy Narratives?

A number of resonant sex scandals have involved members of Hollywood elites. Particularly infamous were Bill Cosby,

"America's Dad"; Harvey Weinstein, a major Hollywood producer; and Les Moonves (CBS) and Matt Lauer (NBC) from the mainstream media. These sex scandals involved dozens of victimized women and teenage girls who were intimidated into silence. It wasn't unreasonable to suspect that there were many more victims out there—and more perpetrators with power, money, and connections to keep the abuse secret. Conspiracy theories build around this existing set of facts, expanding from a natural suspicion into a less reasonable one—adding crazy details (Bosch-esque or *Eyes Wide Shut* orgies and child abuse rituals) and specific celebrities (Tom Hanks, Oprah, Lady Gaga, Hillary Clinton).

Q: Why Are Children at the Center of Conspiracy Theories?

By focusing on babies and children, conspiracy theories anchor their narratives to the most fundamentally "innocent" and "good" beings. Harming babies and children is thus the ultimate evil, and those guilty of this are corrupt beyond redemption. Babies and harm done to them are the foundational axis of good and evil in the normative system that Q-conspiracy theories lay out. It's the lowest common denominator over which they can bond. This QAnon variation on Deep Blue Something's song "Breakfast at Tiffany's" summarizes:

> You'll say, we've got nothing in common
> No common ground to start from
> And we're falling apart
> You'll say, the world has come between us
> Our lives have come between us
> Still I know you just don't care

And I said what about powerful pedophiles?
She said I think that the rumors are true
And I'm sure you'd agree we both really hate it
And I said well that's the one thing we've got

Q: Why Is George Soros So Often Featured in Conspiracy Theories?

Soros was made into a conspiracy theory monster by two (Jewish) political consultants: George Eli Birnbaum and Arthur Finkelstein. Longtime Washington insiders and legends among Republicans for helping elect conservative candidates, Birnbaum and Finkelstein were hired by the Hungarian prime minister, Viktor Orban, for his re-election campaign. The trick of their trade has been attacking their candidate's opponent in a series of negative campaign ads. But Orban had no opposition in Hungary. There was nobody to demonize and terrify voters with, to make them run for safety into the arms of Birnbaum and Finkelstein's candidate, Orban. That's when they decided to create a monster from scratch. They picked Soros, an apolitical and innocuous Hungarian-born Jew, as the subject of their makeover.

Birnbaum and Finkelstein have since claimed that they didn't intentionally use anti-Semitism. However, some of their ads drew from the traditional anti-Semitic repertoire, including references to Soros's double loyalties, claims that he controls governments worldwide, and images of Soros as an octopus wrapping his tentacles around the globe. Tapping into long-standing stereotypes and suspicions, Birnbaum and Finkelstein's anti-Soros campaign became so successful that it went global, spreading like wildfire through parched forest. The anti-Semitic tropes resonated far and wide:

> Finkelstein and Birnbaum had turned Soros into a meme. Right-wing sites like Breitbart, or the Kremlin-controlled Russia Today, could simply adopt the Hungarian campaign, translate it into other languages, and feed it with local arguments. . . . Anti-Soros material is a globalized, freely available, and adaptable open-source weapon.[3]

Even the son of Israeli Prime Minister Benjamin Netanyahu, Yair Netanyahu, reposted an anti-Semitic image of Soros and reptilians controlling the world.[4]

Q: Why Do QAnon Conspiracies Talk About Adrenochrome?

The reference to adrenochrome, like much of folQlore, seems to have been inspired by popular culture. Adrenochrome is featured as a satanic narcotic in Hunter Thompson's book, *Fear and Loathing in Las Vegas*, and in Terry Gilliam's eponymous film adaptation. Adrenochrome is also referenced in Stanley Kubrick's 1971 film *A Clockwork Orange* as "drenchom."[5] In 2017, yet another Hollywood film relied on the fictional power of adrenochrome, called, fittingly, *Adrenochrome*. In short, the film industry, using adrenochrome as a go-to fictional evil drug, has brought it into the popular culture. From there, it seeped into the public subconsciousness, creating fertile ground for Q-conspiracy theories.

Q: Why Do So Many Conspiracy Theories Include Bill Gates?

One explanation has to do with how famously rich Bill Gates is—among the richest people on the planet.[6] As such, he attracts both attention and envy, prompting imaginative conspiratorial thinkers to "uncover" nefarious ways through which Gates amassed his fortune. But other nouveau riche—Warren Buffett, Sergey Brin, J. K. Rowling—don't prompt the same creativity from conspiracy theorists. What, then, is special about Bill Gates?

Possibly, it is Gates's involvement with distributing vaccines (mostly, against malaria) in Africa. Through a version of Pavlovian conditioning, this connection between Gates and vaccinations creates a connection between Gates and feelings of anxiety and suspicion—reactions that many people have toward vaccines. Pairing the idea of Bill Gates with the idea of vaccines results in Bill Gates's name being imbued with suspicion and anxiety, making him a perfect target for conspiracy theories.

One other reason Bill Gates is featured heavily in the folQlore is a widely circulated 2010 video, in which Bill Gates gave a public presentation and talked about unsustainable population growth on our planet. In the same speech, Gates proposed ways to control population growth through medical treatments, including reproductive medicine.[7] This video, poorly understood by those who are not versed in scientific language, likely metamorphized in the collective mind of QAnon followers into a new vision of Bill Gates, a billionaire who got rich off of "vaccines" he produced in order to reduce world population. Bill Gates didn't help the confusion when he spoke, at the beginning of the COVID-19 pandemic, about future "digital certificates"[8] that could help keep track of who had been tested and who had received a future vaccine. The very next day, conspiracy theories sprung up online about microchips that would be injected with COVID-19 vaccine, and the rest was history.

Q: Why Trump?

There are (at least) three reasons: (1) Trump presented as the antithesis to "the system"; (2) Trump presented as the traditional gender role model; (3) Trump was the Conspiracist in Chief.

(1) Trump presented as the antithesis to "the system." Americans who felt cheated by the system were inspired by Trump, who snubs the system and gets away with it. He was a businessman who used bankruptcy laws to benefit himself. He had multiple sexual misconduct allegations against him that never resulted in a trial. As a politician, Trump has disregarded political norms by defying procedures and ignoring precedent. Trump's middle finger to the system embodied the bitterness many of his supporters felt at the system that failed to abide by the norms while enforcing them on "the little guy."

(2) Trump presented as the traditional gender role model. Especially for men who felt insecure in their masculinity, Trump presented as the archetypal manly man:[9] multiple children with multiple wives, not to mention strippers and hookers; chauvinistic talk to convey his low opinion of women's value. Women who supported Trump tended to be more sexist and more racist.[10] To Republican, white women, therefore, Trump appealed as a rich, tall, and blonde Prince Charming who would Make America Great Again by restoring the golden era of their mothers' youth, where men were breadwinners and women homemakers, safe from Black and Brown people.

(3) Trump was the Conspiracist in Chief. Trump's ascent to political power began with him touting a conspiracy theory: that Barack Obama was not born in the United States of America and thus was ineligible to become president (birtherism). This

combined racism and conspiratorial thinking characterized many Trump-supporting women.[11] Trump's love for conspiracies in the media and on the campaign trail has earned him the title "conspiracy theorist in chief."[12]

Q: Why Is Trump the Savior for QAnon Not Just in the United States but Also in Other Countries—the UK, France, Germany, etc.?

QAnon spins "narratives without borders"—the cabal is global, Soros is a Hungarian Jew, Bill Gates wants to reduce population through vaccines all over the "flat earth." For a French or a Russian citizen concerned about the global network of pedophiles, someone who would take it down is a welcome hero, no matter where they come from. And Trump is not an unknown underdog: Hotels advertising Trump's name pierce the sky in Istanbul and Manilla, Panama City and Toronto, and Trump golf courses sprawl over fields in Ireland, Scotland, and Dubai. This international presence of Trump businesses assures QAnon's international followers of Trump's reach and resources.

It is also possible that Trump became a viral "heroic" figure in the folQlore in the same way that Soros became a viral "demonic" figure—with the help of some clever marketing consultants. Many creatives have been applying their talents to boost Trump's appeal, employed by his election campaigns or as private citizens-turned-vigilante fans. Those who wanted Trump to win elections would have benefited greatly from Trump taking on a savior quality. Therefore, it stands to reason that they would have boosted QAnon content of superhero Trump, if not outright creating it. With solid evidence of Russia amplifying QAnon's messages, it's also very likely the Russian troll factories would have translated and transmitted the Trump-as-savior narratives around the world.

Q: Republicans Have Also Been Entangled in Sex Scandals. Why Is QAnon's Outrage Directed at Democrats?

QAnon is comprised mostly of Republican voters. Their bias against Democratic politicians means they hold bigger grudges against Democratic politicians than against Republican ones involved in sex scandals.

Additionally, Republicans who are implicated in violating sexual norms don't achieve the same notoriety as their Democratic colleagues. When they get caught in sexual misconduct, Republicans don't seem compelled to go on talk shows to explain themselves, first denying allegations, then admitting them—as Democrats often do. Republicans spare their audience the embarrassment of witnessing their lies and ultimate confessions. As a result, they leave fewer people angry.

It is also possible that the mass media devotes less coverage to Republican sex scandals than it does to Democratic ones, making these Republican scandals less salient in people's minds.

Q: What's That About Lasers from Space and Microchips in Vaccines?

Part of QAnon's appeal is its acknowledgment and reinforcement of people's mistrust in science. Many people are angry and suspicious—because they have heard real-life stories about unscrupulous pharmaceutical executives charging a fortune for drugs that do more harm than good, or about tech giants who get rich off spying on their clients and selling private information to marketing firms. Instead of ridiculing or talking down to people, QAnon embraces their suspicions and distrust. Stories about lasers from space that cause disasters and about vaccines that would benefit the tech billionaires while violating people's privacy build on fear and offer an outlet for anger.

Q: What Are QAnon Tropes?

Tropes are narrative elements that are common in storytelling. For example, "enemies into lovers" is a timeless trope that was at the heart of Jane Austen's *Pride and Prejudice*. It was also an integral narrative element in James Cameron's movie *Avatar*.

A number of tropes in QAnon's folQlore have circulated for centuries. One is "a global cabal that steals children and tortures/kills them." In the olden days, this trope was used to vilify Jews or Roma. In QAnon's modern retelling, this trope is about the global cabal of powerful politicians and famous celebrities who traffic children in order to torture them, sexually abuse them, and drink their blood.

Another trope is "evil Jews running the world behind the scenes and profiting off gentiles' misery." In QAnon's retelling, this trope is about George Soros (but also about more generic "Jews") who control the mass media and governments to enable the cabal as well as other atrocities, including 5G networks and the lab-made COVID-19.

A third QAnon trope is "a harmful substance that the powerful are seeking to use on the unsuspecting public." In the past, this trope targeted women who were then persecuted for witchcraft, or Jews, who were blamed for "black death." In modern times, QAnon has relied on this trope more than once. First, QAnon claimed that COVID-19 was designed in a lab and used as a bioweapon in order to allow the cabal and the Jews to take over what they haven't yet taken over. Second, QAnon used this trope to suggest the COVID-19 vaccine would carry a micro-tracking device that would allow Bill Gates to kill and/or trace large numbers of people.

A fourth QAnon trope is "some people are not actually people, but a malevolent mix between a human and something disgusting." Traditionally, this trope featured vampires, a human-bat hybrid with blood-drinking habits. Taking a modern twist on this classic, QAnon double-dipped into this trope, too—first, by claiming that there are vampires among high-profile politicians and celebrities, and second, by conjuring lizard people, an evil hybrid between humans and lizards.

Q: Where Does #WWG1WGA (Where We Go One We Go All) Come From?

QAnon influencers on social media (like Martin Geddes[13]) have disseminated the falsehood that "where we go one we go all" (WWG1WGA) is inscribed on the bell on John F. Kennedy's sailboat. They even have a screenshot. This is blatantly untrue. In fact, the image is a still from the film *White Squall* (1996), starring Jeff Bridges.

QAnon makes other efforts to connect the conspiracy to the Kennedy family. In addition to this myth, they also allege that Q might be John F. Kennedy Jr. (disinformation promoted by Liz Crokin,[14] the right-wing conspiracy theorist whom Marjorie Taylor Greene cites as her inspiration to follow Q). In fact, JFK Jr. died in a plane crash off the coast of Martha's Vineyard on July 16, 1999. QAnon also alleges that JFK Jr. was considering a run for a New

York Senate seat and that Hillary Clinton was behind the accident so that she could run for the position.[15] There is no evidence that JKF Jr. was planning a political career: He had started a new political magazine, *George*, and the magazine had just started to make a profit. According to the FolQlore, Kennedy has been hiding in Pittsburgh for the last two decades (as Vincent Fusca) and he's a Trump supporter. QAnon predicted that JFK Jr. would be Trump's running mate in the 2020 election. Needless to say, this was another failed prediction.

Q: Isn't QAnon Just Another Radical Group?

Not really.

With QAnon spread far and wide, it is hard to get good data to represent all of its followers. It seems they are an unusual radical group for several reasons. First, QAnon is different from other U.S. far-right extremist groups because it welcomes women. By contrast, groups like the Proud Boys, Oath Keepers, 3 Percenters, and various neo-Nazi groups are male-dominated and misogynistic.

QAnons are also unusually old for a radical group. The average terrorist tends to be in their early 20s. QAnon followers, on the other hand, are in their late 30s and early 40s.[16]

Additionally, QAnon is a decentralized, "horizontally organized" group—with no leadership hierarchy. Typical radical groups establish a chain of command, and information (propaganda, plans, strategy) flows from top to bottom. But in QAnon, the folQlore can be generated by every group member, with minimal direction from Q or any QAnon super spreader. It is a true grass-roots movement.

Finally, QAnon is unusual among radical groups in its diverse and disjointed ideology. The folQlore is vast and only loosely interrelated. QAnon believers can pick and choose which narratives they believe. As a result, there are subgroups in QAnon who believe in lizard people, but who don't believe in Pizzagate; or those who believe in space lasers directed by Jews to light California forests on fire, but don't believe in flat earth. This kind of liberal approach to ideology—"cherry-picking"—would be unacceptable in a typical radical group, where members must embrace the entire spectrum of the group's ideology.

Q: What Kind of People Believe in QAnon?

As tempting as it might be to view QAnon followers as uneducated or unintelligent,[17] there's no data to support this assumption. Among QAnons cited in this book, there were Harvard graduates and decorated military veterans, small business owners and business executives. Because the number of QAnon followers is so large in the United States (17% of surveyed U.S. adults believe the Q-conspiracy theory about a satanic cabal of pedophiles running the media and government), a good guess is that QAnon is very diverse, including people young and old, rich and poor, highly educated and high school dropouts. What they have in common are not demographic variables but psychological ones.

Anxiety increases conspiratorial thinking.[18] Social isolation and loneliness also increase likelihood that a person would believe a conspiracy theory.[19] People who are depressed, narcissistic, and detached are especially prone to have a conspiratorial mindset.[20] People high on schizotypal personality traits (odd, eccentric, suspicious, and paranoid) and psychopathic traits (manipulative, irresponsible, low on empathy) are more likely to believe conspiracy theories.[21] You may notice a trend in these predictive variables: Belief in conspiracy theory seems to go hand in hand with psychological problems.

In fact, mental illness emerged in many first-person accounts of QAnons profiled in this book. Similarly, an overwhelming number (68%) of QAnons implicated in the Capitol riot had diagnosed mental problems.[22] During the COVID-19 pandemic, loneliness, depression, and anxiety increased for almost everyone, and in doing so, this spurred rapid growth of the QAnon following.[23]

Q: How Do We Deradicalize QAnons?

We shouldn't attempt it.

Radicalization comes in two varieties: radicalization in action and radicalization in opinion. Radicalization in action means breaking the law and/or engaging in political violence. By contrast, radicalization in opinion means supporting illegal/violent political action but not necessarily acting on it. Out of millions who believe Q-conspiracy theories, only a few dozen individuals have ever done anything illegal or violent. These individuals are subjects of police investigations and legal action. For the rest of QAnon believers, radicalization begins and ends inside their head. Research has consistently found that trying to clamp down on radical ideas is counterproductive.[24] It creates grievances that can, over time, actually increase radicalization. In the United States, attempts to deradicalize opinions would also run into constitutional challenges, as the First Amendment guarantees freedom of speech. Thus, deradicalization of QAnons is likely to be counterproductive and logistically difficult.

Conspiracy theories can sound crazy and dangerous. But our own confusion and apprehension of conspiracy talk is not a good reason to isolate, persecute, and further radicalize those who believe in them.

A more fruitful approach would address the sociocultural problems that created a vulnerability to QAnon among millions of Americans and would offer psychological and material support to reduce this vulnerability. Increasing government transparency, reforming healthcare, providing childcare and equal work opportunities for women—these steps would make people more resilient to the allure of conspiracy theories. Given the high prevalence of mental illness among QAnon followers who agreed to be interviewed, and among those who stormed the Capitol on January 6, it seems the best strategy to address their radical opinions would be to offer counseling and therapy.

Q: If QAnon Are, for the Most Part, Not Dangerous to the Public, Then Why Should We Worry About Them?

After January 6, 2021, failed to bring "the Storm" and fulfill "the plan," many QAnons became Doubters, seeking comfort and guidance online. Right-wing radical groups saw this as a recruitment opportunity. With QAnon vulnerable, dangerous and violent groups, such as neo-Nazis and Proud Boys, positioned themselves to bring these lost sheep into their ranks. So, although QAnon "membership" didn't pose a sizable threat, when QAnon prophecies failed, followers became marks for radicalization into much more dangerous groups. Because conspiracy theories spun by QAnon are not true, its followers will likely face reality checks in the future, every time creating an opportunity for their recruitment and radicalization to violent groups lurking online. With QAnon followers numbering in the millions, this risk is too high to leave the QAnon problem unattended.

Another risk presented by QAnon is the spread of misinformation that can influence behavior of people outside QAnon. Facebook conducted a massive study of its users and discovered that a relatively small number of accounts associated with QAnon spread messages that promoted hesitancy about COVID-19 vaccines.[25] Although this content is not prohibited by Facebook and cannot be sanctioned, it is nonetheless capable of causing harm. For example, if QAnon influencers' Facebook content can stop their Facebook followers from getting a COVID-19 vaccine, a number of these followers can get infected with the virus and might even die as a result. This avoidable harm would have been the result of the disinformation spread by QAnon accounts.

To mitigate these risks, we proposed several measures in Chapter 4, including enhancing social media filters, changing content-recommending algorithms, and offering treatments to willing Doubters.

Q: My Loved One Is a Defector. How Can I Help Them?

Life after QAnon can be difficult: Many relationships are damaged or lost, and the emotional trauma of having been misled and manipulated is haunting. The most important role you can play is that of a supportive and nonjudgmental presence. Social isolation is the reason that many people turned to QAnon in the first place. Now that they are out, they need a social network outside QAnon in order to begin rebuilding their life. The best chance for successful recovery is to take advantage of the resources laid out in Chapter 4: cognitive therapy, mindfulness training, volunteering, and engagement with support groups. However, keep in mind that your loved one has to arrive at the realization that they need these resources by themselves. Nobody can be helped by therapy unless they want to be helped. As the joke goes, "It takes only one psychologist to change a lightbulb, but the lightbulb has to WANT to be changed."

Q: My Loved One Is a Diehard, Deep into QAnon. How Can I Help Them?

Avoid directly challenging them or arguing—that would actually strengthen their beliefs. Instead, practice empathetic listening while communicating with your loved one.

A helpful thing to say is, "I understand how you *feel*." Saying this doesn't mean you agree with the Diehard's beliefs. You don't have to believe in a satanic cannibalistic cabal to understand that someone who does would be scared. You don't need to agree with the Diehard's belief in Donald Trump's ability to save us all to understand the Diehard's need to hope. You can relate to your loved one on the emotional plane, leaving the cognitive plane aside for the time being. Research shows that validating someone's feeling by simply saying "I understand why you feel this way" decreases their negative emotions and increases their positive affect.[26]

If and when your loved one asks for help, suggest online resources for people who have left QAnon, such as r/Qult_Headquarters or r/ReQuovery on Reddit or sites like IGotOut (https://www.igotout.org). The former cult member-turned therapist, Steve Hassan, created a website that has a variety of helpful resources: https://freedomofmind.com.

Having a loved one deeply entrenched in an unhealthy mindset can be very difficult for *you*. Maybe you feel responsible for them and feel guilty for not doing enough to get them out. Maybe you feel angry. Maybe you feel sad for your relationship, damaged by their QAnon addiction. All of these difficult emotions take a toll on your own quality of life, on your other relationships, and on your ability to make good choices for yourself. If your loved one is deep in QAnon, we suggest mindfulness training for yourself, such as MBSR training summarized in Chapter 4. Mindfulness can help with stress, difficult emotions, and negative thoughts.

Q: My Loved One Is a Doubter. How Can I Help Them?

Don't argue with a Doubter about QAnon conspiracies. You might turn them into a Diehard by doing so. Don't ostracize them for their beliefs, and don't make fun of them. Isolation is likely to propel a Doubter into the QAnon community where they would feel welcome.

Instead, socialize with the Doubter, if you can. Your company and acceptance can be the only human contact in their lives, a lifeline to sanity and a reality check. Invite them for a walk in nature. Recent research discovered that nature can offer the kind of awe that QAnons experienced while "connecting the dots." What's more, in experimental studies, people who experienced awe from being in nature became less radical in their political views.[27] A simple walk in the park might be the tiny shift needed for a Doubter to be open to a change in their views. Wait for the Doubter to ask questions. Rather than asserting your opinion, question theirs.

Tread lightly.

"How do you know?" is a useful question. "How do you know Trump is fighting against the cabal?" "How do you know Q is not misleading you on purpose?" "How do you know what Q says is true when so many previous drops were lies?" It's best to quit when they pause at your question. Give them a moment, and, if the answer is not forthcoming, it's your clue that you planted the seed of reason. Change the subject and move on. With any luck, the Doubter will germinate the seed and connect the dots into a more realistic worldview.

Q: Why Is Q So Popular in the United States?

Americans are more physically isolated than, for example, Europeans, and they are lonelier. Social isolation and loneliness make more Americans resort to social media, as compared to Europeans, and that makes Americans more likely to encounter Q-conspiracy theories. In addition, many Americans feel disillusioned with the government and suspicious of political and cultural elites. For that reason, they are more accepting of stories about behind-the-scenes shenanigans featuring these powerful players. Finally, Americans are less cynical about online content and are less likely to suspect malfeasance in stories they read on social media, because the United States does not teach Internet literacy and critical thinking as part of its school curriculum, as many European countries do. All of these factors make Americans a lot more likely to engage with fake stories online, and, click by click, to become consumed by QAnon content.

Q: How Can Someone Spewing QAnon Conspiracies, Like Marjorie Taylor Greene or Lauren Boebert, Be Elected to Congress?

While it's tempting to view these politicians as an aberration, they represent a long tradition of radical right women in U.S. politics. In the Jim Crow era, most white women in the south were against integration and racial equality.[28] More recently, Sarah Palin embodied the kind of feminized fascism: "aw shucks" folksiness and overt ignorance masking ruthless political instincts. Sarah Palin's supporters helped elect Donald Trump. They are now cheering on this political legacy in the celebrity of Greene and Boebert.

The mass media and old school political circles have dismissed Palin, Trump, Greene, and Boebert as ridiculous—to our peril. These performance politicians' popularity points to a strong demand for the qualities they flaunt: racism, anti-Semitism, and disdain for science and democracy. Their apparent weaknesses are decoys, used to destruct the outsiders while they dog whistle to their loyal base, rousing support and amassing donations. As long as the mainstream media remains fooled by these wolves in sheep's clothing, they have the upper hand.

It's not an accident Greene and Boebert were elected. It's a reflection of a deeply fractured society. In the 2020 election cycle, there were more than two dozen QAnon-supporting candidates to Congress.[29] Greene and Boebert's success stories will encourage others like them to seek public office. Without a concerted effort to heal the fault lines that separate Americans who see QAnon as ridiculous from Americans who see them as righteous, the number of U.S. politicians taking advantage of this cultural rift will continue to increase.

Q: Is QAnon a Uniquely American Phenomenon?

Far from it.

In fact, QAnon has spread around the world, with a documented following on every continent. In Europe, QAnon followings have been gaining ground in France and Germany;[30] in Poland[31] and Hungary;[32] in Russia;[33] Finland,[34] and the Netherlands;[35] in Portugal,[36] Italy,[37] and Spain;[38] in Serbia and Croatia;[39] in Ukraine and in Romania.[40] In Asia, QAnon followings have been growing in Japan,[41] Kazakhstan,[42] and Pakistan.[43] In Africa, QAnon has a significant presence in South Africa,[44] Algeria, and Egypt. In North America, QAnon has followings in the United States and Canada.[45] In Australia and New Zealand,[46] QAnon groups have been active online. QAnon is also in Latin America: in Costa Rica, Argentina, Colombia, Mexico, Guatemala, Panama, Brazil, and Uruguay.[47]

QAnon Qontagion is spreading.

NOTES

CHAPTER 1

1. Amanda Seitz, "QAnon's 'Save the Children' Morphs into Popular Slogan," *AP News* (October 28, 2020). https://apnews.com/article/election-2020-donald-trump-child-trafficking-illinois-morris-aab978bb7e9b89cd2cea151ca13421a0

2. Q sensitive allows access to special nuclear material (SNM) category 1. An employee with a Q sensitive clearance has access to nuclear weapons design, manufacture, or use data; disclosure could cause exceptionally grave damage to the nation. Q nonsensitive allows access to special nuclear material (SNM) category 2. The higher the SNM category, the more readily the material could be converted to a nuclear explosive device. Categories 1 and 2 require special protection, such as armed guards. "DOE Classification and Security," (n.d.). https://fas.org/sgp/classdoe.htm; Izabella Kaminska, "Is QAnon a Game Gone Wrong? | FT Film," *Financial Times* (October 16, 2020). https://www.ft.com/video/372cac40–0f6f-498b-8c19–7b635142296e

3. Kevin Roose, "What Is QAnon, the Viral Pro-Trump Conspiracy Theory?" *New York Times* (March 4, 2021). https://www.nytimes.com/article/what-is-qanon.html

4. "The Making of QAnon: A Crowdsourced Conspiracy," *Bellingcat* (January 7, 2021). https://www.bellingcat.com/news/americas/2021/01/07/the-making-of-qanon-a-crowdsourced-conspiracy/

5. https://www.4chan.org/

6. Roose, "What Is QAnon?"

7. Will Sommer, "Inside the Completely Nutso Universe of QAnon: An Explainer for the Conspiracy Theory That's Taking over the GOP," *Daily Beast* (August 21, 2020). https://www.thedailybeast.com/what-is-qanon-a-deep-look-inside-the-nutso-conspiracy-theory-infecting-our-politics

8. Ramona Duoba, "QAnon: The Search for Q," *Provokr* (January 26, 2021). https://www.provokr.com/tv/QAnon-the-search-for-q/

9. David Gilbert, "The Democrats' Lazy QAnon Attack Ad Will Only Make Things Worse," *Vice News* (February 3, 2021). https://www.vice.com/en/article/epd8d4/the-democrats-lazy-qanon-attack-ad-will-only-make-things-worse

10. Marc-André Argentino, "Twitter / @_MAArgentino: Congresswomen, Lawyers, Doctors . . . " (February 3, 2021). https://twitter.com/_MAArgentino/status/1356834269738467328?s=20

11. Daniel Morrison, "Evidence of the People Responsible for 'Qanon' Being Responsible for 'Qanon,'" *Medium* (January 26, 2021). https://daniel-ed-morrison.medium.com/evidence-of-the-people-responsible-for-qanon-being-responsible-for-qanon-779c357da8ae

12. Duoba, "QAnon: The Search for Q"; Cullen Hoback, *Q: Into the Storm*, HBO, 2021. https://www.hbo.com/q-into-the-storm

13. Mike Pesca, "What ISIS Can Tell US About QAnon," *Slate* (September 15, 2020). https://slate.com/news-and-politics/2020/09/qanon-clint-watts-isis-comparisons-gist-transcript.html

14. "Dread Pirate Roberts," Princess Bride Wiki, *Fandom.com* (n.d.). https://princessbride.fandom.com/wiki/Dread_Pirate_Roberts

15. Brandy Zadrozny and Ben Collins, "How Three Conspiracy Theorists Took 'Q' and Sparked Qanon," *NBC News* (August 14, 2018). https://www.nbcnews.com/tech/tech-news/how-three-conspiracy-theorists-took-q-sparked-QAnon-n900531

16. Duoba, "QAnon: The Search for Q."

17. Kaminska, "Is QAnon a Game Gone Wrong?"

18. Great Big Story, "Cracking the Code of Cicada 3301," *YouTube* (August 14, 2019). https://www.youtube.com/watch?v=RatbYqc0-jE

19. Izabella Kaminska, "The 'Game Theory' in the Qanon Conspiracy Theory," *Financial Times* (October 16, 2020). https://www.ft.com/content/74f9d20f-9ff9-4fad-808f-c7e4245a1725

20. Kaminska, "Is QAnon a Game Gone Wrong?"

21. Reed Berkowitz, "A Game Designer's Analysis of QAnon," *The Street* (January 22, 2021). https://www.thestreet.com/phildavis/news/a-game-designers-analysis-of-qanon

22. Morrison, "Evidence of the People Responsible for 'Qanon' Being Responsible for 'Qanon.'"

23. Conspirador Norteño, "Twitter / @conspirator0: #FollowTheWhiteRabbit . . . " (November 18, 2017). https://twitter.com/conspirator0/status/931983301597913088?s=20

24. Zadrozny and Collins, "How Three Conspiracy Theorists Took 'Q' and Sparked Qanon."

25. Conspirador Norteño, "Twitter / @conspirator0: The #UraniumOne hashtag . . . " (November 2, 2017). https://twitter.com/conspirator0/status/926277839430848513?s=20

26. William Turton and Joshua Brustein, "QAnon Was on the Fringe Until This Citigroup Executive Came Along," *Financial Review* (October 14, 2020). https://www.afr.com/world/north-america/qanon-was-on-the-fringe-until-this-citigroup-executive-came-along-20201013-p564j7

27. Duoba, "QAnon: The Search for Q."

28. Kaminska, "The 'Game Theory' in the Qanon Conspiracy Theory."

29. "Protected: Q Files: Manual Chavez III Interviewed," *Samizdat* (March 13, 2020). https://therealsamizdat.com/tag/QAnon/

30. Ibid.

31. Patrick Lucas Austin, "What Is 8chan? Shooter Left Racist Screed on Message Board," *Time* (August 5, 2019). https://time.com/5644314/8chan-shootings/; Brian Dunning, "How to Extract Adrenochrome from Children," "Skeptoid" podcast #750 (October 20, 2020). https://skeptoid.com/episodes/4750?gclid=Cj0KCQiA34OBBhCcARIsAG32uvMnCIuSn4pOdHmnzKwIlqwuQQiA3mWQVRzNMV16YjuiWzv9s90vedEaAjSdEALw_wcB; Tanner Sherlock, "The Legacy of GamerGate. How an Online Mob Catalyzed the Alt-Right," *Medium* (October 22, 2020). https://medium.com/engl-201/gamergate-and-trump-how-a-small-internet-movement-gave-rise-to-the-alt-right-a6cb8509c3e

32. Hoback, *Q: Into the Storm.*

33. Duoba, "QAnon: The Search for Q."

34. A.J. Vicens and Alie Breland, "QAnon Is Supposed to Be All About Protecting Kids. Its Primary Enabler Appears to Have Hosted Child Porn Domains." https://www.motherjones.com/politics/2020/10/jim-watkins-child-pornography-domains/

35. William Turton and Joshua Brustein, "Who Is QAnon Evangelist, QMap Creator, and Former Citigroup Exec Jason Gelinas?," *Bloomberg* (October 7, 2020). https://www.bloomberg.com/news/features/2020%E2%80%9310%E2%80%9307/who-is-qanon-evangelist-qmap-creator-and-former-citigroup-exec-jason-gelinas

36. Craig Silverman and Jane Lytvynenko, "The Owner of 8chan Has Created a News Source for Internet Trolls," *BuzzFeed News* (February 22, 2017). https://www.buzzfeednews.com/article/craigsilverman/meet-the-online-porn-pioneer-who-created-a-news-site-for-int

37. Ibid.

38. Reddit Calm Before the Storm r/CBTS_Stream, https://

web.archive.org/web/20180111150259/https://www.reddit.com/r/CBTS_Stream/

39. Zadrozny and Collins, "How Three Conspiracy Theorists Took 'Q' and Sparked Qanon."

40. Duoba, "QAnon: The Search for Q."

41. Zadrozny and Collins, "How Three Conspiracy Theorists Took 'Q' and Sparked Qanon."

42. Duoba, "QAnon: The Search for Q"; Hoback, *Q: Into the Storm*.

43. Duoba, "QAnon: The Search for Q."

44. "Reddit Bans QAnon Subreddits for Inciting 'Violence,'" *Daily Beast* (September 12, 2018). https://www.thedailybeast.com/reddit-bans-qanon-subreddits-for-inciting-violence

45. Zadrozny and Collins, "How Three Conspiracy Theorists Took 'Q' and Sparked Qanon."

46. Kevin Roose, "'Shut the Site Down,' Says the Creator of 8chan, a Megaphone for Gunmen," *New York Times* (August 4, 2019). https://www.nytimes.com/2019/08/04/technology/8chan-shooting-manifesto.html

47. Makena Kelly, "8chan 'Has No Intent of Deleting Constitutionally Protected Hate Speech,' Owner Tells Congress," *The Verge* (September 5, 2019). https://www.theverge.com/2019/9/5/20850791/8chan-hate-speech-delete-jim-watkins-infinitechan-el-paso-shooting-racist-white-supremacist

48. Ibid.

49. https://www.christchurchcall.com/

50. Turton and Brustein "Who Is QAnon Evangelist . . . "

51. Ibid.

52. Turton and Brustein "QAnon Was on the Fringe . . . "

53. Turton and Brustein, "Who Is QAnon Evangelist . . . "

54. James Walker, "The QAnon Super PAC Was a Flop," *Washington Monthly* (November 18, 2020). https://washingtonmonthly.com/2020/11/18/the-QAnon-super-pac-was-a-flop/

55. Alex Kaplan, "Here Are the QAnon Supporters Running for Congress in 2020," *Media Matters* (January 7, 2020). https://www.mediamatters.org/qanon-conspiracy-theory/here-are-qanon-supporters-running-congress-2020

56. Chris Francescani, "The Men Behind QAnon," *ABC News* (September 22, 2020). https://abcnews.go.com/Politics/men-qanon/story?id=73046374

57. "Country of Liars," "Reply All" podcast #166 (September 18, 2020), https://gimletmedia.com/shows/reply-all/llhe5nm

58. Rachel E Greenspan, "Who Is Q: Why People Think Jim Watkins Leads QAnon Conspiracy Theory," *Insider* (October 7, 2020).

https://www.insider.com/who-is-q-why-people-think-jim-watkins-qanon-8chan-2020-10

59. Jacob Silverman, "Is This Q? A New HBO Documentary Investigates the First Family of QAnon," *New Republic* (March 23, 2021). https://newrepublic.com/article/161775/q-qanon-hbo-ron-watkins

60. Martin Geddes, "10 Essays of 'On Q' with Robert David Steele" (August 20, 2020). https://www.martingeddes.com/10-essays-of-on-q-with-robert-david-steele/

61. Komorusan 714, "Going After Child Hunters—Robert David Steele," *YouTube* (November 28, 2018). https://www.youtube.com/watch?v=ODZo21ge-8g

62. Ibid.

63. https://www.itv.com/news/2018-11-22/lucky-17-q-and-the-tippy-top-president-how-conspiracy-theories-are-being-turbo-charged-into-donald-trumps-america

64. https://mikeflynndefensefund.org/ has been disabled. The content is described by the *Daily Mail*: Nikki Schwab, "Mike Flynn Endorses QAnon Merchandise," *Daily Mail* (December 30, 2020). https://www.dailymail.co.uk/news/article-9100139/Mike-Flynn-endorses-selling-QAnon-merchandise-pays-legal-defense-fund.html

65. Will Sommer, "Michael Flynn Is Now Selling QAnon Merch," *Daily Beast* (November 29, 2020).

66. Correspondence with presidential historian Douglas Brinkley who asked the Kennedy family. Dr. Joseph Brown also checked the boat himself and confirmed with the archivist at the JFK Library that neither of JFK's two boats, the *Victura* (on the UMB campus) or the other sailboat, the *Honey Fitz*, ever contained a bell.

67. Adrienne LaFrance interview with Anderson Cooper, "CNN Special Reports: Inside the QAnon Conspiracy," (February 6, 2021). Transcript available at http://transcripts.cnn.com/TRANSCRIPTS/2102/06/csr.01.html

68. The tweet is now deleted as the account has been suspended. @D3Mo_Anon (August 6, 2018). https://twitter.com/D3Mo_Anon/status/1026464797133422593

69. "Trump Aide Michael Flynn Jnr out After 'Pizzagate' Tweets," *BBC News* (December 7, 2016). https://www.bbc.com/news/world-us-canada-38231532

70. Salvador Hernandez, "Russian Trolls Spread Baseless Conspiracy Theories Like Pizzagate and QAnon After the Election," *Buzzfeed News* (August 15, 2018). https://www.buzzfeednews.com/article/salvadorhernandez/russian-trolls-spread-baseless-conspiracy-theories-like

71. Anna Merlan, "The Conspiracy Singularity Has Arrived," *Vice*

News (July 17, 2020). https://www.vice.com/en/article/v7gz53/the-conspiracy-singularity-has-arrived

72. However not all Catholics accept the second Vatican. Mel Gibson, for example, does not and neither does his 2004 film *The Passion of the Christ*, which reinforced the centuries-old myths about Jewish culpability for the millions of moviegoers who watched it.

73. "Blood Libel," in *Holocaust Encyclopedia*. The United States Holocaust Memorial Museum (n.d.). https://encyclopedia.ushmm.org/content/en/article/blood-libel

74. Andrew Desiderio, "Franken Compares Trump Ad to Elders of Zion," *Daily Beast* (April 13, 2017). https://www.thedailybeast.com/cheats/2016/11/06/franken-compares-trump-ad-to-elders-of-zion

75. Jason Stanley, "Movie at the Ellipse: A Study in Fascist Propaganda," *Just Security* (February 14, 2021). https://www.justsecurity.org/74504/movie-at-the-ellipse-a-study-in-fascist-propaganda

76. "Why Is Billionaire George Soros a Bogeyman for the Hard Right?" *BBC News* (September 7, 2019). https://www.bbc.com/news/stories-49584157

77. Victoria Bekiempis, "Cesar Sayoc, Who Sent Pipe Bombs to Trump Critics, Gets 20 Years in Prison," *The Guardian* (August 5, 2019). https://www.theguardian.com/us-news/2019/aug/05/cesar-sayoc-sentencing-pipe-bombs-targets-trump-critics

78. Dunning, "How to Extract Adrenochrome from Children."

79. Ibid.

80. Anti-Defamation League, "Blood Libel: A False, Incendiary Claim Against Jews" (n.d.). https://www.adl.org/education/resources/glossary-terms/blood-libel

81. BlueTooth Truther. "Jew Ritual BLOOD LIBEL Sacrifice is #ADRENOCHROME Harvesting," *YouTube* (September 9, 2015). https://www.youtube.com/watch?v=PYCG30D8lkg

82. Roland Betancourt, "What the QAnon of the 6th Century Reveals About Conspiracies," *Time* (February 3, 2021). https://time.com/5935586/QAnon-6th-century-conspiracies/

83. Anti-Defamation League, "Blood Libel."

84. "Blood Libel," in *Holocaust Encyclopedia*.

85. Niv M. Sultan, "The Story of America's First—and Only—Blood Libel," *NYU News* (September 10, 2019). https://www.nyu.edu/about/news-publications/news/2019/september/berenson-on-massena-blood-libel.html

86. "Daily Life: Food Laws—Practices in Judaism," *BBC—Bitesize* (n.d.). https://www.bbc.co.uk/bitesize/guides/zv626yc/revision/8

87. Leviticus 7:26–27: https://biblehub.com/leviticus/17-14.htm

88. Marvin Perry and Frederick M. Schweitzer, eds., *Anti-Semitic*

Myths: A Historical and Contemporary Anthology (Bloomington: Indiana University Press, 2008), 3.

89. Sommer, "Inside the Completely Nutso Universe of QAnon."

90. Ibid.

91. Seek Truth, "Adrenochrome Users Exposed: #RobertDavidSteele #Davidicke #Billcooper #Adrenochrome #Childtrafficking," *YouTube* (May 7, 2020). https://www.youtube.com/watch?v=rQ7-xDsC2KE

92. MrLen, "Did Icke Rip Off the Old 'V' TVSeries?" *CosmoQuest Forums* (May 7, 2004). https://forum.cosmoquest.org/showthread.php?11257-Did-Icke-rip-off-the-old-quot-V-quot-tv-series

93. Ben Collins, "QAnon's Dominion Voter Fraud Conspiracy Theory Reaches the President," *NBC News*, November 13, 2020.*NBC News* (November 13, 2020). https://www.nbcnews.com/tech/tech-news/q-fades-qanon-s-dominion-voter-fraud-conspiracy-theory-reaches-n1247780

94. https://www.youtube.com/watch?v=9tjdswqGGVg&list=PLr4E97YzUfEMIr23hzOBmk9mg-z8TDOXj

CHAPTER 2

1. Marissa L. Jang, "Trump Supporters Plan DC Rally on Day Congress Certifies Election Results," *Washington Post* (December 22, 2020). https://www.washingtonpost.com/local/dc-trump-rally-january-6-protests/2020/12/22/1c94ab7a-447a-11eb-a277–49a6d1f9dff1_story.html; Atlantic Council DFRLab, "#Stop the Steal Timeline of Social Media and Extremist Activities Leading to 1/6 Insurrection," *Just Security* (February 10, 2021). https://www.justsecurity.org/74622/stopthesteal-timeline-of-social-media-and-extremist-activities-leading-to-1–6-insurrection/

2. David Kirkpatrick, Mike MacIntire, and Christian Triebert, "Fundraisers Piled Up Cash for Caravans to DC," *New York Times* (January 17, 2021). https://www.arkansasonline.com/news/2021/jan/17/fundraisers-piled-up-cash-for-caravans-to-dc/

3. Lili Loofbourow, "It Makes Perfect Sense That QAnon Took off with Women This Summer," *Slate* (September 18, 2020). https://slate.com/news-and-politics/2020/09/QAnon-women-why.html

4. Luke Mogelson, "A Reporter's Video from Inside the Capitol Siege," *New Yorker* (January 17, 2021). https://www.newyorker.com/video/watch/a-reporters-footage-from-inside-the-capitol-siege

5. Donie O'Sullivan, "Watch CNN Go Inside a Gathering of QAnon Followers," *CNN Business* (February 5, 2021). https://www.cnn.com/videos/business/2021/02/05/inside-qanon-culture-meeting-donie-osullivan-pkg-ctn-vpx.cnn

6. Seth G. Jones and Martin C. Libicki, *How Terrorist Groups End: Lessons for Countering al Qa'ida*. Santa Monica, CA: RAND Corporation, 2008.

7. Elizabeth Gillespie McRae, "Marjorie Taylor Greene Is Just the Latest White Radical Woman Poisoning Politics," *Washington Post* (February 26, 2021). https://www.washingtonpost.com/outlook/2021/02/06/marjorie-taylor-greene-is-just-latest-radical-white-woman-poisoning-politics/

8. Seyward Darby, *Sisters in Hate: American Women on the Front Lines of White Nationalism*. New York: Little Brown, 2020.

9. Seyward Darby, cited in E. J. Dickson, "How Do Women Become White Supremacists?" *Rolling Stone* (July 15, 2020). https://www.rollingstone.com/culture/culture-features/seyward-darby-sisters-in-hate-female-white-supremacists-1029109/

10. Mona Eltawahy, "White Women Storm the Capitol," *Feminist Giant* (January 10, 2021). https://www.feministgiant.com/p/white-women-storm-the-capitol

11. Craig Silverman, Jane Lytvynenko, and Pranav Dixit, "How 'The Women for America First' Bus Tour Led to the Capitol Coup Attempt," *BuzzFeed News* (January 26, 2021). https://www.buzzfeednews.com/article/craigsilverman/maga-bus-tour-coup

12. Drew Harwell, Isaac Stanley-Becker, Razzan Nakhlawi, and Craig Timberg, "QAnon Reshaped Trump's Party and Radicalized Believers: The Capitol Siege May Just Be the Start," *Washington Post* (January 14, 2021). https://www.washingtonpost.com/technology/2021/01/13/qanon-capitol-siege-trump/

13. Ellen Barry, Nicholas Bogel-Burroughs, and Dave Philipps, "Woman Killed in Capitol Embraced Trump and QAnon," *New York Times* (January 20, 2021). https://www.nytimes.com/2021/01/07/us/who-was-ashli-babbitt.html

14. Ibid.

15. Facebook. https://www.facebook.com/ProtestAccess/posts/246152553795723

16. Anna North, "White Women's Role in White Supremacy Explained," *Vox* (January 15, 2021). https://www.vox.com/2021/1/15/22231079/capitol-riot-women-QAnon-white-supremacy

17. Evan Hill, Arielle Ray, and Dahlia Kozlowsky, "Videos Show How Rioter Was Trampled in Stampede at Capitol," *New York Times* (January 15, 2021). https://www.nytimes.com/2021/01/15/us/rosanne-boyland-capitol-riot-death.html

18. Ibid.

19. Wayne Drash and Sarah Rose, "Kennesaw Woman Who Died Amid DC Chaos Was Among Trump's 'Biggest Fans,'" *Geor-*

gia Public Broadcasting (January 8, 2021). https://www.gpb.org/news/2021/01/08/kennesaw-woman-who-died-amid-dc-chaos-was-among-trumps-biggest-fans

20. Aneesa Miller, "Say Her Name," *Sentinel Tribune*, letter to the editor (January 19, 2021), https://www.sent-trib.com/opinion/say-her-name-roseanne-boyland/article_0854de4a-5a74–11eb-863d-eb20b9bf0f9a.html

21. Reuters, "Trump to Blame for the Death of Woman Trampled in Capitol Riot" (January 8, 2021). https://www.reuters.com/article/us-usa-election-deaths/trump-to-blame-for-death-of-woman-trampled-in-capitol-riot-family-member-says-idUSKBN29D2B1

22. Drash and Rose, "Kennesaw Woman Who Died Amid DC Chaos . . ."

23. Mea Watkins, Meghan Packer, and Rhiannon Youngbauer, "Kennesaw Woman Among People Who Died at D.C. Riot," *CBS46* (January 7, 2021). https://www.cbs46.com/news/kennesaw-woman-among-people-who-died-at-d-c-riot/article_1a7950a8-5112-11eb-bbe7-37a8f7f03703.html#:~:text=Washington%20D.C.%20Metropolitan%20Police%20Department,medical%20emergency%20during%20the%20protests.

24. Mariel Padilla, "The Spread of Conspiracies and Disinformation by Women on Social Media," *19th News* (October 19, 2020). https://19thnews.org/2020/10/19th-explains-women-disinformation-election-2020/

25. Ciaran O'Connor, "TikTok Fails to Stop the Spread of QAnon Conspiracies on Its Platform," *ISD* (October 16, 2020). https://www.isdglobal.org/digital_dispatches/tiktok-fails-to-stop-spread-of-QAnon-conspiracy/

26. Facebook, "An Update to How We Address Movements and Organizations Tied to Violence" (August 19, 2020).

27. Ibid.

28. Conversations with Erin Saltman and Dina Hussein at Facebook as part of the Global Internet Forum to Counter Terrorism and the author.

29. Harwell, Stanley-Becker, Nakhlawi, and Timberg, "QAnon Reshaped Trump's Party . . ."

30. Parler data collected by the Evidence Based Cyber Security research group. The Parler post linked to a local news story: https://www.kusi.com/kusi-news-confirms-identity-of-woman-shot-and-killed-inside-us-capitol/

31. Marc-André Argentino and Adnan Raja, "Ashli Babbitt: A Far-Right Martyr of the Insurrection." *GNET* (January 13, 2021). https://gnet-research.org/2021/01/13/ashli-babbitt-a-far-right-martyr-of-the-insurrection/

32. Ibid.

33. Eltawahy, "White Women Storm the Capitol."

34. Rob O'Dell and Richard Ruelas, "QAnon, False Flags, and Baby-Eating Liberals," *Arizona Republic* (October 1, 2020). https://www.azcentral.com/in-depth/news/local/arizona-investigations/2020/10/01/how-arizona-patriots-have-built-community-around-conspiracy-theories/3486382001/

35. Lois Beckett, "QAnon: A Timeline of Violence Linked to the Conspiracy Theory," *The Guardian* (October 16, 2020). https://www.theguardian.com/us-news/2020/oct/15/qanon-violence-crimes-timeline

36. Sarah Jean Green, "God Told Me He Was a Lizard," *Seattle Times* (January 8, 2019). https://www.seattletimes.com/seattle-news/crime/god-told-me-he-was-a-lizard-seattle-man-accused-of-killing-his-brother-with-a-sword/

37. "He Wasn't Seeking to Kill a Mob Boss, He Was Trying to Help," *New York Times* (July 21, 2019). https://www.nytimes.com/2019/07/21/nyregion/gambino-shooting-anthony-comello-frank-cali.html

38. Brittany Shammas, "A Mother Teamed Up Qanon Followers to Kidnap Her Son, " *Washington Post* (January 8, 2020). https://www.washingtonpost.com/crime-law/2020/01/08/mother-teamed-up-with-qanon-followers-kidnap-her-son-protective-custody-police-say/

39. Ibid.

40. Will Sommer, "QAnon Believer Teamed Up with Conspiracy Theorists to Plot Kidnapping, Police Say," *Daily Beast* (January 4, 2020). https://www.thedailybeast.com/cynthia-abcug-qanon-conspiracy-theorist-charged-in-kidnapping-plot

41. Richard Winton, "FBI Looks for Ties to Extremist Groups in Train Derailment Near Hospital Ship *Mercy*," *LA Times* (April 2, 2020). https://www.latimes.com/california/story/2020–04–02/fbi-train-derailment-mercy-naval-ship-extremist-groups

42. Larry Celona and Kenneth Garger, "Ranting Illinois Stripper Carrying 18 Knives Livestreams Arrest Outside USS *Intrepid*," *New York Post* (April 30, 2020). https://nypost.com/2020/04/30/illinois-stripper-live-streams-arrest-outside-the-uss-intrepid/

43. Jim Hagerty, "Former Illinois Woman Arrested with Knives: 'I am the Coronavirus,'" *Rock River Times* (May 15, 2020). http://rockrivertimes.com/2020/05/15/former-illinois-woman-arrested-with-knives-i-am-the-coronavirus/

44. "Exotic Fire Dancer, QAnon Follower Arrested Near USNS *Comfort* with Car Full of Knives," *NBC4 NY* (April 30, 2020). https://www.nbcnewyork.com/news/local/exotic-fire-dancer-arrested-in-nyc-outside-usns-comfort-with-car-full-of-knives/2396217/

45. "Corey Hurren Accused in Rideau Hall Attack," *CBC News* (July 17, 2020). https://www.cbc.ca/news/politics/corey-hurren-rideau-date-for-bail-hearing-1.5653252

46. Julian Feeld, "Texas QAnon Supporter Used Car to Attack Strangers She Believed Were 'Pedophiles,'" *Right Wing Watch* (August 20, 2020). https://www.rightwingwatch.org/post/texas-qanon-car-attack-cecilia-fulbright/

47. Facebook. https://www.facebook.com/mcsoflorida/posts/3670231042997477

48. Will Sommer, "Another QAnon Mom Has Allegedly Kidnapped Her Kid," *Daily Beast* (October 1, 2020). https://www.thedailybeast.com/another-qanon-mom-has-allegedly-kidnapped-her-kid?ref=author

49. Rebekah Sager, "Mother of Infamous Horned Shirtless Capitol Rioter Says Her Son Is a Great Patriot," *KNX Newsradio 1070* (January 11, 2021). https://www.radio.com/knx1070/news/national/mother-of-capitol-rioter-says-her-son-is-a-great-patriot

50. Farnoush Amiri and Dan Sewell, "'Just Shocked': a Town Reckons with Charges in Capitol Riot," *Associated Press* (January 29, 2021). https://apnews.com/article/capitol-siege-columbus-media-social-media-ohio-b033c3b44e9a260a26dc10172dc7e7cd

51. "Former Left-Wing Extremist Tried for Failed Attacks in the 1980s," *Deutche Welle* (April 13, 2007). https://www.dw.com/en/former-left-wing-extremist-tried-for-failed-attacks-in-1980s/a-2438945

52. Rote Zora, "Resistance Is Possible: Interview with Two Members of Rote Zora," *Freilassung* (June 1984). http://www.freilassung.de/otherl/arm/rzora84.htm

53. Carrie Hamilton, "Why Do Women Become ETA Terrorists?" *The Guardian* (21 October 2009). http://www.telegraph.co.uk/news/worldnews/europe/spain/6397643/Iratxe-Sorzabal-Diaz-why-do-women- become-ETA-terrorists.html

54. Nick Meo and Fiona Govan, "ETA Resurgent on 50th Anniversary as Women Come to the Fore," *The Telegraph* (August 2, 2009). http://www.telegraph.co.uk/news/worldnews/europe/spain/5956832/Eta-resurgent-on-50th- anniversary-as-women-come-to-the-fore.html

55. Interviews conducted by the author, Belfast 2009.

56. Julie Peteet, *Gender in Crisis: Women and the Palestinian Resistance Movement*. New York: Columbia University Press, 1992, 155.

57. Mia Bloom, *Dying to Kill: The Allure of Suicide Terrorism*. New York: Columbia University Press, 2005.

58. Darby, *Sisters in Hate,* 11.

59. Annie Kelly, "Mothers for QAnon." *New York Times* (September 10, 2020)., https://www.nytimes.com/2020/09/10/opinion/qanon-women-conspiracy.html

60. Brian Friedberg, "The Dark Virality of Hollywood Blood Harvesting Conspiracy," *Wired* (July 31, 2020). https://www.wired.com/story/opinion-the-dark-virality-of-a-hollywood-blood-harvesting-conspiracy/

61. Paris Martineau, "How Chrissy Teigen and John Legend Became Victims of a Horrible New Conspiracy Theory," *New York Magazine* (January 2, 2018). https://nymag.com/intelligencer/2018/01/what-happened-with-chrissy-teigen-on-twitter-an-explainer.html

62. Sopan Deb, "Roseanne Barr's Tweets Didn't Come out of Nowhere," *New York Times* (May 29, 2018). https://www.nytimes.com/2018/05/29/arts/television/twitter-posts-roseanne-barr.html

63. Marjorie Taylor Greene's videos posted to Travis View's (real name: Logan Strain) Twitter timeline. https://twitter.com/travis_view/status/1345792096339456004?s=20

64. Asawin Suebsaeng and Will Sommer, "Team Trump Finally Disavows Pizzagate Theorist Who Boasted of Being on 2020 Board," *Daily Beast* (January 23, 2019). https://www.thedailybeast.com/team-trump-finally-disavows-pizzagate-theorist-who-boasted-of-being-on-2020-board

65. Criminal complaint for the Superior Court of the District of Columbia, case UI6036846, Pizzagate incident reprinted in *New York Times* (December 5, 2016). https://www.nytimes.com/interactive/2016/12/05/us/document-Edgar-Welch-Criminal-Complaint-Comet-Ping-Pong.html

66. Gabrielle Bruney, "Unpacking QAnon: A Batsh*t Conspiracy Theory Tailor-Made for the Trump Era," *Esquire* (July 24, 2020). https://www.esquire.com/news-politics/a22646546/q-anon-trump-conspiracy-theory-explained/

67. Spencer S. Hsu, "Pizzagate Gunman Says He Was Foolish, Reckless, Mistaken—and Sorry," *Washington Post* (June 14, 2017). https://www.washingtonpost.com/local/public-safety/pizzagate-shooter-apologizes-in-handwritten-letter-for-his-mistakes-ahead-of-sentencing/2017/06/13/f35126b6-5086-11e7-be25-3a519335381c_story.html

68. E. J. Dickson, "The Birth of QAmom," *Rolling Stone* (September 2, 2020). https://www.rollingstone.com/culture/culture-features/qanon-mom-conspiracy-theory-parents-sex-trafficking-qamom-1048921/

69. Quoted in Kelly, "Mothers for QAnon."

70. Snejana Farberov, "QAnon Supporters Charged with DWI and Assault," *Daily Mail* (August 21, 2020). https://www.dailymail.co.uk/news/article-8651451/Drunk-QAnon-supporter-30-chased-two-motorists-thought-pedophiles.html

71. Ibid.

72. Sabrina Tavernise, "'Trump Just Used Us and Our Fear': One Woman's Journey out of QAnon," *New York Times* (January 30, 2021). https://www.nytimes.com/2021/01/29/us/leaving-qanon-conspiracy.html?smid=tw-share

73. Kelly, "Mothers for QAnon."

74. Ibid.

75. Beckett, "QAnon: A Timeline of Violence Linked to the Conspiracy Theory."

76. Bridget Johnson, "Wray Explains Antifa, Qanon, Boogaloo, and Racially Motivated Violence at Threats Hearing," *Homeland Security Today* (September 18, 2020). https://www.hstoday.us/subject-matter-areas/counterterrorism/wray-explains-antifa-QAnon-boogaloo-and-racially-motivated-violence-at-threats-hearing/

77. Tavernise, "'Trump Just Used Us and Our Fear.'"

78. Michael Jensen and Sheehan Kane, "QAnon Offenders in the United States," Study of Terrorism and the Responses to Terrorism (START) (2021). https://www.start.umd.edu/pubs/START_PIRUS_QAnon_Feb2021_0.pdf

79. Ibid.

80. Hallie Jackson and Dareh Gregorian, "RNC Cancels Speaker Mary Ann Mendoza After She Promoted QAnon Anti-Semitic Conspiracies," *NBC News* (August 25, 2020). https://www.nbcnews.com/politics/2020-election/rnc-cancels-speaker-mary-ann-mendoza-after-she-promoted-qanon-n1238109

81. Will Sommer, "RNC Speaker Cancelled After Boosting QAnon Conspiracy About Jewish Plot to Enslave the World," *Daily Beast* (August 27, 2020). https://www.thedailybeast.com/rnc-speaker-boosts-qanon-conspiracy-theory-about-jewish-plot-to-enslave-the-world-1

82. Over the past year, I have accessed QAnon Telegram chatrooms as part of my research on terrorism and social media. See also Loofbourow, "It Makes Perfect Sense That QAnon Took off with Women This Summer."

83. Loofbourow, "It Makes Perfect Sense That QAnon Took off with Women This Summer."

84. Reed Berkowitz, "A Game Designer's Analysis of QAnon," *The Street* (January 22, 2021). https://www.thestreet.com/phildavis/news/a-game-designers-analysis-of-qanon

85. Dickson, "The Birth of QAmom."

86. Rachel E. Greenspan, "Lifestyle Influencers Using COVID-19 to Spread QAnon Conspiracy Theory," *Insider* (May 15, 2020). https://www.insider.com/lifestyle-influencers-using-covid-19-to-spread-qanon-conspiracy-theory-2020-5

87. Berkowitz, "A Game Designer's Analysis of QAnon."

88. Ibid.

89. Fareed Zakaria interview with Bill Gates, *CNN GPS* (February 28, 2021). https://www.cnn.com/videos/tv/2021/02/28/exp-gps-0228-bill-gates-covid-19.cnn

90. Izabella Kaminska, "The 'Game Theory' in the Qanon Conspiracy Theory," *Financial Times* (October 16, 2020). https://www.ft.com/content/74f9d20f-9ff9-4fad-808f-c7e4245a1725

91. Greenspan, "Lifestyle Influencers Using COVID-19 to Spread QAnon Conspiracy Theory."

92. Tavernise, "'Trump Just Used Us and Our Fear.'"

93. Ibid.

94. Rachel E. Greenspan and Gabby Landsverk, "How QAnon Infiltrated the Yoga World," *Insider* (November 11, 2020). https://www.insider.com/qanon-conspiracy-theory-yoga-influencer-took-over-world-2020-11

95. Eli Pariser, *The Filter Bubble: What the Internet Is Hiding from You*. London: Penguin, 2011.

96. Daniel Kahneman, *Thinking, Fast and Slow*. New York: Penguin, 2011.

97. Union College, "Who Believes in Conspiracy Theories: New Research Offers a Theory," *Science Daily* (September 25, 2018). https://www.sciencedaily.com/releases/2018/09/180925075108.htm

98. Tavernise, "'Trump Just Used Us and Our Fear.'"

99. Sue Greenwood, "How British Grannies Are Spreading QAnon Conspiracy Theory Memes on Facebook," *The Conversation* (September 25, 2020). https://ray.yorksj.ac.uk/id/eprint/4781/1/how-british-grannies-are-spreading-QAnon-conspiracy-theory-memes-on-facebook-145820

100. Anne Helen Petersen, "The Real Housewives of QAnon: How QAnon Used #SaveTheChildren to Lure Suburban Moms," *Elle* (October 29, 2020). https://www.elle.com/culture/a34485099/qanon-conspiracy-suburban-women/

101. Christopher Wray, "Worldwide Threats to the Homeland," statement before the House Homeland Security Committee (September 17, 2020). https://www.fbi.gov/news/testimony/worldwide-threats-to-the-homeland-091720

102. Travis M. Andrews, "She Fell into QAnon and Went Viral for Destroying a Target Mask Display. Now She's Rebuilding Her Life," *Washington Post* (November 11, 2020). https://www.washingtonpost.com/technology/2020/11/11/masks-QAnon-target-melissa-rein-lively/

103. Ibid.

104. Padilla, "The Spread of Conspiracies and Disinformation by Women on Social Media."

105. North, "White Women's Role in White Supremacy Explained."

106. Haiyan Jia, an assistant journalism professor at Lehigh University, cited in Padilla, "The Spread of Conspiracies and Disinformation by Women on Social Media."

107. Jennifer Senior, "The Women Who Paved the Way for Marjorie Taylor Greene," *New York Times* (February 7, 2021). https://www.nytimes.com/2021/02/07/opinion/marjorie-taylor-greene-republican-women.html

108. Kaylen Ralph, "Marjorie Taylor Greene and Lauren Boebert Are the Women of Trump's Republican Party," *Teen Vogue* (February 5, 2021). https://www.teenvogue.com/story/marjorie-taylor-green-lauren-boebert-republican-women-congress

109. Daniel A. Cox and John Halpin, "Conspiracy Theories, Misinformation, COVID-19, and the 2020 Election," Survey Center on American Life (October 13, 2020). https://www.americansurveycenter.org/research/conspiracy-theories-misinformation-covid-19-and-the-2020-election/

110. Loofbourow, "It Makes Perfect Sense That QAnon Took off with Women This Summer."

111. Greenspan and Landsverk, "How QAnon Infiltrated the Yoga World."

112. Casey Newton, "How the 'Plandemic' Video Hoax Went Viral," *The Verge* (May 12, 2020). https://www.theverge.com/2020/5/12/21254184/how-plandemic-went-viral-facebook-youtube

113. Davey Alba, "Virus Conspiracists Elevate a New Champion," *New York Times* (May 9, 2020). https://www.nytimes.com/2020/05/09/technology/plandemic-judy-mikovitz-coronavirus-disinformation.html

114. Ibid.

115. Jane Lytvynenko, "The 'Plandemic' Video Has Exploded Online—And It Is Filled with Falsehoods," *BuzzFeed News* (May 7, 2020). https://www.buzzfeednews.com/article/janelytvynenko/coronavirus-plandemic-viral-harmful-fauci-mikovits

116. Greenspan and Landsverk, "How QAnon Infiltrated the Yoga World."

117. Ibid.

118. Adam Lewental, "I Think Dan Brown Turned My Parents into QAnoners," *Salon* (December 19, 2020). https://www.salon.com/2020/12/18/QAnon-conspiracy-dan-brown-da-vinci-code/

119. Mama Wolf, Facebook. https://www.facebook.com/informedmamawolf/posts/173081114193987

120. Greenwood, "How British Grannies Are Spreading QAnon Conspiracy Theory Memes on Facebook."

121. Mama Wolf, Facebook. https://www.facebook.com/informedmamawolf/posts/173081114193987

122. Kimi Robinson, "Why Is Wayfair Accused of Trafficking Children?" *Arizona Republic* (August 17, 2020). https://www.azcentral.com/story/entertainment/life/2020/08/17/wayfair-child-sex-trafficking-conspiracy-theory-reddit-qanon-facts-myths/3345421001/

123. Jonathon Chait, "GOP Congresswomen Blames Wildfires on Secret Jewish Space Laser," *New York Magazine,* (January 28, 2021). https://nymag.com/intelligencer/article/marjorie-taylor-greene-qanon-wildfires-space-laser-rothschild-execute.html

124. Kelly, "Mothers for QAnon."

125. Petersen, "The Real Housewives of QAnon."

126. Daniel A. Cox, "After the Ballots Are Counted: Conspiracies, Political Violence, and American Exceptionalism," Survey Center on American Life (February 11, 2021). https://www.americansurveycenter.org/research/after-the-ballots-are-counted-conspiracies-political-violence-and-american-exceptionalism/

CHAPTER 3

1. Stephen Marche, "Swallowing the Red Pill: A Journey to the Heart of Modern Misogyny," *The Guardian* (April 14, 2016). https://www.theguardian.com/technology/2016/apr/14/the-red-pill-reddit-modern-misogyny-manosphere-men

2. Sabrina Tavernise, "'Trump Just Used Us and Our Fear': One Woman's Journey out of QAnon," *New York Times* (January 30, 2021). https://www.nytimes.com/2021/01/29/us/leaving-qanon-conspiracy.html

3. Clark McCauley and Sophia Moskalenko, Friction: How Conflict Radicalizes Them and Us. New York: Oxford University Press, 2016, ch. 7.

4. Richard Gunther, Erik C. Nisbet, and Paul Beck, "Trump May Owe His 2016 Victory to 'Fake News,'" *The Conversation* (February 15, 2018). https://theconversation.com/trump-may-owe-his-2016-victory-to-fake-news-new-study-suggests-91538

5. Christine R. Harris, "Embarrassment: A Form of Social Pain," *American Scientist, 94* (6)(2006): 524–533. http://charris.ucsd.edu/articles/Harris_AS2006.pdf

6. A. Small, L. Teagno, and K. Selz, "The Relationship of Sex Role to Physical and Psychological Health," *Journal of Youth and Adolescence, 9* (4) (1980): 305–314. https://pubmed.ncbi.nlm.nih.gov/24318152/

7. John Sabini, *Social Psychology,* 2nd ed. New York: Norton, 1995, ch. 12.

8. Bette L. Bottoms, "Individual Differences in Perceptions of Child Sexual Assault Victims" (1993). http://citeseerx.ist.psu.edu/viewdoc/download?doi=10.1.1.414.8837&rep=rep1&type=pdf

9. L. S. Maule and R. K. Goidel, "Adultery, Drugs, and Sex: An Experimental Investigation of Individual Reactions to Unethical Behavior by Public Officials," *Social Science Journal, 40* (1) (2003): 65–78.

10. Bette L. Bottoms, et al., "Explaining Gender Differences in Jurors' Reactions to Child Sexual Assault Cases," *Behavioral Sciences and the Law, 32* (6) (2014): 789–812.

11. Richard Gunther, Paul A. Beck, and Erik C. Nisbet, "Fake News *Did* Have a Significant Impact on the Vote in the 2016 Election" (2018). https://cpb-us-w2.wpmucdn.com/u.osu.edu/dist/d/12059/files/2015/03/Fake-News-Piece-for-The-Conversation-with-methodological-appendix-11d0ni9.pdf

12. "Bill Cosby: From 'America's Dad' to Disgraced Comic," *BBC News* (September 25, 2018). https://www.bbc.com/news/entertainment-arts-30194819

13. Chiqui Esteban and Manuel Roig-Franzi, "Bill Cosby's Accusers Now Number 58. Here's Who They Are," *Washington Post* (May 23, 2016). https://www.washingtonpost.com/graphics/lifestyle/bill-cosby-women-accusers/

14. Ben Kaye, "Harvey Weinstein Faces New Lawsuit for Sexually Assaulting Underaged Girl," *CoS* (December 29, 2019). https://consequenceofsound.net/2019/12/harvey-weinstein-sexual-assault-lawsuit-underage-girl/

15. David Klepper, "Checked by Reality, Some QAnon Supporters Seek a Way Out," *AP News* (January 29, 2021). https://apnews.com/article/qanon-conspiracy-theory-recovery-4ea47c2966a41b30ae678e5f471f6070

16. Moira Donegan, "QAnon Conspiracists Believe in a Vast Pedophile Ring," *The Guardian* (September 20, 2020). https://www.theguardian.com/commentisfree/2020/sep/20/qanon-conspiracy-child-abuse-truth-trump

17. Dave DeNatale, Phil Trexler, and Will Ujek, "Former Cleveland Schools Employee Charged for Alleged Role in Riot at U.S. Capitol," *WKYC Studios* (January 14, 2021). https://www.wkyc.com/article/news/crime/christine-priola-federal-charges-riot-united-states-capitol-cleveland-schools-therapist/95-d5138c4d-f3a3-476d-a834-07c28695a9bd#:~:text=According%20to%20documents%20filed%20in,unlawful%20activities%20on%20Capitol%20grounds

18. Katherine Schaeffer, "Among U.S. Couples, Women Do More Cooking and Grocery Shopping Than Men," *PEW Research*

Center (September 24, 2019). https://www.pewresearch.org/fact-tank/2019/09/24/among-u-s-couples-women-do-more-cooking-and-grocery-shopping-than-men/

19. Maria Cohut, "Women 'Spend More Time on Housework, Childcare Than Men,'" *Medical News Today* (October 10, 2017). https://www.medicalnewstoday.com/articles/319687

20. Family Caregiver Alliance, "Women and Caregiving: Facts and Figures" (n.d.). https://www.caregiver.org/women-and-caregiving-facts-and-figures/

21. Gabrielle Jackson, "The Female Problem: How Male Bias in Medical Trials Ruined Women's Health," *The Guardian* (November 13, 2019). https://www.theguardian.com/lifeandstyle/2019/nov/13/the-female-problem-male-bias-in-medical-trials

22. Hayley Hudson, "How Purdue Pharma and the Sackler Family Perpetrated the Opioid Crisis," *Addiction Center* (June 30, 2020). https://www.addictioncenter.com/community/how-purdue-pharma-sackler-family-perpetrated-opioid-crisis/

23. Julia Craven, "Meet the Latest Republican Nominee to Have Expressed Support for QAnon," *Slate* (September 16, 2020). https://slate.com/news-and-politics/2020/09/meet-lauren-witzke-the-qanon-friendly-senate-nominee-in-delaware.html

24. Eliza Relman, "A Republican Who Posed in a QAnon Shirt and Tweeted the Conspiracy Theory's Hashtag Just Won a Senate Primary in Delaware," *Business Insider* (September 16, 2020). https://www.businessinsider.in/politics/world/news/a-republican-who-posed-in-a-qanon-shirt-and-tweeted-the-conspiracy-theorys-hashtag-just-won-a-us-senate-primary-in-delaware/articleshow/78151205.cms

25. E. J. Dickson, "Why Are Fewer Women Than Men Planning to Get a Covid-19 Vaccine," *Rolling Stone* (December 4, 2020). https://www.rollingstone.com/culture/culture-news/women-men-covid-19-vaccine-1099020/

26. Ronan Farrow, "A Pennsylvania Mother's Path to Insurrection," *New Yorker* (February 1, 2021). https://www.newyorker.com/news/news-desk/a-pennsylvania-mothers-path-to-insurrection-capitol-riot

27. Ibid.

28. Ibid.

29. Wikipedia, "Catholic Church Sexual Abuse Cases" (n.d.). https://en.wikipedia.org/wiki/Catholic_Church_sexual_abuse_cases

30. Linda Stasi, "Secrets and Lies: Sexual Abuse in the World of Orthodox Judaism," *Harper's* (October 2019). https://harpers.org/archive/2019/10/secrets-and-lies-sexual-abuse-orthodox-jews/

31. Stephanie Russell-Kraft, "The Survivor Who Broke the Shambhala Sexual Assault Story," *Columbia Journalism Review* (May 7, 2019).

https://www.cjr.org/the_profile/shambhala-buddhist-project-sunshine.php

32. Lauren Gilger, "Female Bloggers Led the Push Against Sexual Abuse in Protestant Churches." *KJZZ* (June 24, 2019). https://kjzz.org/content/1023106/female-bloggers-led-push-against-sexual-abuse-protestant-churches

33. Jalal Baig, "The Perils of #MeToo as a Muslim," *The Atlantic* (December 21, 2017). https://www.theatlantic.com/international/archive/2017/12/tariq-ramadan-metoo/548642/

34. Nancy Dillon, "Ashtanga Yoga Guru Pattabhi Jois Accused of Sexual Assault in New Photo," *New York Daily News* (October 9, 2018). https://www.nydailynews.com/news/ny-news-ashtanga-founder-photos-allege-sex-assault-20181009-story.html

35. Adrian Horton, "'He Got Away with It': How the Founder of Bikram Yoga Built an Empire on Abuse," *The Guardian* (November 20, 2019). https://www.theguardian.com/film/2019/nov/20/bikram-choudhury-yoga-founder-abuse-netflix-documentary

36. Manuel Roig-Franzia, "Scandal Contorts Future of John Friend, Anusara Yoga," *Washington Post* (March 28, 2012). https://www.washingtonpost.com/lifestyle/style/scandal-contorts-future-of-john-friend-anusara-yoga/2012/03/28/gIQAeLVThS_story.html?hpid=z2

37. Kate Shellnutt, "1 in 10 Young Protestants Have Left a Church over Abuse," *Christianity Today* (May 21, 2019). https://www.christianitytoday.com/news/2019/may/lifeway-protestant-abuse-survey-young-christians-leave-chur.html

38. ABC News/ Washington Post, "Seven in 10 Catholics See a Church in Crisis" (May 2002). https://abcnews.go.com/images/PollingUnit/879a2%20Church%20in%20Crisis.pdf

39. S. J. Rossetti, "The Impact of Child Sexual Abuse on Attitudes Toward God and the Catholic Church," *Child Abuse & Neglect, 19* (12), (1995): 1469–1481. https://www.sciencedirect.com/science/article/abs/pii/014521349500100I

40. Ibid.

41. Morgan Lee, "Why Someone You Love Might Join QAnon," *Christianity Today* (September 9, 2020). https://www.christianitytoday.com/ct/2020/september-web-only/QAnon-evangelicals-global-conspiracy-theory.html; Katelyn Beaty, "QAnon: The Alternative Religion That's Coming to Your Church," *Religion News Service* (August 17, 2020). https://religionnews.com/2020/08/17/QAnon-the-alternative-religion-thats-coming-to-your-church/

42. Reuters Staff, "Fact Check: Article Falsely Reports Arrest of Pope Francis" (January 12, 2021). https://www.reuters.com/article/

uk-factcheck-pope-francis-not-arrested/fact-check-article-falsely-reports-arrest-of-pope-francis-idUSKBN29H2KO

43. Reuters Staff, "Fact Check: Misleading Claims About Tom Hanks, Ellen DeGeneres, and Oprah Winfrey" (August 5, 2020). https://www.reuters.com/article/uk-factcheck-tom-hanks-ellen-oprah/fact-check-misleading-claims-about-tom-hanks-ellen-degeneres-and-oprah-winfrey-idUSKCN2511WY

44. Molly Ball, "Donald Trump Didn't Really Win 52% of White Women in 2016," *Time* (October 18, 2018). https://time.com/5422644/trump-white-women-2016/

45. Kaylen Ralph, "White Women's Support for Trump Remains High in 2020 Election," *Teen Vogue* (November 10, 2020). https://www.teenvogue.com/story/white-women-support-trump

46. Aliya Hamid Rao, "Even Breadwinning Wives Don't Get Equality at Home," *The Atlantic* (May 12, 2019). https://www.theatlantic.com/family/archive/2019/05/breadwinning-wives-gender-inequality/589237/

47. Sonam Sheth, "7 Charts That Show the Glaring Gap Between Men's and Women's Salaries in the US," *Business Insider* (March 31, 2020). https://markets.businessinsider.com/news/stocks/gender-wage-pay-gap-charts-2017-3-1029049751

48. Linda Gorman, "New Evidence on Gender Differences in Promotions and Pay," *National Bureau of Economic Research* (February 2007). https://www.nber.org/digest/feb07/new-evidence-gender-differences-promotions-and-pay

49. Taylor D. Roebig, "How Gender Discrimination Affects Women in the Workplace" (August 4, 2020). https://florinroebig.com/workplace-discrimination-women/

50. Axios, "Trump Praises QAnon Supporters: 'I Understand They Like Me Very Much'" (August 20, 2020). https://www.axios.com/trump-praises-qanon-supporters-i-understand-they-like-me-very-much-42146fb3-bd69-4943-8e80-2f0bcf4b0b17.htm

51. Mariel Padilla, "The Spread of Conspiracies and Disinformation by Women on Social Media," 19th News (October 19, 2020). https://19thnews.org/2020/10/19th-explains-women-disinformation-election-2020/

52. Donie O'Sullivan, "She Was Stunned by Biden's Inauguration. How This South Carolina Mom Escaped QAnon," *Madison.com* (March 12, 2021). https://madison.com/lifestyles/technology/she-was-stunned-by-bidens-inauguration-how-this-south-carolina-mom-escaped-QAnon/article_fafa0b24-ae41-55e2–8192-dbf5c0aa8dc9.html

53. Ibid.

54. Sky Palma, "'Hateful Moron': Trump Supporter's Business Faces the Internet's Wrath After Her Anti-Gay Tirade Goes Viral," *Raw Story* (December 1, 2020). https://www.rawstory.com/2020/12/hateful-moron-trump-supporters-business-faces-the-internets-wrath-after-her-anti-gay-tirade-goes-viral/

55. Sky Palma, "Beverly Hills Salon Owner Charged with 7 Counts of 'Aiding and Abetting' Capitol Riot," *Dead State* (February 2, 2021). https://deadstate.org/beverly-hills-salon-owner-charged-with-7-counts-of-aiding-and-abetting-capitol-riot/

56. Karen M. Douglas, Robbie M. Sutton, and Aleksandra Cichocka, "The Psychology of Conspiracy Theories," *Current Directions in Psychological Science*, *26* (6) (2017): 538–542. https://journals.sagepub.com/doi/pdf/10.1177/0963721417718261

57. Ana Aleixo, et al., "A Review of Empirical Studies Investigating Narrative, Emotion and Meaning-Making Modes and Client Process Markers in Psychotherapy," *Journal of Contemporary Psychotherapy*, *51* (2021): 31–40. https://link.springer.com/article/10.1007/s10879-020-09472-6

58. Gilad Hirschberger, "Collective Trauma and the Social Construction of Meaning," *Frontiers in Psychology*, *9* (2018): 1441. https://doi.org/10.3389/fpsyg.2018.01441

59. Kate Feldman, "Oklahoma Man Tied to QAnon's #SaveOurChildren Accused of Murdering Girlfriend's Baby," *New York Daily News* (September 29, 2020). https://www.nydailynews.com/news/crime/ny-oklahoma-QAnon-save-our-children-murder-20200929-gi42kkngkbfndfwu56ubhte2ka-story.html

60. S. Gramling, "Tweets Suggest Mom Isn't Giving up After She's Arrested for Reportedly Teaming up with a Far-Right Conspiracy Group to Kidnap Her Own Son," *Mamas Uncut* (February 5, 2020). https://mamasuncut.com/mom-far-right-conspiracy-group-kidnap-own-son/step1/

61. Tavernise, "'Trump Just Used Us and Our Fear.'"

62. Celeste Kidd and Benjamin Y. Hayden, "The Psychology and Neuroscience of Curiosity," *Neuron*, *88* (3) (2015): 449–460. https://www.ncbi.nlm.nih.gov/pmc/articles/PMC4635443/

63. S. M. A. Moin, "Storytelling for Minds: Neuroscience's Approaches to Branding," in *Brand Storytelling in the Digital Age* (pp. 41–51). London: Palgrave Macmillan, Cham, 2020.

64. Statista, "Population Density of the United States from 1790 to 2017 in Residents per Square Mile of Land Area" (March 11, 2021). https://www.statista.com/statistics/183475/united-states-population-density/

65. World Atlas, "European Countries by Population Density"

(2021). https://www.worldatlas.com/articles/european-countries-by-population-density.html.

66. Belden Russonello & Stewart LLC, "The 2011 Community Preference Survey: What Americans Are Looking for When Deciding Where to Live," *Opinion Research Strategic Communication* (March 2011). https://www.builderonline.com/money/economics/80-percent-of-americans-prefer-single-family-homeownership_o

67. Wendell Cox, "America Is More Small Town Than We Think," *New Geography*, *9* (2008). https://www.newgeography.com/content/00242-america-more-small-town-we-think

68. Chris Isidore and Tami Luhby, "Turns Out Americans Work Really Hard . . . but Some Want to Work Harder," *CNN Money* (July 9, 2015). https://money.cnn.com/2015/07/09/news/economy/americans-work-bush/index.html

69. Alexa Lardieri, "Study: Many Americans Report Feeling Lonely, Younger Generations More So," *U.S. News & World Report* (May 1, 2018). https://www.usnews.com/news/health-care-news/articles/2018-05-01/study-many-americans-report-feeling-lonely-younger-generations-more-so

70. Euronews, "Which Is Europe's Loneliest Country?" (June 29, 2017). https://www.euronews.com/2017/06/29/what-is-europes-loneliest-country

71. Srikant Devaraj and Pankaj Patel, "Change in Psychological Distress in Response to Changes in Residential Mobility During COVID-19 Pandemic: Evidence from the US," *SSRN* (May 20, 2020). https://papers.ssrn.com/sol3/papers.cfm?abstract_id=3603746

72. Damaris Graeupner and Alin Coman, "The Dark Side of Meaning-Making: How Social Exclusion Leads to Superstitious Thinking," *Journal of Experimental Social Psychology*, *69* (2017): 218–222. https://www.princeton.edu/~acoman/Publications_files/The%20Dark%20Side%20of%20Meaning%20Making-Graeupner%20&%20Coman.pdf

73. Melissa G. Hunt, Rachel Marx, Courtney Lipson, and Jordyn Young, "No More FOMO: Limiting Social Media Decreases Loneliness and Depression," *Journal of Social and Clinical Psychology, 37* (10) (December 2018): 751–768.

74. Yocov Rofé, "Stress and Affiliation: A Utility Theory," *Psychological Review*, *91* (2) (1984): 235. https://psycnet.apa.org/record/1984-17740-001

75. Moonshot CVE. @MoonshotCVE (February 21, 2021). https://twitter.com/moonshotcve/status/1357043632705011717?s=21. Worryingly, we found high volumes of conversation about suicide and self-harm among QAnon supporters on 8kun around Election Day.

76. Ronan Farrow, "An Air Force Combat Veteran Breached the

Senate," *New Yorker* (January 8, 2021). Retrieved https://www.newyorker.com/news/news-desk/an-air-force-combat-veteran-breached-the-senate

77. Patrizia Rizzo, "DYNAMIC DUO: Who Are Eric Munchel and Lisa Eisenhart," *The Sun* (January 11, 2021). https://www.the-sun.com/news/2118042/eric-munchel-lisa-eisenhart-capitol-riot-trump/

78. Robert A. Pape and Keven Ruby, "The Capitol Rioters Aren't Like Other Extremists," *The Atlantic* (February 2, 2021). https://www.theatlantic.com/ideas/archive/2021/02/the-capitol-rioters-arent-like-other-extremists/617895/

79. Ibid.

80. Sophia Moskalenko and Clark McCauley, *Radicalization to Terrorism: What Everyone Needs to Know*. New York: Oxford University Press, 2020.

81. Morty Bernstein and Faye Crosby, "An Empirical Examination of Relative Deprivation Theory," *Journal of Experimental Social Psychology, 16* (5) (1980): 442–456. https://www.sciencedirect.com/science/article/abs/pii/0022103180900505

82. Tatjana Schnell, "The Sources of Meaning and Meaning in Life Questionnaire (SoMe): Relations to Demographics and Well-Being," *Journal of Positive Psychology, 4* (6) (2009): 483–499. https://www.researchgate.net/publication/301231622_Sources_of_Meaning_and_Meaning_in_Life_Questionnaire_SoMe_English_version

83. Huanhuan Zhao, et al., "Why Are People High in Dispositional Awe Happier? The Roles of Meaning in Life and Materialism," *Frontiers in Psychology, 10* (May 2019): 1208. https://www.frontiersin.org/articles/10.3389/fpsyg.2019.01208/full#:~:text=Those%20who%20perceive%20their%20lives,of%20life%20easier%20for%20them.

84. Tavernise, "'Trump Just Used Us and Our Fear.'"

85. Joseph Menn, Elizabeth Culliford, Katie Paul, and Carrie Monahan, "'No Plan, No Q, Nothing': QAnon Followers Reel as Biden Inaugurated," *Reuters* (January 20, 2021). https://www.reuters.com/article/us-usa-biden-QAnon/no-plan-no-q-nothing-QAnon-followers-reel-as-biden-inaugurated-idUSKBN29P2VO

86. Ben Collins and Brandy Zadrozny, "Some QAnon Followers Lose Hope After Inauguration," *NBC News* (January 20, 2021). https://www.nbcnews.com/tech/internet/some-QAnon-followers-struggle-inauguration-day-n1255002

CHAPTER 4

1. Drew Harwell, "QAnon Believers Seek to Adapt Their Extremist Ideology for a New Era: 'Things Have Just Started,'" *Washington*

Post (January 21, 2021). https://www.washingtonpost.com/technology/2021/01/21/qanon-faithful-biden-trump/

2. Julia Carrie Wong, "QAnon's 'Great Awakening' Failed to Materialize. What's Next Could Be Worse," *The Guardian* (January 20, 2021). https://www.theguardian.com/us-news/2021/jan/20/qanon-biden-inauguration-trump-antisemitism-white-nationalism

3. Ibid.

4. Kevin Roose, "'I'm the Meme Queen': A QAnon Digital Soldier Marches On," *Irish Times* (January 18, 2021). https://www.irishtimes.com/news/world/us/i-m-the-meme-queen-a-qanon-digital-soldier-marches-on-1.4461146

5. Elliot Aronson, "Back to the Future: Retrospective Review of Leon Festinger's—A Theory of Cognitive Dissonance," *American Journal of Psychology, 110* (1) (1997): 127. https://www.jstor.org/stable/1423706?seq=1

6. Michael Kunzelman, Amanda Seitz, and David Klepper, "Inauguration Sows Doubt Among QAnon Conspiracy Theorists," *Associated Press* (January 20, 2021). https://www.abc27.com/news/us-world/national/inauguration-sows-doubt-among-qanon-conspiracy-theorists/

7. Sean Everton, "When Prophecies Fail: The Future of QAnon," *God, Politics, and Baseball* (January 22, 2021). http://godpoliticsbaseball.blogspot.com/2021/01/when-prophecies-fail-future-of-qanon.html

8. Jack Brewster, "QAnon Traffic Declined After Facebook Cracked Down," *Forbes* (September 10, 2020). https://www.forbes.com/sites/jackbrewster/2020/09/10/qanon-traffic-declined-after-facebook-cracked-down/?sh=7977bc384fb0

9. James Hale, "Social Media Platforms See 73% Drop in Election Misinformation After Trump's Ban (Study)," *Tubefilter.com* (January 18, 2021). https://www.tubefilter.com/2021/01/18/social-media-misinformation-twitter-trump-ban/

10. Kunzelman, Seitz, and Klepper, "Inauguration Sows Doubt Among QAnon Conspiracy Theorists."

11. Ali Breland, "On Telegram, White Nationalists Are Trying to Radicalize Those Fleeing Parler," *Mother Jones* (January 11, 2021). https://www.motherjones.com/politics/2021/01/on-telegram-white-nationalists-are-trying-to-radicalize-those-fleeing-parler/

12. Ibid.

13. Harwell, "QAnon Believers Seek to Adapt Their Extremist Ideology for a New Era."

14. Todd C. Frankel, "A Majority of the People Arrested for Capitol Riot Had a History of Financial Trouble," *Washington Post* (February 10, 2021). https://www.washingtonpost.com/business/2021/02/10/capitol-insurrectionists-jenna-ryan-financial-problems/

15. Tina Nguyen and Mark Scott, "Trump Leaves QAnon and the Online MAGA World Crushed and Confused," *Politico* (January 20, 2021). https://www.politico.com/news/2021/01/20/trump-qanon-inauguration-day-460926

16. Bronte Lord and Richa Naik, "He Went Down the QAnon Rabbit Hole for Almost Two Years. Here's How He Got Out.," *CNN* (October 18, 2020). https://www.cnn.com/2020/10/16/tech/qa-non-believer-how-he-got-out/index.html

17. Travis M. Andrews, "She Fell into QAnon and Went Viral for Destroying a Target Mask Display. Now She's Rebuilding Her Life," *Washington Post* (November 11, 2020). https://www.washingtonpost.com/technology/2020/11/11/masks-QAnon-target-melissa-rein-lively/

18. NPR/Ipsos Poll, "More Than 1 in 3 Americans Believe a 'Deep State' Is Working to Undermine Trump" (December 30, 2020). https://www.ipsos.com/en-us/news-polls/npr-misinformation-123020

19. Ibid.

20. Jesselyn Cook, "'I Miss My Mom': Children of QAnon Believers Are Desperately Trying to Deradicalize Their Own Parents," *HuffPost.com* (February 11, 2021). https://www.huffpost.com/entry/children-of-qanon-believers_n_601078e9c5b6c5586aa49077

21. Jane Lytvynenko, "Friends and Family Members of QAnon Believers Are Going Through a 'Surreal Goddamn Nightmare,'" *BuzzFeed News* (September 18, 2020). https://www.buzzfeednews.com/article/janelytvynenko/qanon-families-friends

22. Cecilia S. Watt, "The QAnon Orphans: People Who Have Lost Loved Ones to Conspiracy Theories," *The Guardian* (September 23, 2020). https://www.theguardian.com/us-news/2020/sep/23/qanon-conspiracy-theories-loved-ones

23. Joseph Menn, "Russian-Backed Organizations Amplifying QAnon Conspiracy Theories, Researchers Say," *Reuters* (August 24, 2020). Aug 24. https://www.reuters.com/article/us-usa-election-qanon-russia/russian-backed-organizations-amplifying-qanon-conspiracy-theories-researchers-say-idUSKBN25K13T

24. Ibid.

25. Tony Romm and Kurt Wagner, "Facebook Says 126 Million People in the U.S. May Have Seen Posts Produced by Russian-Government-Backed Agents," *Vox* (October 30, 2017). https://www.vox.com/2017/10/30/16571598/read-full-testimony-facebook-twitter-google-congress-russia-election-fake-news

26. Craig Timberg and Tony Romm, "New Report on Russian Disinformation, Prepared for the Senate, Shows the Operation's Scale and Sweep," *Washington Post* (December 17, 2018). https://www.washing-

tonpost.com/technology/2018/12/16/new-report-russian-disinformation-prepared-senate-shows-operations-scale-sweep/

27. NBC News, "NBC News Signal Presents Factory of Lies: Democracy Under Attack," Video (November 5, 2018). https://www.nbcnews.com/video/nbc-news-signal-presents-factory-of-lies-democracy-under-attack-1362496579619?v=raila&.%5b%5bAU

28. Kevin Poulsen, "Americans Are Easy Marks for Russian Trolls, According to New Data," *Daily Beast* (October 31, 2018). https://www.thedailybeast.com/americans-are-easy-marks-for-russian-trolls-new-data-prove

29. Eric W. Dolan, "People Who Believe COVID-19 Conspiracy Theories Tend to Struggle with Scientific Reasoning, Study Finds," *PsyPost* (February 25, 2021). https://www.psypost.org/2021/02/people-who-believe-covid-19-conspiracy-theories-tend-to-struggle-with-scientific-reasoning-study-finds-59801

30. Natalie Grover, "People with Extremist Views Less Able to Do Complex Mental Tasks, Research Suggests," *The Guardian* (February 21, 2021). https://www.theguardian.com/science/2021/feb/22/people-with-extremist-views-less-able-to-do-complex-mental-tasks-research-suggests

31. Eliza Macintosh and Edward Kiernan, "Finland Is Winning the War on Fake News. What It's Learned May Be Crucial to Western Democracy," *CNN.com* (2019). https://edition.cnn.com/interactive/2019/05/europe/finland-fake-news-intl/

32. Julian McDougall, Marketa Zezulkova, M., Barry van Driel, and Dalibor Sternadel, "Teaching Media Literacy in Europe: Evidence of Effective School Practices in Primary and Secondary Education," NESET Analytic Report, (2018). https://nesetweb.eu/en/resources/library/teaching-media-literacy-in-europe-evidence-of-effective-school-practices-in-primary-and-secondary-education/

33. Scott O. Lilienfeld and Hal Arkowitz, "Why "Just Say No" Doesn't Work," *Scientific American* (January 1, 2014). https://www.scientificamerican.com/article/why-just-say-no-doesnt-work/

34. Kathrin F. Stanger-Hall and David W. & Hall, "Abstinence-Only Education and Teen Pregnancy Rates: Why We Need Comprehensive Sex Education in the US," *PloS One*, *6* (10) (2011): e24658. https://www.ncbi.nlm.nih.gov/pmc/articles/PMC3194801/

35. W. J. McGuire and D. Papageorgis, "The Relative Efficacy of Various Types of Prior Belief-Defense in Producing Immunity Against Persuasion," *Journal of Abnormal and Social Psychology*, *62* (2) (1961): 327. https://psycnet.apa.org/doiLanding?doi=10.1037%2Fh0042026

36. Christopher J. Bryan, David S. Yeager, and Cintia P. Hinojosa, "A Values-Alignment Intervention Protects Adolescents from the Ef-

fects of Food Marketing," *Nature Human Behaviour*, *3* (6) (2019): 596–603. https://www.nature.com/articles/s41562-019-0586-6

37. Kurt Braddock, "Vaccinating Against Hate: Using Attitudinal Inoculation to Confer Resistance to Persuasion by Extremist Propaganda," *Terrorism and Political Violence* (2019): 1–23. https://www.tandfonline.com/doi/abs/10.1080/09546553.2019.1693370?journalCode=ftpv20

38. Craig Timberg and Elizabeth Dwoskin, "Misinformation Dropped Dramatically the Week After Twitter Banned Trump," *Washington Post* (January 16, 2021). https://www.seattletimes.com/nation-world/misinformation-dropped-dramatically-the-week-after-twitter-banned-trump/

39. Issie Lapowsky, "How Cambridge Analytica Sparked the Great Privacy Awakening," *Wired* (March 17, 2018). https://www.wired.com/story/cambridge-analytica-facebook-privacy-awakening/

40. Neil MacFarquhar, "Inside the Russian Troll Factory: Zombies and a Breakneck Pace," *New York Times* (February 18, 2018). https://www.nytimes.com/2018/02/18/world/europe/russia-troll-factory.html

41. Verlin B. Hinsz and James H. Davis, "Persuasive Arguments Theory, Group Polarization, and Choice Shifts," *Personality and Social Psychology Bulletin*, *10* (2) (1984): 260–268. https://journals.sagepub.com/doi/10.1177/0146167284102012.

42. Clark McCauley and Sophia Moskalenko, *Friction: How Conflict Radicalizes Them and Us*. New York: Oxford University Press, 2016.

43. Irving L. Janis, "Groupthink," *IEEE Engineering Management Review*, *36* (1) (2008): 36. https://ieeexplore.ieee.org/document/4490137

44. Douglas Guilbeault, Andrea Baronchelli, and Damon Centola, "Experimental Evidence for Scale-Induced Category Convergence Across Populations," *Nature Communications*, *12* (1) (2021): 1–7. https://www.nature.com/articles/s41467-020-20037-y

45. Nirmita Panchal, Rabah Kamal, Cynthia Cox, and Rachel Garfield, "The Implications of COVID-19 for Mental Health and Substance Use," *KFF* (February 10, 2021). https://www.kff.org/coronavirus-covid-19/issue-brief/the-implications-of-covid-19-for-mental-health-and-substance-use/

46. Eric Levitz, "QAnon Is Madness. But Believing in It Can Be Rational," *New York Magazine* (September 23, 2020). https://nymag.com/intelligencer/2020/09/why-qanon-pandemic-popular-trump.html.

47. Michael Jensen and Sheehan Kane, "QAnon Offenders in the United States," *NC-START* (2021). https://www.start.umd.edu/sites/

default/files/publications/local_attachments/START_PIRUS_QAnon_Mar2021.pdf

48. Johns Hopkins Medicine, "Mental Health Disorder Statistics" (2020). https://www.hopkinsmedicine.org/health/wellness-and-prevention/mental-health-disorder-statistics

49. Aaron T. Beck, "Cognitive Therapy: Past, Present, and Future," *Journal of Consulting and Clinical Psychology, 61* (2) (1993): 194. https://psycnet.apa.org/record/1993-34412-001

50. Lord and Naik, "He Went Down the QAnon Rabbit Hole for Almost Two Years."

51. Steven Hassan, "Trump's QAnon Followers Are a Dangerous Cult. How to Save Someone Who's Been Brainwashed," *NBC News* (September 11, 2020). https://www.nbcnews.com/think/opinion/trump-s-qanon-followers-are-dangerous-cult-how-save-someone-ncna1239828

52. www.freedomofmind.com

53. Sophia Moskalenko and Clark McCauley, *The Marvel of Martyrdom: The Power of Self-Sacrifice in a Selfish World*. New York: Oxford University Press, 2018.

54. McCauley and Moskalenko, *Friction*.

55. John Kabat-Zinn, *Full Catastrophe Living: Using the Wisdom of Your Body and Mind to Face Stress, Pain, and Illness*. New York: Bantam Dell, 2013.

CHAPTER 5

1. David Lawrence and Gregory Davis, "QAnon in the UK: The Growth of a Movement," *Hope Not Hate* (October 8, 2020). https://www.hopenothate.org.uk/wp-content/uploads/2020/10/qanon-report-2020-10-FINAL.pdf

2. Anne Helen Petersen, "The Real Housewives of QAnon: How QAnon Used #SaveTheChildren to Lure Suburban Moms," *Elle* (October 29, 2020). https://www.elle.com/culture/a34485099/qanon-conspiracy-suburban-women/

3. Aoife Gallagher, Jacob Davey, and Mackenzie Hart, "The Genesis of a Conspiracy Theory: Key Trends in QAnon Activity Since 2017," *ISD* (July 2020). https://www.isdglobal.org/isd-publications/the-genesis-of-a-conspiracy-theory/

4. Ibid.

5. Daniel A. Cox, "After the Ballots Are Counted: Conspiracies, Political Violence, and American Exceptionalism," Survey Center on American Life (February 11, 2021). https://www.americansurveycenter.org/research/after-the-ballots-are-counted-conspiracies-political-violence-and-american-exceptionalism/

6. Jack Jenkins, "Survey: More Than a Quarter of White Evangelicals Believe Core QAnon Conspiracy Theory," *Religion News Servies* (February 11, 2021). https://www.sltrib.com/religion/global/2021/02/11/survey-more-than-quarter/

7. Adrienne LaFrance, "The Prophecies of Q: American Conspiracy Theories Are Entering a Dangerous New Phase," *The Atlantic* (May 14, 2020). https://medium.com/the-atlantic/the-prophecies-of-q-10c59d85f88b

8. Lawrence and Davis, "QAnon in the UK."

9. "How QAnon Conspiracy Is Spreading in Christian Communities Across the U.S," *NPR—All Things Considered* (August 21, 2020). https://www.npr.org/2020/08/21/904798097/how-qanon-conspiracy-is-spreading-in-christian-communities-across-the-u-s

10. Katelyn Beaty, "QAnon: The Alternative Religion That's Coming to Your Church," Religion News Service (August 17, 2020). https://religionnews.com/2020/08/17/QAnon-the-alternative-religion-thats-coming-to-your-church/

11. Lesley Stahl, "QAnon's Corrosive Impact on the U.S.," *CBS—60 Minutes* (February 21, 2021). https://www.cbsnews.com/news/qanon-conspiracy-united-states-60-minutes-2021-02-21/

12. Michiko Kakutani, "'The Death of Expertise' Explores How Ignorance Became a Virtue," *New York Times* (March 21, 2017). https://www.nytimes.com/2017/03/21/books/the-death-of-expertise-explores-how-ignorance-became-a-virtue.html

13. Marc-André Argentino, "The Church of QAnon: Will Conspiracy Theories Form the Basis of a New Religious Movement?" *The Conversation* (May 18, 2020). https://theconversation.com/the-church-of-qanon-will-conspiracy-theories-form-the-basis-of-a-new-religious-movement-137859

14. "How QAnon Conspiracy Is Spreading."

15. "'Unholy' Examines the Alliance Between White Evangelicals and Trump ," *NPR—Fresh Air* (July 8, 2020). https://www.npr.org/2020/07/08/888906337/unholy-examines-the-alliance-between-white-evangelicals-and-trump

16. Sarah Posner, *Unholy: Why White Evangelicals Worship at the Altar of Donald Trump.* New York: Random House, 2020.

17. Kevin Roose, "How the Biden Administration Can Help Solve Our Reality Crisis," *New York Times* (February 2, 2021). https://www.nytimes.com/2021/02/02/technology/biden-reality-crisis-misinformation.html

18. Daniel A. Cox, "Rise of Conspiracies Reveals an Evangelical Divide in the GOP," Survey Center on American Life (February 12,

2021). https://www.americansurveycenter.org/rise-of-conspiracies-reveal-an-evangelical-divide-in-the-gop/

19. Richard Ruelas, "QAnon Interpreter, Praying Medic, Off Facebook After Q Crackdown," *Arizona Central* (October 8, 2020). https://www.azcentral.com/story/news/local/arizona-investigations/2020/10/08/qanon-interpreter-praying-medic-off-facebook-after-q-crackdown/5917183002/

20. Jan Jaben-Eilon, "QAnon Attracts Jewish Believers Despite Anti-Semitic Leanings," *Atlanta Jewish Times* (February 3, 2021). https://atlantajewishtimes.timesofisrael.com/qanon-attracts-jewish-believers-despite-anti-semitic-leanings/

21. In July 2020, Twitter removed 7,000 QAnon accounts and "limited" 150,000 others, reducing its reach and limiting its ability to gain new followers. Facebook and Instagram in August 2020 removed 900 QAnon groups and pages and limited over 10,000 accounts. QAnon slogans could no longer trend.

22. Craig Timberg, "Twitter Banished the Worst QAnon Accounts. But More Than 93,000 Remain on the Site, Research Shows," *Washington Post* (October 3, 2020). https://www.washingtonpost.com/technology/2020/10/03/twitter-banished-worst-qanon-accounts-more-than-93000-remain-site-research-shows/

23. Lawrence and Davis, "QAnon in the UK."

24. Mack Lamoureaux, "QAnon Has Gone Global," *Vice* (July 29, 2020). https://www.vice.com/en/article/pkym3k/qanon-conspiracy-has-gone-global

25. Ibid.

26. Marc-André Argentino, "Twitter / @_MAArgentino: Lets Talk About QAnon Worldwide . . . " (August 8, 2020).

27. Max Zimmerman, "QAnon's Rise in Japan Shows Conspiracy Theory's Global Spread," *Bloomberg* (November 29, 2020). https://www.bloomberg.com/news/articles/2020-11-29/qanon-s-rise-in-japan-shows-conspiracy-theory-s-global-spread

28. Ibid.; Chine Labbe, et al., "QAnon's Deep State Conspiracies Spread to Europe," *News Guard* (2021). https://www.newsguardtech.com/special-report-qanon/

29. Japan has long been a breeding ground for conspiratorial thought. In 1877, when the authorities tried to vaccinate the general population for an outbreak of cholera, rumors circulated that the government was stealing people's livers to sell to foreigners. After the Great Kanto earthquake of 1923, Koreans were blamed for the disaster, and thousands of Koreans were lynched. In 1995, an apocalyptic religious sect called Aum Shinrikyo instigated a nerve gas attack on the Tokyo subway. In the official magazine of the sect, the group's leader declared

"war on the shadow world government" as "his supporters killed 14 people and wounded 6,000 others." Matt Allen, "Why QAnon Flopped in Japan," *New York Times* (March 26, 2021). https://www.nytimes.com/2021/03/26/opinion/qanon-japan-janon.html

30. Zimmerman, "QAnon's Rise in Japan."

31. Allen, "Why QAnon Flopped in Japan."

32. Katrin Bennhold, "QAnon Is Thriving in Germany. The Extreme Right Is Delighted," *New York Times* (November 3, 2020). https://www.nytimes.com/2020/10/11/world/europe/qanon-is-thriving-in-germany-the-extreme-right-is-delighted.html

33. Lawrence and Davis, "QAnon in the UK," 19.

34. Bennhold, "QAnon Is Thriving in Germany"

35. Gregory Stanton, "QAnon Is a Nazi Cult, Rebranded," Just Security (November 9, 2020). https://www.justsecurity.org/72339/qanon-is-a-nazi-cult-rebranded/

36. Network Contagion, "The QAnon Conspiracy: Destroying Families, Dividing Communities, Undermining Democracy" (n.d). https://networkcontagion.us/wp-content/uploads/NCRI-%E2%80%93-The-QAnon-Conspiracy-FINAL.pdf

37. Stanton, "QAnon is a Nazi Cult, Rebranded.".

38. Lydia Morrish, "How QAnon Content Endures on Social Media Through Visuals and Code Words," *First Draft News* (December 3, 2020). https://firstdraftnews.org/latest/how-qanon-content-endures-on-social-media-through-visuals-and-code-words/

39. Emily Rauhala and Loveday Morris, "In the United States, QAnon Is Struggling. The Conspiracy Theory Is Thriving Abroad," *Washington Post* (November 13, 2020). https://www.washingtonpost.com/world/qanon-conspiracy-global-reach/2020/11/12/ca312138-13a5-11eb-a258-614acf2b906d_story.html

40. Anna Merlan, "The Conspiracy Singularity Has Arrived," *Vice News* (July 17, 2020). https://www.vice.com/en/article/v7gz53/the-conspiracy-singularity-has-arrived

41. Rauhala and Morris, "In the United States, QAnon Is Struggling."

42. Petersen, "The Real Housewives of QAnon."

43. Mark Scott, "QAnon Goes European," *Politico* (November 23, 2020). https://www.politico.eu/article/qanon-europe-coronavirus-protests/

44. Chine Labbe, et al., "QAnon's Deep State Conspiracies Spread to Europe," *News Guard* (2021). https://www.newsguardtech.com/special-report-qanon/

45. Scott, "QAnon Goes European."

46. Matthew Remski, "When QAnon Came to Canada," *The Wal-*

rus (December 3, 2020). https://thewalrus.ca/when-qanon-came-to-canada/

47. Ibid.

48. "Corey Hurren, Alleged Rideau Hall Intruder, Pleads Guilty to 8 Charges," *Global News* (February 5, 2021). https://globalnews.ca/news/7622570/corey-hurren-rideau-hall-plea/

49. Petersen, "The Real Housewives of QAnon."

50. "Ivanka Trump on Human Trafficking," U.S. Department of State. https://statedept.brightcovegallery.com/detail/video/5849934794001/ivanka-trump-on-human-trafficking

51. Author interview with State Department ambassador, October 9, 2020.

52. Darlene Superville, "Trump Gives $35 Million to Aid Human Trafficking Victims," *AP News* (August 4, 2020). https://apnews.com/article/ivanka-trump-politics-william-barr-human-trafficking-virus-outbreak-89347d1b618ab522ec6d13aa114f4e92

53. Rauhala and Morris, "In the United States, QAnon Is Struggling."

54. Etienne Jacob, "QAnon, Cette Mouvance Pro-Trump Conspirationniste Qui Touche La France," *Le Figaro* (February 14, 2021). https://www.lefigaro.fr/actualite-france/qanon-cette-galaxie-venue-d-amerique-qui-touche-la-france-20210214

55. The original website for French QAnon is no longer available. It was https://qanon-fr.com/. Reference to the material can be found on https://www.newsguardtech.com/special-report-qanon/

56. DimancheEnPolitique, "Twitter / @DimPolitique: @MarlenSchiappa s'inquiète de l'emergence en France . . . " (January 10, 2021).

57. Tom Wheeldon, "'Stakes Are High' as QAnon Conspiracy Phenomenon Emerges in France," *France 24* (February 20, 2021). https://www.france24.com/en/france/20210220-stakes-are-high-as-qanon-conspiracy-phenomenon-emerges-in-france

58. Steven Hassan, "Episode 69: Exiting the Cult Feat," *QAnon Anonymous* (2020). https://soundcloud.com/qanonanonymous/episode-69-exiting-the-cult-feat-steven-hassan

59. Scott, "QAnon Goes European."

60. Melanie Smith, "Interpreting Social Qs: Implications of the Evolution of QAnon," *Graphika* (August 9, 2020). https://graphika.com/reports/interpreting-social-qs-implications-of-the-evolution-of-qanon/

61. Ibid., 10.

62. Franklin Foer, "Putin Is Well on His Way to Stealing the Next Election: RIP Democracy," *The Atlantic* (May 11, 2020). https://

www.theatlantic.com/magazine/archive/2020/06/putin-american-democracy/610570/

63. Luke Mogelson, "Among the Insurrectionists at the Capitol," *New Yorker* (January 15, 2021). https://www.newyorker.com/magazine/2021/01/25/among-the-insurrectionists

64. Amar Diwakar, "Why the Far-Right Conspiracy Theory QAnon Is Going Global," *Frontier Post* (August 27, 2020). https://thefrontierpost.com/why-the-far-right-conspiracy-theory-qanon-is-going-global/

65. Joseph Menn, "QAnon Received Earlier Boost from Russian Accounts on Twitter, Archives Show," *Reuters* (November 2, 2020). https://www.reuters.com/article/us-usa-election-qanon-cyber/qanon-received-earlier-boost-from-russian-accounts-on-twitter-archives-show-idUSKBN27I18I

66. Gallagher et al., "The Genesis of a Conspiracy Theory."

67. Felix Light, "QAnon Gains Traction in Russia," *Moscow Times* (November 30, 2020). https://www.themoscowtimes.com/2020/11/30/qanon-gains-traction-in-russia-a72180

68. Ibid.

69. Scott Neuman, "Referendum in Russia Passes, Allowing Putin to Remain President Until 2036," *NPR* (July 1, 2020). https://www.npr.org/2020/07/01/886440694/referendum-in-russia-passes-allowing-putin-to-remain-president-until-2036

70. "Putin's Stasi Spy ID Pass Found in Germany," *BBC News* (December 11, 2018). https://www.bbc.com/news/world-europe-46525543

71. Glenn Curtis, "An Overview of Psychological Operations (PSYOP)," Defense Technical Iinformation Center (1989). https://apps.dtic.mil/sti/citations/ADA302389

72. Federal Security Service of the Russian Federation (FSB), Федеральная служба безопасности Российской Федерации

73. Curtis, "An Overview of Psychological Operations."

74. Gabriel Gatehouse, "Marine Le Pen: Who's Funding France's Far Right?" *BBC News* (April 3, 2017). https://www.bbc.com/news/world-europe-39478066

75. Andrew Roth, "Ukraine's Ex-President Viktor Yanukovych Found Guilty of Treason," *The Guardian* (January 25, 2019). https://www.theguardian.com/world/2019/jan/25/ukraine-ex-president-viktor-yanukovych-found-guilty-of-treason

76. John R. Schindler, "Is Vladimir Putin Behind Right-Wing Riots in Chemnitz Germany?" *Observer* (August 30, 2018). https://observer.com/2018/08/is-vladimir-putin-behind-right-wing-riots-in-chemnitz-germany/

77. Carol Matlack and Robert Williams, "France to Probe Possi-

ble Russian Influence on Yellow Vest Riots," *Bloomberg* (December 7, 2018). https://www.bloomberg.com/news/articles/2018-12-08/pro-russia-social-media-takes-aim-at-macron-as-yellow-vests-rage

78. iSans, "Propaganda in Time of Plague: In Between Reptilians and the Lifting of Sanctions" (March 21, 2020). https://isans.org/articles-en/propaganda-in-time-of-plague-in-between-reptilians-and-the-lifting-of-sanctions.html

79. "Powerful 'Putin's Chef' Prigozhin Cooks up Murky Deals," *BBC News* (November 4, 2019). https://www.bbc.com/news/world-europe-50264747

80. "Washington Puts Putin's Friend Prigozhin on Wanted List," *UAWire* (February 27, 2021). http://uawire.org/washington-puts-putin-s-friend-prigozhin-on-wanted-list

81. Medet Yesimkhanov, "WHO, Dulles, Rockefeller, World Government and Population Control—Conspiracy Theory Breakdown," *Factcheck.KZ* (October 23, 2020). https://factcheck.kz/claim-checking/verdict/voz-dalles-rokfeller-mirovoe-pravitelstvo-i-kontrol-rosta-naseleniya-razbor-teorii-zagovora/

82. Network Contagion, 8.

83. Kaleigh Rogers, "Why Qanon Has Attracted So Many White Evangelicals." *FiveThirtyEight* (March 4, 2021). https://fivethirtyeight.com/features/why-qanon-has-attracted-so-many-white-evangelicals/

CHAPTER 6

1. Anne Helen Petersen, "The Real Housewives of QAnon: How QAnon Used #SaveTheChildren to Lure Suburban Moms," *Elle* (October 29, 2020). https://www.elle.com/culture/a34485099/qanon-conspiracy-suburban-women/

2. Joanne R. Cantor, Dolf Zillmann, and Jennings Bryant, "Enhancement of Experienced Sexual Arousal in Response to Erotic Stimuli Through Misattribution of Unrelated Residual Excitation," Journal of Personality and Social Psychology, 32 (1) (1975): 69. https://psycnet.apa.org/record/1975-26821-001

3. Hannes Grassegger, "The Unbelievable Story of the Plot Against George Soro," *BuzzFeed News* (January 20, 2019). https://www.buzzfeednews.com/article/hnsgrassegger/george-soros-conspiracy-finkelstein-birnbaum-orban-netanyahu

4. Hagay Hacohen, "Netanyahu's Son Sparks Outrage After Posting Antisemitic-Themed Meme," *Jerusalem Post,* (September 9, 2017). https://www.jpost.com/Israel-News/Netanyahus-son-lashes-out-via-internet-again-504620

5. Josie Adams, "The Truth About Adrenochrome," *The Spinoff*

(April 7, 2020). https://thespinoff.co.nz/society/07-04-2020/explainer-adrenochrome-the-drug-that-doesnt-exist/

6. Jane Wakefield, "How Bill Gates Became the Voodoo Doll of Covid Conspiracies," *BBC News* (June 6, 2020). https://www.bbc.com/news/technology-52833706

7. Aigerim Mekisheva and Pavel Bannikov, "Infotrash: Operation Coronavirus 2020, Adrenochrome, and Satanic Pedophiles," *Factcheck.kz* (February 12, 2020). https://factcheck.kz/claim-checking/verdict/false/infotresh-operaciya-koronavirus-2020-adrenoxrom-i-pedofily-satanisty/

8. Christopher James Blythe, "Bill Gates' Comments on COVID-19 Vaccine Enflame 'Mark of the Beast' Worries in Some Christian Circles," *Religion Dispatches* (May 4, 2020). https://religiondispatches.org/bill-gates-comments-on-covid-19-vaccine-enflame-mark-of-the-beast-worries-in-some-christian-circles/

9. Sarah H. DiMuccio and Eric D. Knowles, "Precarious Manhood Predicts Support for Aggressive Policies and Politicians," *Personality and Social Psychology Bulletin* (October 13, 2020). https://journals.sagepub.com/doi/abs/10.1177/0146167220963577

10. Mark Setzler and Alixandra B. Yanus, "Why Did Women Vote for Donald Trump?" *Political Science & Politics*, *51* (3) (2018): 523–527. https://www.mrsteadman.com/uploads/1/2/6/6/126648902/why_did_women_vote_for_donald_trump.pdf

11. Dan Cassino, "Emasculation, Conservatism, and the 2016 Election," *Contexts*, *17*(1) (2018): 48–53. https://journals.sagepub.com/doi/full/10.1177/1536504218766551

12. Adam M. Enders and Joseph E. Uscinski, "On Modeling the Psychological Foundations of Support for Donald Trump" (n.d.). https://www.joeuscinski.com/uploads/7/1/9/5/71957435/trump_factor.pdf

13. Martin Geddes, "WWG1WGA: The Greatest Communications Event in History" (July 11, 2018). https://www.martingeddes.com/wwg1wga-the-greatest-communications-event-in-history/?fbclid=IwAR1uVoDlD1ToyBXGYUVVXF2_HaKEz9v1qBxCouVYNSRmayjAoRJc8YjPUDI

14. E. J. Dickson, "QAnon Followers Think JFK Jr. Is Coming Back on the 4th of July," *Rolling Stone* (July 3, 2019). https://www.rollingstone.com/culture/culture-features/qanon-jfk-jr-conspiracy-theory-854938/

15. John C. Moritz, "Fact Check: Hillary Clinton, JFK Jr. and the 2000 New York Senate Race," *USA Today* (October 21, 2020). https://www.usatoday.com/story/news/factcheck/2020/10/21/fact-check-hillary-clinton-jfk-jr-and-2000-new-york-senate-race/5993292002/

16. Robert A. Pape and Keven Ruby, "The Capitol Rioters Aren't

Like Other Extremists," *The Atlantic* (February 2, 2021). https://www.theatlantic.com/ideas/archive/2021/02/the-capitol-rioters-arent-like-other-extremists/617895/

17. Osita Nwanevu, "The Democratic Party Has a Fatal Misunderstanding of the QAnon Phenomenon," *New Republic* (February 5, 2021). https://newrepublic.com/article/161266/qanon-classism-marjorie-taylor-greene

18. Monika Grzesiak-Feldman, "The Effect of High-Anxiety Situations on Conspiracy Thinking," *Current Psychology, 32* (2013): 100–118. https://psycnet.apa.org/record/2013-02867-001

19. Damaris Graeupner and Alin Coman, "The Dark Side of Meaning-Making: How Social Exclusion Leads to Superstitious Thinking," *Journal of Experimental Social Psychology, 69* (2017): 218–222. https://www.princeton.edu/~acoman/Publications_files/The%20Dark%20Side%20of%20Meaning%20Making-Graeupner%20&%20Coman.pdf

20. Shauna M. Bowes, et al., "Under the Tinfoil Hat: Clarifying the Personological and Psychopathological Correlates of Conspiracy Beliefs," *Journal of Personality* (January 27, 2020). https://onlinelibrary.wiley.com/doi/abs/10.1111/jopy.12588

21. Evita March and Jordan Springer, "Belief in Conspiracy Theories: The Predictive Role of Schizotypy, Machiavellianism, and Primary Psychopathy," *PloS One, 14* (12) (2019): e0225964. https://journals.plos.org/plosone/article?id=10.1371/journal.pone.0225964

22. Michael Jensen and Sheehan Kane, "QAnon Offenders in the United States," *NC-START* (2021). https://www.start.umd.edu/sites/default/files/publications/local_attachments/START_PIRUS_QAnon_Mar2021.pdf

23. Deepa Seetharaman, "QAnon Booms on Facebook as Conspiracy Group Gains Mainstream Traction," *Wall Street Journal* (August 13, 2020). https://www.wsj.com/articles/qanon-booms-on-facebook-as-conspiracy-group-gains-mainstream-traction-11597367457

24. Clark McCauley and Sophia Moskalenko, "Understanding Political Radicalization: The Two-Pyramids Model, *American Psychologist, 72* (3) (2017): 205. https://psycnet.apa.org/record/2017-13879-002

25. Elizabeth Dwoskin, "Massive Facebook Study on Users' Doubt in Vaccines Finds a Small Group Appears to Play a Big Role in Pushing the Skepticism," *Washington Post* (March 19, 2021). https://www.washingtonpost.com/technology/2021/03/14/facebook-vaccine-hesistancy-qanon/

26. Cinthia Benitez, Kristen P. Howard, and Jennifer S. Cheavens, "The Effect of Validation and Invalidation on Positive and Negative Affective Experiences," *Journal of Positive Psychology* (2020): 1–13. https://www.tandfonline.com/doi/full/10.1080/17439760.2020.1832243

27. Daniel M. Stancato and Dacher Keltner, "Awe, Ideological Conviction, and Perceptions of Ideological Opponents," *Emotion, 21* (1) (2021): 61–72. https://pubmed.ncbi.nlm.nih.gov/31403808/

28. Chauncey Devega, "White Women and the Racist Right: Marjorie Taylor Greene Is Not an Aberration," *Salon* (March 1, 2021). https://www.salon.com/2021/03/01/white-women-and-the-racist-right-marjorie-taylor-greene-is-not-alone/

29. Em Steck, Nathan McDermott, and Christopher Hickey, "The Congressional Candidates Who Have Engaged with the QAnon Conspiracy Theory," *CNN.com* (October 30, 2020). https://www.cnn.com/interactive/2020/10/politics/qanon-cong-candidates/

30. Carol Schaeffer, "How Did a Fringe Corona Conspiracy Theory in Germany Grow to a Nationwide Movement?" *The Local* (June 26, 2020). https://www.thelocal.de/20200626/in-depth-how-did-germanys-largest-conspiracy-theory-group-gain-momentum

31. Nad'a Kovalcikova and Caitlyn Ramsey, "QAnon and Anti-Vax Conspiracy Theories Pose a Threat to Democracy Beyond National Borders. Alliance for Securing Democracy" (March 17, 2021). https://securingdemocracy.gmfus.org/qanon-and-anti-vax-conspiracy-theories-pose-a-threat-to-democracy-beyond-national-borders/

32. Mack Lamoureaux, "QAnon Has Gone Global," *Vice* (July 29, 2020). https://www.vice.com/en/article/pkym3k/qanon-conspiracy-has-gone-global

33. Felix Light, "QAnon Gains Traction in Russia," *Moscow Times* (November 30, 2020). https://www.themoscowtimes.com/2020/11/30/qanon-gains-traction-in-russia-a72180.

34. Tahira Sequeira, "QAnon and the Looming Threat of Misinformation in Finland," *Helsinki Times* (November 3, 2020). https://www.helsinkitimes.fi/finland/finland-news/domestic/18262-qanon-and-the-looming-threat-of-misinformation-in-finland.html

35. Diederik Baazil, "Dutch Fall for COVID Conspiracies in Warning to Europe's Leaders," *Bloomberg* (November 3, 2020). https://www.bloomberg.com/news/articles/2020-11-03/dutch-fall-for-covid-conspiracies-in-warning-to-europe-s-leaders

36. "There are 250 Portuguese Fans of QAnon" *Al Khaleej Today* (2020). https://alkhaleejtoday.co/international/5177520/There-are-250-Portuguese-fans-of-QAnon-Authorities-guarantee-to.html

37. Nicola Righetti, "QAnon in Italy: A Growing Phenomenon?" (May 10, 2020). http://www.nicolarighetti.net/research/qanon-in-italy-a-growing-phenomenon/

38. Alyssa McMurtry, "Spanish Conspiracy Theorists Funded on Patreon: Study," *Anadolu Agency* (December 12, 2020). https://www.

aa.com.tr/en/europe/spanish-conspiracy-theorists-funded-on-patreon-study/2081604

39. Mladen Obrenovic, "QAnon Gets Foothold in Balkans, Claiming COVID-19 'Does Not Exist,'" *Balkan Insight* (September 7, 2020). https://balkaninsight.com/2020/09/07/qanon-gets-foothold-in-balkans-claiming-covid-19-does-not-exist/

40. Aoife Gallagher, "How Did the QAnon Conspiracy Go Global? *Al Jazeera* (February 10, 2021). https://www.aljazeera.com/podcasts/2021/2/10/how-did-the-qanon-conspiracy-go-global

41. Alex Silverman, "QAnon Is Alive and Well in Japan," *The Diplomat* (January 29, 2021). https://thediplomat.com/2021/01/qanon-is-alive-and-well-in-japan/

42. Katia Patin, "In Kazakhstan, Coronavirus Conspiracies Are the Latest Celebrity Craze," *Coda* (July 17, 2020). https://www.codastory.com/disinformation/information-war/kazakhstan-celebrity-conspiracies/

43. Umar Farooq, "Pakistan's COVID Vaccine Drive Needs Antidote to Conspiracy Theories," *Reuters* (December 8, 2020). https://www.reuters.com/article/us-health-coronavirus-pakistan-vaccine/pakistans-covid-vaccine-drive-needs-antidote-to-conspiracy-theories-idUSKBN28I1B4

44. Rebecca Davis, "QAnon Originated in South Africa—Now That the Global Cult Is Back Here We Should All Be Afraid," *Daily Maverick* (September 26, 2020). https://www.dailymaverick.co.za/article/2020–09–26-qanon-originated-in-south-africa-now-that-the-global-cult-is-back-here-we-should-all-be-afraid/.

45. Mack Lamoureaux, "Armed Man Who Allegedly Stormed Trudeau's Residence Appears to Have Posted QAnon Content," *Vice* (July 3, 2020). https://www.vice.com/en/article/z3ez39/armed-man-corey-hurren-who-allegedly-stormed-justin-trudeaus-residence-rideau-hall-appears-to-have-posted-qanon-content

46. Amy Gunia, "The U.S. Exported QAnon to Australia and New Zealand. Now It's Creeping into COVID-19 Lockdown Protests," *Time* (September 30, 2020). https://time.com/5894139/qanon-australia-new-zealand-conspiracy-theory/

47. Arturo Wallace, "QAnon in Latin America: How and Why Groups Associated with This Controversial Conspiracy Theory Have Multiplied in the Region," *BBC News World* (August 28, 2020). https://translate.google.com/translate?hl=en&sl=es&u=https://www.bbc.com/mundo/noticias-america-latina-53936695&prev=search&pto=aue.

INDEX